WRONGFUL CONVICTION

WRONGFUL CONVICTION

From Prevention to the Reversal of Injustice

By

JOHN A. HUMPHREY

and

KAITLYN M. CLARKE

CHARLES C THOMAS • PUBLISHER, LTD.
Springfield • Illinois • U.S.A.

Published and Distributed Throughout the World by

CHARLES C THOMAS • PUBLISHER, LTD.
2600 South First Street
Springfield, Illinois 62704

ISBN 978-0-398-09206-1 (paper)
ISBN 978-0-398-09207-8 (ebook)

With THOMAS BOOKS *careful attention is given to all details of manufacturing
and design. It is the Publisher's desire to present books that are satisfactory as to their
physical qualities and artistic possibilities and appropriate for their particular use.*
THOMAS BOOKS *will be true to those laws of quality that assure a good name
and good will.*

Printed in the United States of America

TO-C-1

Library of Congress Cataloging-in-Publication Data

Names: Humphrey, John A., author. | Clarke, Kaitlyn M., author.
Title: Wrongful conviction : from prevention to the reversal of injustice /
    By John A. Humphrey and Kaitlin M. Clarke.
Description: Springfield, Illinois : Charles C. Thomas, 2017. | Includes
    bibliographical references and index.
Identifiers: LCCN 2017043265 (print) | LCCN 2017043304 (ebook) | ISBN
    9780398092078 (ebook) | ISBN 9780398092061 (pbk.)
Subjects: LCSH: Judicial error--United States. | Trials--United States. |
    Criminal justice, Administration of--United States.
Classification: LCC KF9756 (ebook) | LCC KF9756 .H86 2017 (print) | DDC
    345.73/0122--dc23
LC record available at https://lccn.loc.gov/2017043265

To the convicted innocents yet to be exonerated
and their struggle that inspire us to seek justice.

PREFACE

The precipitants of wrongful convictions are well-documented in the United States and around the world. Eyewitness misidentification, false confessions, flawed forensics, police and prosecutorial misconduct, the use of jailhouse informants, and inadequate defense counsel have been considered in a growing number of research papers, law review articles, and monographs. In addition, the arduous and lengthy exoneration process has been described in books and documentaries dealing with high profile cases of wrongful conviction.

What is missing in the literature on wrongful conviction is a book that provides an understanding of the legal remedies, organizational reforms and policy changes that have been proposed, and implemented, in various jurisdictions to reduce the likelihood of a wrongful conviction. The proposed book does just that.

Legal and organizational reforms and changes in criminal justice policy are considered at three key junctures of the process: (1) the investigation, evidence gathering and forensic analysis, (2) prosecutorial decision-making, and (3) judicial review and the exoneration of a wrongfully convicted defendant.

Each chapter opens with a vignette of a wrongful conviction case that illustrates the reform strategies being considered. For example, the chapter on the investigatory process begins with the case of Ronald Cotton who was identified in a police photo lineup, an in-person lineup, and at two trials by Jennifer Thompson, a college student who was raped in Burlington, North Carolina. Reforms in the manner in which the police process eyewitness identifications are then analyzed in detail. Eyewitness misidentification cases are used throughout the chapter to highlight the procedural errors that led to the conviction of an innocent person.

Each of the key precipitants of wrongful conviction during the processing of a criminal case is considered in separate chapters and discussed in relation to reforms and policy changes that been implemented or proposed in various jurisdiction around the country. Scientific advances and U.S. Supreme Court rulings that led to these reforms and policy changes are also explored.

This book, then, will be of particular interest to the law enforcement community, prosecutors and defense attorneys, judges, advocates for the wrongfully convicted and criminal justice policymakers. In addition, this book will contribute to academic courses in the fields of criminology, criminal justice, law and society, and social justice. In sum, anyone concerned with how our system of justice functions each day will be interested in this book.

J.H
K.M.C

CONTENTS

ILLUSTRATIONS

WRONGFUL CONVICTION

PART I

Chapter 1

INTRODUCTION

Mr. Forman, has the jury reached a verdict?

Yes, your Honor. We find the defendant guilty of rape in the first degree.

Is this your verdict so say you all?

Yes, your Honor.

I'm numb–this just can't be. I'm innocent, what happened. I just attended my own funeral. They are all wrong . . . . I didn't do anything . . . I'm innocent.

My lawyer is anxious to leave the courtroom. He has been whining about being overworked, too many cases to deal with and far too little time or no help from the Public Defender's Office here. He is mumbling something about what will happen next and that he would try to do what he can. I don't believe a word he is saying.

The bailiff is now leading me to a holding cell in the courthouse. I will soon be transported to the maximum security prison, about 90 miles from here to start a life sentence.

The numbness and confusion are beginning to lift as I am being led to the holding cell in the basement of the courthouse. I'm trying to piece together how I got here.

I certainly am no angel. My friends and I were well-known to the police for a variety of reasons: vandalism, graffiti, shoplifting, groping girls, smoking dope, a lot of "little" stuff. No doubt I was thought by the police to be a constant annoyance – someone who they would like to get rid of.

Things got far more serious after I dropped out of school when I was working as a dishwasher in a restaurant and that girl accused me of sexually assaulting her. I was arrested, booked, and held overnight in the county jail. A few days later she decided not to press charges against me and I was released.

Now this . . .

A forcible rape occurred in my hometown. The police showed up at my home very early in the morning and asked if I would come with them to the station to answer a few questions. The victim, an innocent, naive, college sophomore, was shown an array of photos to possibly identify her rapist. My picture appeared in most of the photo arrays. She told the police that my picture looked familiar. I was then asked to participate in a lineup with other young black men. Being innocent of any wrongdoing, I agreed to assist the police. Unfortunately, the victim seemed to recognize me. The more she talked to the police, the more convinced she was that I had raped her.

The police then focused on me exclusively as the perpetrator of this horrible crime. I was taken into custody, there was mention of Miranda rights, which I have half-heard in the confusion of being told that I was under arrest for forcible rape, and that arrangements could be made for me to talk to a lawyer.

The media went wild: the suspected rapist has been found, an arrest has been made, and justice will be served.

I was placed in an interrogation room, no windows, door locked, two detectives began questioning me about the rape. I was trapped. They were angry and insisted that I confess. Conviction was certain, a life sentence was inevitable. But if I was willing to confess to the rape, then the police would make sure that the district attorney would accept a plea to a lesser charge and my sentence would be drastically reduced. If I choose not to admit my guilt, all bets were off and I would die in prison.

I was alone, in shock, unable to think, completely intimidated by their hostile accusations and demands that I confess to committing the rape. They made no sense to me, but their unrelenting harassment, was more than I could take. I was told that not only had the victim positively identified me, but the forensic evidence gathered from the victim and the crime scene was conclusive. I was indeed the rapist.

No doubt I became more compliant with the police than I wanted to be. I repeated specifics about the crime that they screamed at me. Things only the rapist would know. My confession was recorded and presented to me for my signature. I agreed they were my words just to stop their haranguing. It is amazing what you will admit to in your worst nightmare.

My public defender arrived the next day just before my probable cause hearing. It was a rushed meeting; he said bail would probably be too high and that he would try meet me in my jail cell in the next few days. Bail could not possibly be met, and I was returned to jail to think.

It was not too long before a cellmate arrived. He was no stranger to being locked up, a real talker who was very curious about how I got there, and how I planned to beat the rap. I had no idea. But my cellmate seemed to know how best to handle the situation. With an absentee lawyer, I was more than willing to tell him about myself and the mess I was in. He, in turn, talked endlessly about his many "brushes with the law."

My lawyer showed up a few days after my cellmate was moved to another lockup. My phantom lawyer was nothing but doom and gloom. The evidence against me was overwhelming and the only course of action was to try to strike a plea bargain with the district attorney. The prosecution's case included: a positive identification by the victim, footprint evidence, hair, and threads from a tee-shirt from the crime scene, my partial confession given to the police, and the testimony of a jailhouse snitch. Yes, my cellmate friend was planted by the district attorney to gather incriminating evidence against me. He is even willing to say that he heard me scream in my sleep that I raped the girl.

My lawyer assured me that, as strange as it seems, jailhouse snitch testimony is very likely to be believed by the jury. He then began to complain endlessly about being overburdened with cases with few if any resources to conduct an independent investigation in the case. He must rely on the prosecuting attorney to provide a list of witnesses, access to police records, and forensic evidence to prepare an adequate defense. Given the situation that we are in the best strategy is to try to strike a deal with the prosecuting attorney and to plead guilty to the charge that carries the shortest prison term. Since I am innocent, admitting guilt and allowing me to be incarcerated for decades made no sense. My solution to the problem was to plead not guilty and go to trial. This angered everyone, including my own lawyer. My strategy failed miserably.

It would take more than 12 years before DNA evidence con-
clusively showed that I was not the rapist found guilty at trial. The
actual rapist has never been arrested, convicted, nor incarcerated.

Any one of the reasons for this wrongful conviction may well have
been enough for a jury to convict the defendant. Eyewitness misidentification is the most common legal cause for a wrongful conviction, followed by invalid forensic evidence and coerced false confessions.[1]
Police and prosecutorial misconduct and inadequate counsel often co-
occur with the leading causes of wrongful conviction. Singularly, or
most often in combination, these precipitants of wrongful conviction
account for the vast majority of the incarceration of innocent persons.

Evidence mounts daily that the innocents across the country and
around the world are arrested, convicted, and incarcerated for extended periods of time. Yet, until the advent of the use of DNA analysis
in forensic investigations, wrongful convictions were considered anomalies, events of little interest to criminologists and legal scholars.

WRONGFUL CONVICTION RESEARCH:
THE BEGINNINGS

The work of Yale Professor Edwin M. Bouchard was the first serious
scholarly effort to call attention to wrongful convictions. In 1932, 20
years after his paper on European errors in criminal justice, he published *Convicting the Innocent: Errors of Criminal Justice* (Bouchard, 1932).
This book focused attention on the most common errors that lead
to the conviction of innocent persons in the United States: eyewitness
misidentification, false confessions, circumstantial evidence, and overzealous prosecutors.

Fifty-five years passed before Hugo Bedau, Michael Radelet and
Constance Putnam conducted their investigation of wrongful conviction. They argued that in the twentieth century 350 persons had been
wrongfully convicted, including possible death penalty cases (Bedau,
Radelet & Putnam, 1992). The work of Bedau, Radelet and Putnam
sparked considerable attention to the possibility that wrongful convic-

---

1. For more information see: Innocence Project. (n.d.k). *The causes of wrongful conviction.*
New York: Innocence Project. Retrieved from http://www.innocenceproject.org/
causes-wrongful-conviction.

tions were far more common than had been imagined. Case study books and scholarly efforts to understand the causes of wrongful conviction began appearing in bookstores around the country and in professional academic journals.

However, it was not until the DNA revolution that the plight of the wrongfully convicted was significantly advanced. DNA testing made it possible for law enforcement agents to genetically link the alleged perpetrator with the victim, or conversely exclude the accused from involvement in the crime. Far less reliable forensic methods, fingerprints, hair analysis, and bite marks were superseded by the incontrovertible evidence provided by DNA testing.

In 1992, Barry Scheck and Peter Neufeld launched the Innocence Project at Yeshiva University's Cardozo Law School. The Innocence Project is an advocacy program limited to cases where there is a claim of actual innocence and for which DNA evidence is available for testing. Since its inception, DNA testing has exonerated more than 350 innocent persons.[2] Additionally, a network of innocence projects and commissions has been established around the country to advance the work of Scheck and Neufeld in New York. The Innocence Network established in 2004 includes 56 members in the United States and Puerto Rico and 13 additional countries around the world (The Innocence Network, n.d.). In 2006, North Carolina established the first in the nation Innocence Inquiry Commission to "investigate and evaluate post-conviction claims of factual innocence" (North Carolina Innocence Inquiry Commission, 2016). Subsequently, Pennsylvania, Connecticut, New York, California, Wisconsin, and Illinois have established similar commissions.

In 2012, Samuel Gross founded the National Registry for Exonerations at the University of Michigan to gather statistical information on exonerations in the United States. Wrongfully conviction cases included in the National Registry are not limited to DNA exonerations, but include convictions based often on a combination of false confessions, official misconduct, guilty pleas, and the absence of any criminal activity (National Registry for Exonerations, 2017). As of July 17, 2017 there have been 2,065 cases of wrongful conviction documented in the National Registry.

---

2. As of July 17, 2017, for more information see: Innocence Project. (n.d.a). *All cases.* New York: Innocence Project. Retrieved from https://www.innocenceproject.org/all-cases/#exonerated-by-dna.

THE EXTENT OF WRONGFUL CONVICTIONS

Dan Simon argues that the "true" rate of wrongful conviction is "unknowable" (Simon, 2012). And, Barry Scheck and Peter Neufled, cofounders of the Innocence Project in New York, are often quoted as saying that the known cases of wrongful conviction are "just the tip of the iceberg" (1996). What we do know about the conviction of the innocent is largely limited to two kinds of crimes: murder and rape, simply because DNA evidence is far more likely to be available for testing in these crimes.

What is figuratively "below the water line" has been the subject of various attempts to scientifically establish the prevalence of wrongful conviction. This is a daunting task at best. Criminal justice practitioners are understandably reluctant to admit that egregious errors have been made in the process of convicting an innocent person.

Estimates of Wrongful Conviction

While certainly not without drawbacks, two kinds of studies have been undertaken to gauge the extent of wrongful conviction. The most common type of study is largely speculative, relying on criminal justice officials for their estimate of wrongful conviction. Huff, Rattner and Sagarin's survey of 41 attorney generals from around the country and 53 prosecutors, 59 sheriffs and chiefs of police, and 21 public defenders from seven Ohio cities found that more than seven in 10 estimated that wrongful convictions were evident in 1 percent or less of the felony cases, while two in 10 believed they occurred 5 to 10 percent, and 6 percent believed they never occurred (Huff, Rattner, Sagarin, MacNamara, 1986; Huff et al., 1996). Because most respondents surveyed thought that wrongful convictions occurred in 1 percent or less of criminal cases, Huff and his colleagues decided that .5 percent of criminal convictions were erroneous. The result of this early effort to measure the extent of wrongful conviction is not surprising given that it was conducted prior to the onset of DNA exonerations.

Similarly, Ramsey and Frank (2007) studied sheriffs and police chiefs, prosecutors, defense attorneys, and judges in Ohio. Their findings are strikingly similar to those of Huff and his colleagues. Taken together, the criminal justice professions estimated that between 0.5 and 1.0 percent of felony defendants were wrongfully convicted in their jurisdictions. However, they thought that 1 to 3 percent of persons convicted of a felony across the United States were wrongfully convicted.

Perceptions of wrongful conviction varied across criminal justice professionals. Defense attorneys most often believed that wrongful convictions occurred 1 to 3 percent of the time, compared to judges 0.5 to 1.0 percent of the time. Police and prosecutors did not differ in the perceptions of wrongful conviction. Both held that wrongful convictions occurred in less than 0.5 percent of the time (Ramsey & Frank, 2007, pp. 452-453).

Zalman, Smith, and Kiger (2008) replicated the Ramsey and Frank's Ohio study among criminal justice practitioners in Michigan. The findings are strikingly similar: (1) overall criminal justice professions, police, prosecutors, defense attorneys, and judges, estimated a wrongful conviction rate of between 0.5 and 1 percent of felony cases, and (2) the estimated rate was highest among defense attorneys, and lowest among police and prosecutors with judges falling between the two, and (3) 20 percent of the respondents thought that wrongful convictions never happen. More specially, 41 percent of the police and 48 percent of the prosecutors report that wrongful convictions never occurred, compared to 5.3 percent of judges and none of the defense attorneys. Ninety-three percent of defense attorneys believed that wrongful convictions occurred at least 1 percent of the time, and more than half of the defense attorneys (51.8%) thought wrongful convictions occurred 6 percent of the time or more, compared to 9.8 percent of judges (Zalman, Smith, & Kiger, 2008, p. 84).

Zalman and his colleagues attribute these striking differences in the perception of wrongful conviction to the professional socialization of the various participants in the criminal justice system. In an adversarial system of justice, the participants hold distinct views of the process of "seeking the truth." The police and prosecutors are pitted against the defense in resolving any criminal case. Each side of the adversarial process has a vested interest in its outcome. Judges seek to ensure that the procedural rules are followed and the defendant is provided a "fair" hearing as defined by adherence to these procedural guidelines. Each of the participants in the legal contest is a member of a larger professional subculture, which shapes their perceptions of their adversaries and strategies for gaining an advantage in the adjudicatory process. Judges themselves are drawn from the ranks of the legal profession.

Typically, they have served as prosecutors, defense attorneys, or both. Socialization into professional subcultures with distinct views of "justice" may well account for the differences in the perception of wrongful conviction.

Smith, Zalman, and Kiger (2011) extend the replication of Ramsey and Frank's survey on criminal justice professionals to include their perceptions of: (1) the reliability of eyewitness and forensic experts, and (2) their belief that reforms in criminal procedure are necessary. Not unexpectedly, defense attorneys view of errors in the adjudication of a criminal case were markedly different from police and prosecutors, and less so from judges. Defense attorneys reported that errors occurred across the spectrum of criminal justice practitioners, including themselves. Defense attorneys were also more likely to advocate reforms at each stage of the processing of a criminal case, from the initial police investigation through the adjudicatory process. Police and prosecutors tend to oppose any reforms that may be advantageous to the interests of the defense. Judges were more balanced in their advocacy for reform.

Earlier Poveda (2001) used multiple methods to estimate wrongful convictions. He focused on court-ordered discharges, and incarcerated offenders' self-reports of their criminal liability. His analysis of court-ordered discharges in New York State showed that 1.4 percent of defendants were later found to be wrongfully convicted. The self-report findings were considerably different from the analysis of the court-ordered discharges. Overall, 15.4 percent of inmates claimed that they did not commit the crime that led to their incarceration. This finding did not vary appreciably across the three sites studied: Michigan (14.1%), California (14.65), and Texas (16.7%). Denial of criminal liability was highest for rapist and sex offenders (37.7% to 26.9%), and lowest for drug and nonviolent offenders (about 7%), violent offenders – murders, weapons violations, assault and robbery fell into the middle range of criminal denial (17.5%-11.5%) (Poveda, 2001, p. 701).

Risinger (2007) has undertaken a particularly ambitious effort to document the rate of wrongful convictions. He notes that his study establishes "the first such empirically justified wrongful conviction rate ever for a significant universe of real world serious crimes; capital rape-murders in the 1980s" (Risinger, 2007, p. 761). He compared DNA exonerations in capital rape-murder cases from 1982 through 1989 and a subsample of 2235 sentences for capital crimes over the same time period. Data on DNA exonerations between 1982 and 1989 were provided by the Innocence Project in New York. After careful analysis, 11 DNA rape-murder exonerations were documented during this time period. Risinger adjusted the number of cases by one in 20 (or .5) that an exonerated case might, in fact, be guilty. A numerator of 10.5 wrongfully convicted rape-murder cases was determined. A subsample of 479 rape-murder convictions during the same period was identified. Because two-thirds cases of rape-murder brought to the attention of the Innocence Project included usable DNA evidence, the 479 rape-murder convictions were reduced by one-third to yield a denominator of 319 cases. Dividing the 10.5 DNA exonerations by the 319 convictions for rape-murder for which DNA was likely available resulted in a wrongful conviction rate of 3.3. A 3.3 error rate for rape-murder is considerably above the estimates of wrongful conviction in felony cases overall.

SITUATIONAL APPROACH TO WRONGFUL CONVICTIONS

Most of human behavior takes place in recognizable situations. These situations occur, intentionally or not, with others. Palmer defines a situation as: "an episode of interaction between two or more individuals . . . [T]he reciprocal stimulation and response is interaction" (Palmer, 1970, p. 19). The intensity of the interaction defines the situation. Criminal events, e.g., murder, rape, robbery are examples of high intensity situational behavior. The interaction between the offender and victim define the criminal event.

A criminal situation typically triggers another situational reaction. The police are summoned and an investigation ensues. The investigatory process involves, to a greater or lesser degree, intense interaction among line officers, detectives, forensic experts, and others. Interviews are conducted with witnesses and the victim (if possible): circumstantial evidence and physical evidence is also gathered. The immediate goal is to identify and locate the perpetrator of the crime. The longer the offender is unknown, the less likely an arrest will be made, and a convictable case presented to the prosecutor.

In a sense the criminal situation flows into the investigatory situation. The initial definition of the criminal situation by the police affects the actions of the police. While each criminal event may have unique characteristics, they tend to fit into patterns of behavior generally understood by the police. Murders of domestic partners, drug dealers, or gangbangers tend to have common characteristics, as do the abduction and forcible rape of an innocent victim by a stranger, or the robbery of a convenience store late at night in a high crime neighborhood. Characteristics of a likely perpetrator emerge from the initial investigation and an assessment of the solvability of the case. Solvability factors typically include: "a witness to the crime, naming, location, and identification of a suspect, description of a vehicle associated with the crime, identification of stolen property, physical evidence, and unique crime methods" (Hirschy, 2003).

Palmer (1970) notes that: "a social situation is institutionalized to the extent that interaction is patterned and follows the grooves marked out in similar past situations" (p. 21). In a very real sense, the crime itself dictates its own investigation shaped in large part by previous investigations of similar criminal events. As Thomas and Thomas (1928) posit: "If men define situations as real, they are real in their consequences" (p. 572). The definition of the situation is vital to understanding the behavior of various actors within the situation. Thomas (1923) explains the definition of the situation in this way:

> Preliminary to any self-determined act of behavior there is always a stage of examination and deliberation which we may call the *definition of the situation*. And actually not only concrete acts are dependent on the definition of the situation, but gradually a whole life policy and the personality of the individual himself follow from a series of such definitions. (p. 42)

The definition of the situation then precedes the actions of its participants and largely determines its outcome. Criminal cases are successfully processed largely in routine ways by the police and prosecutors. Arrests are made of a suspect who actually committed the crime: evidence is then gathered, analyzed and presented to the prosecutor. Most often the case results in a plea bargain with the defendant, far less often the case goes to trial. However, similar criminal situations, processed in routine ways by the agents of the criminal justice system may result in a plea bargain or conviction at trial of an innocent person. In short, similar criminal situations, processed in similar ways, may result in vastly different outcomes.

The Structure of the Legal Case

Donald Black's (1976) innovative work on the behavior of law provides a way to understand the influence of the criminal situation on its legal processing and likelihood of a wrongful conviction. Black (1976) defines law as governmental social control (p. 2). That is, the more involvement of the agents of the criminal justice system, e.g., the police, prosecutors, trial and appellate judges, the greater the governmental social control. Arresting a suspect is more law than not arresting one; as is charging, indicting, resolving the case by a plea bargain or trial. Law then behaves as do other physical and social phenomena.

Black (1976) argues that the structure of the legal case-*who does what to whom*-affects the behavior of law. The structure of the legal case defines the criminal situation. The characteristics of the suspected offender vis-à-vis the victim predicts the extent of involvement of the government in the case. Black's theory of the behavior of law includes 29 propositions, three of which are particularly important for the understanding of wrongful convictions. Three variables: *relative status*, respectability and relational distance of the offender and victim are most relevant for our discussion. Relative status refers to the socioeconomic status of the offender compared to the victim; *respectability* is how well-regarded the offender and victim are in the community; and *relational distance*, means the closeness of their relationship (e.g. family member, friend, acquaintance, or stranger).

Black hypothesizes that:

Relative Status: *(1) The higher the status of the victim compared to that of the offender, the greater the governmental social control. (2) The higher the status of the offender compared to that of the victim, the less the governmental social control.*

Respectability: *(1) The greater the respectability of the victim compared to the suspected offender, the greater the governmental social control. (2) The greater the respectability of the suspected offender compared to the victim, the less the governmental control.*

Relational Distance: *(1) The greater the relational distance between the suspected offender and the victim, the greater the governmental social*

*control. (2) The less the relational distance between the suspected offender
and the victim, the less the governmental social control.*

In sum, when the victim is perceived to be more socioeconomically
advantaged and more respected in the community than the offender,
and when they are less well-known to one another, there will be more
investment of the criminal justice system in securing a conviction. In
short, Black argues that the structure of the legal case defines the
situation which, in turn, affects the time, effort, and resources expended
by the government in the case.

Media Attention

Media attention to the case can also markedly influence the vigor-
ousness of the investigation by the police and the commitment to "go
forward" by the prosecution. Extensive coverage of the circumstances
surrounding the case, the background of an "innocent" victim tends to
fuel political involvement in the case. Action must be taken by the
police and prosecutors for a quick resolution. Trust and confidence in
the criminal justice system is being threatened by the failure to bring
closure to the case. In short, a "convictable" suspect must be identified
and brought to justice without unnecessary delay.

Perception of Convictability

Whereas prosecutors are ethically obliged to seek the truth, in an
adversarial system of justice, the "truth" is invariably equated with a
conviction in the case. Frohmann (1997) defines convictability as the
"likelihood of a guilty verdict at trial" (p. 531). Case convictability then
becomes a "decision-making standard" for prosecutors (Frohmann
(1997, p. 531). Black's structure of the legal case defines certain defendants as particularly convictable. As we have seen, Black argues that
the quantity of law, or the extent of governmental social control, systematically varies with the structure of the legal case. He further con-
tends that the social structure of a legal case – the web of social
positions and relationships – predicts the amount of law the case will
involve. He writes: ". . . this structure is crucial to understanding legal
variation from one technically identical case to another" (Black, 1989,
p. 8). If an innocent person is perceived to be convictable, then the
odds of a wrongful conviction are significantly increased.[3]

---

3. See Chapter 7 for an additional discussion of Black's theory.

Decision-making Process

Criminal justice decision-making takes place largely outside the public view. Distinct police and prosecutorial subcultures exist to facilitate their work. These subcultures are characterized by secrecy, information control, and internal loyalty. Police and prosecutors do not want their day-to-day activities to be scrutinized by public officials, citizen review boards, or any entity outside the criminal justice system. Justice is, in a sense, administered in cloistered environments, subject to their own policies and procedures.

It is within these subcultures that criminal justice professionals are socialized into the day-to-day working of their agency, the expectations for their performance; and appropriate definitions of crime related situations. Perceptions are shaped, and evaluations are made of the circumstance of the crime, including the victims, suspects, and available evidence. The prosecutor's decision to "go forward" with the case is made in collaboration with the police and the viability of the case. Based on convictions of similar cases in the past, and the perceived "credibility" of the evidence provided by the police, the decision to prosecute the case is made. In a sense the subcultures of the police and prosecutors flow into one another to shape the decision to proceed with the prosecution of the defendant. The mutual self-dependency of the police and prosecutor determine much of their decision-making.

Stateless Locations and Self-Help

To Black (1983) stateless locations are places that typically function outside the constraints of a formal legal system. Rather informal controls are used to address grievances and wrongdoing. Black argues that much of what is currently defined as criminal is rather "moralistic and involves the pursuit of justice" (p. 34). In a sense, self-help is a form of informal social control. Black (1983) defines self-help as the "expression of a grievance by unilateral aggression" (p. 34). Formal legal action by the police and prosecutors is not available in all situations of wrongdoing. Many times the offender is known to the victim, but may be unwilling or unable to provide the evidence to support an arrest. In these cases self-help behaviors are more common. Retaliation against the suspected offender is used to address the wrongdoing. This reversion to the principle of Lex Talionis – an eye for an eye, a tooth for a tooth – underlies the self-help approach to justice. Black's analysis of stateless locations may be extended to the context for criminal justice decision-making.

Decision-making by police and prosecutors takes place largely outside the scrutiny of the public. In the broadest sense, they are charged with establishing the moral order, by redressing a wrong against the victim, and by exacting justice. The decisions made in pursuit of these lofty goals are shaped by the rather mundane practicalities of police and prosecutorial work. The goal is very simple, to arrest, convict, and sentence the offender. The means to this goal are often quite murky: witnesses contradict each other and sometimes themselves, physical evidence is compromised, its validity is lost, and the persons with knowledge of the crime refuse to cooperate with the police.

Police and prosecutors often rely on self-help to effect a conviction. Certainty is imposed on an uncertain situation. These self-help strategies may well expedite the processing of the case and support a "convictable" case against the accused. However, they increase the odds of an innocent person being convicted. In short the self-help strategies employed by criminal justice professionals, while perhaps well-meaning, are the leading causes of wrongful conviction.

CAUSES OF WRONGFUL CONVICTIONS

Most of the causes of wrongful conviction identified to date involve some form of self-help by the police and prosecutors. There is general consensus that wrongful convictions are the result of the following:

- Tunnel Vision
- Eyewitness Misidentification
- Coerced Confessions
- Invalid Forensic Evidence
- Police Misconduct
- Prosecutorial Misconduct
- Perjured Informant Testimony (e.g. Use of Jailhouse Snitches)
- Inadequate Defense Counsel[4,5]

---

4. For more informs see: Borchard, 1932; Garrett, 2011; Gould, Carrano, Leo, & Hall-Jares, 2014; Gould & Leo, 2010.
5. Each of these "causes" of wrongful conviction will be discussed in detail in the following chapters.

Richard Leo (2005, 2017) notes that these "causes" were largely identified by lawyers and journalist and do not adequately explain the genesis of wrongful convictions. He argues that what must be understood is not simply "why" a person was wrongfully convicted, e.g., eyewitness misidentification, false confession, but "how" was it possible that the erroneous evidence was gathered, and presented to the prosecutor. We must understand the "root cause" that is, the decision-making process engaged in by criminal justice professions that underlies the assembly of faulty evidence. The causes are rooted in the routine decision-making intended to identify convictable defendants and eliminate those not likely to be found guilty by a jury.[6] Wrongful convictions are then the result of the flawed processing of a criminal case. In sum, Leo (2005) writes:

> One of the most surprising, and yet perhaps predictable, aspects of wrongful conviction is that each miscarriage of justice typically involves a series of actors whose decisions were, in all likelihood, made in the good faith belief that the suspect or defendant was guilty, although later those beliefs turned out to be wrong. (p. 215)

Lofquist (as cited in Westervelt and Humphrey, 2001, pp. 174-196) considered two possible explanations for compromising the legal processing of a criminal case: rational choice or agency, and organizational processing or structure. Rational choice perspective focuses on the aberrant behavior of the actors in the criminal justice system, while the organizational perspective considers the day-to-day routine behaviors of actors as they carry out the processing of criminal cases. Lofquist rejects the idea that wrongful convictions are the result of the willful intent of the criminal justice professionals to "frame" an innocent person simply to dispose of the case. The rational choice perspective would involve the conspiratorial misdeeds of several agents of the criminal justice system to effectively explain wrongful convictions. Rather, he finds that the organizational framework provides a better understanding of an erroneous processing of a criminal matter. Lofquist (2001) describes a wrongful conviction as:

> . . . the product of the normal, day-to-day routine operations of decision makers acting free of conspiratorial intent or wrongdoing: the outcome

---

6. For further discussion see: Packer, H. (1968). *The limits of the criminal sanction.* Stanford, CA: Stanford University Press.

was generated by the structures and routines in which actors act . . . Although lacking the drama, linearity, and storytelling power of the agency model, this perspective accords with the mundane nature of daily life and work. (p. 192)

PACKER'S MODELS OF CRIMINAL SANCTIONS

Herbert Packer (1968) sets for two models for the understanding "how" the criminal justice system operates. The two models – *Crime Control* and *Due Process* – are each premised on competing value systems. The crime control model emphases the quick, efficient, and final resolution of a criminal matter, while the skepticism, and strictly adhering to the Constitutional and procedural safeguard of the accused characterize the due process model. The central values of the crime control model then are: efficiency, speed, informality, uniformity, finality, and the presumption of guilt. Efficiency refers to the "capacity to apprehend, try, convict, and dispose of a high proportion of criminal offenders whose offenses become known" (Packer, 1968, p. 158). The value of efficiency depends on speed and finality. Since the volume of crime invariably exceeds the capacity to handle it, cases must be processed through the system and a final resolution reached without delay. Obstacles to the smooth functioning of the system must be removed. The values of informality and uniformity expedite the processing of a criminal case. Informality means that the police and prosecutors are permitted wide latitude in decision making during the investigation, evidence gathering, and charging phases of the process. Uniformity refers to following routine, time honored procedures in framing the case against the accused. Efficiency and speed in the processing of a case are greatly enhanced by the use of informal and uniform practices. The values of finality and the presumption of guilt drive much of the decision-making by practitioners committed to the crime control model. If a "convictable" suspect is identified and taken into custody, then a conviction must be sought as expeditiously as possible.

The values that underlie the due process model are diametrically opposed to those of the crime control model. Rather than accelerating the processing of a criminal case, the due process model values a slow, deliberate, and ponderous process to ensure that the legal safeguards of the accused are provided. The key values of the due process model are: reliability of fact-finding, establishment of legal guilt, equality, skepticism, and morality and utility. Reliability of fact-finding recognizes the possibility of error in the gathering of testimonial, physical, and circumstantial evidence. Therefore, advocates of the due process model are adamant about a "formal, adjudicative, adversary fact-finding process in which the factual case against the accused is publicly heard by an impartial tribunal and is evaluated only after the accused has had full opportunity to discredit the case against him" (Packer, 1968, pp. 163-164). Legal guilt relies on the ability of the government to convince a jury that the defendant is criminally liable. The presumption of innocence prevails until a finding of guilt is rendered by the court. Equity refers to the financial ability of the accused to mount a defense commensurate with the criminal charge. Justice is not served if adequate defense counsel is not possible at each stage of the adjudicatory process. Skepticism is the value of questioning the decision-making at each stage of the criminal justice process. Issues related morality and utility are intertwined with the pursuit of justice. To what extent are the decisions made by criminal justice professionals, and sentencing decisions made by the courts morally defensible? Do the outcomes of the adjudicatory process serve a useful purpose? Or, would justice be better served by considering alternative forms to address criminal offending? Packer (1968) posits that:

> The two models merely afford a convenient way to talk about the operation of process whose day–to-day functioning involves a constant series of minute adjustments between the competing demands of two values systems and whose normative future likewise involves a series of resolutions of the tensions between competing claims. (p. 153)[7]

THEME OF THE BOOK

The systemic tension within the criminal justice system between the goal of an efficient and final resolution to a crime, i.e., an arrest, prosecution, and conviction, and the goal to ensure that justice has been served underlies the conviction of the innocent. Reforms intended to reduce the likelihood of a wrongful conviction must significantly lessen the tension between the goal of efficiency and finality in the processing of a criminal case and the ultimate goal of achieving a just outcome.

---

7. See Chapter 6 for an additional discussion of Packer's models.

Reforms must be undertaken on two fronts: the legal-changes in the procedural rules that derive from the due process rights of the accused, and the culture of the agents of the adversarial system of justice. Changes in procedural rule alone are not sufficient because the rules are interpreted within the crime control subcultures of police and prosecutors. These subcultures must be encouraged to adopt values that reduce the tension between the goals of crime control and those of due process. The goals and interests of the agents of the adversarial system must be redefined through revamping law enforcement and legal educational programs to define a balance between the goals and interests of the state and those of the defendant.

ORGANIZATION OF THE BOOK

This book considers key junctures in the criminal justice process that give rise to wrongful convictions. Each chapter begins with a vignette of case that illustrates typical procedures and policies that may well lead to an erroneous outcome. The procedural error(s) are then explained in detail.

The book is organized in the following way. Part I includes the introductory chapter which provides an overview of the field of wrongful convictions, discusses the theme of the book and its organizational structure. Chapter 2 considers the investigatory process routinely employed to gather evidence and identify a suspect. Analysis of forensic evidence is considered in Chapter 3. Included are issues related to the forensic evidence gathering, chain of custody, contamination of the evidence, its misinterpretation, and the falsification of the forensic reports.

Part II includes Chapters 4, 5 and 6 which focus the agents of the court – the prosecutors, defense attorneys, judges and juries. Chapter 4 considers prosecutorial misconduct. Included here are: plea bargaining strategies, coaching witnesses, violations of the rules of discovery, use of jailhouse snitches, and other deceptive practices. Inadequate defense counsel is considered in Chapter 5. The failure to provide an adequate defense may be the result of lack of preparation of the attorney, lack of adequate resources to mount an effective defense, or the burden of far too many cases assigned to a public defender. The influence of judges and juries on wrongful convictions is covered in Chapter 6. Misinterpretation of the law and the failure of instructing jurors about the potential drawbacks of certain kinds of evidence, e.g., eyewitness identification, forensic analysis, and even confessions of the accused may well lead to a wrongful conviction.

In Part III, Chapters 7, 8 and 9 analyze the processes involved in the reversal of wrongful convictions. Chapter 7 reviews post-conviction remedies: judicial review, obstacles encountered in the exoneration process. Chapter 8 deals with the possibility of compensation for a wrongful conviction. Included here are the principles governing compensation, variations in compensations by state, and proposals for reforms in wrongful conviction reforms. In the final chapter, we consider the future of criminal justice reforms and criminal justice policies that affect wrongful convictions.

This book then provides an analytical overview of the criminal justice processes involved in a wrongful conviction and the reforms that are needed to prevent and reverse injustices. We consider the source of the reforms, obstacles to their adoption, and evidence of their impact on averting wrongful convictions. We conclude with recommendations for the continued development of promising strategies for criminal justice reform.

Chapter 2

INVESTIGATORY PROCESS

To maintain at all times a relationship with the public that gives reality to the historic tradition that the police are the public and that the public are the police, the police being only members of the public who are paid to give full-time attention to duties which are incumbent on every citizen in the interests of community welfare and existence.

– Sir Robert Peel, *Nine Principles of Policing*

THE CASE OF JULIA REA

Julia was at home with Joel, her 10-year old-son who was asleep in his bedroom. Following a particularly nasty divorce, her ex-husband, a police officer, was awarded physical custody of their son on the grounds that Julia, a psychology doctoral student, allegedly traveled "too much." Because Julia only saw Joel on the weekends, she treasured the time with him. At about 4:00 in the morning, Julia heard a violent scream, she ran to Joel's bedroom, but he was not there. In a panic she ran from room to room – no Joel. Out of the darkness she was suddenly grabbed by a man. She broke free, chased him into the backyard, screaming for help. Where was he? Julia was hit in the back of her head and shoved into the ground. She remembers seeing the man take off his mask under a streetlight to be seen no more.

The police were on the scene within moments to find Julia with a bloody cut on her arm and a badly scraped forehead. Joel was found dead inside the home having been stabbed several times in the chest. Julia and her ex-husband were "persons of interest" to the police. The ex-husband was quickly dismissed as a suspect because he was elsewhere at the time of the crime.

There was no evidence that Julia's injuries were self-inflicted. There was no blood on her clothing. Her fingerprints were not found on the knife used to stab Joel. And yet, without another suspect, the police focused on Julia as the only suspect in the murder of her son. A circumstantial case was constructed to support a charge of willful and intentional killing of her son. The circumstantial case involved the following elements: (1) her ex-husband testified that Julia wanted to have an abortion and only reluctantly gave birth to their son – an assertion refuted by Julia's obstetrician who testified that she was confined to bed for a month to prevent a spontaneous abortion before Joel was born, (2) Julia's ex-husband further testified that she was "emotionally unstable" and given to unpredictable behavior, and (3) witnesses reported that her demeanor at the crime scene seemed inconsistent with the tragic death of her son.

Despite Julia's vehement and repeated claim that she did not kill her son, she was indicted three years after the crime occurred. As special state prosecutor Ed Parkinson argued: "To believe her, you would have to believe that this assailant came into her home in the middle of the night, in dark clothes, hiding his identity by the use of a mask, for the sole purpose of killing a 10-year-old boy. And after he accomplished his result he pulled off the mask to reveal his identity to her. Nonsense."[1]

Julia's attorney did not call her as a witness in her own defense. The jury deliberated five hours before finding Julia guilty of first degree murder – her sentence was 65 years.

The Reversal

An unlikely series of events led to the exoneration of Julia Rea. Diane Fanning was working on a book about serial killer Tommy Lynn Sells, currently on death row in Texas. She happened to see an *ABC 20/20* report on Julia's case and became curious about its outcome. In a letter to Sells, Diane mentioned her doubt that Julia murdered her son and her concern that she was wrongfully convicted. She said: "didn't tell him who she was, I didn't tell him where it happened, I didn't tell him when it happened, nothing." Sells wrote back: "Was that murder you were talking about one that happened two days before the one I did in Springfield, Mo.? Say maybe on the 13th?"[2] Sells

1. Sherr, L., Redmond, L., & St. John, C. (2007, May 8). Untangling a murder mystery. *ABC News*. Retrieved from http://www.abc.news.go.cpm/20/20/story/id.2931404&page.
2. Sherr, L., Redmond, L., & St. John, C. (2007, May 8). Untangling a murder mystery. *ABC News*. Retrieved from http://www.abc.news.go.cpm/20/20/story/id.2931404&page

admitted entering a stranger's house, stabbing a sleeping boy multiple times, and fighting with a woman before he left.

Two years later, a new trial was held, Sells' confession was admitted, some of Julia's ex-husband's biased testimony about Julia's emotional well-being was excluded, and Julia testified on her own behalf. After a two-week trial, Julia was found not guilty of all charges.

The case of Julia Rea illustrates the potentially adverse effects of tunnel vision – the premature focus on a criminal suspect to the exclusion of all others. Tunnel vision shapes all subsequent investigatory and prosecutorial decisions. Witness reports are interpreted as validating the culpability of the suspect, forensic evidence is selectively gathered and analyzed, and the prosecutor is presented with a carefully crafted case that supports the guilt of the suspect. Prosecutors typically respond to the public's sense of urgency.[3]

HOW CRIMES ARE SOLVED

More than nine in 10 crimes are solved as a result of the cooperation of the suspect and the subsequent plea bargain. The first goal of the police is to identify a "convictable suspect." Compelling evidence against the accused depends on a coherent, consistent, and integrated narrative of the case. The narrative must be readily understandable and convincing to any potential juror. Jurors tend to be convinced by the eyewitness identification of the offender, particularly by the victim, and/or by the suspect's confession. Ironically, what seems to be the most compelling evidence to the jury – eyewitness identification and confessions – is highly unreliable and most likely to result in a wrongful conviction.

Clearance Rates

Clearance rates refer to the number of crimes for which a suspect has been arrested and charged (Federal Bureau of Investigation [FBI], 2016). Clearance rates provide an approximate measure of the effectiveness of the police carrying out their crime related responsibilities. Police agencies across the country have difficulty in identifying and

---

3. For more information see: Bluhm Legal Clinic, Center on Wrongful Convictions. (n.d.b). Julia Rea. Retrieved from http://www.uis.edu/illinoisinnocenceproject/exonores/jrea/.

arresting criminal offenders. Data from the most recent Federal Bureau of Investigation's Uniform Crime Report (2016) shows that clearance rates are the highest for murder and non-negligent manslaughter (61.5%) and aggravated assault (54%). Other crimes against the person, while not particularly high, rank above crimes against property. Forcible rape is cleared by arrest (37.8%) of the time, while robbery is only cleared in (29.3%) of the cases. The clearance rates for property crimes are markedly lower. Larceny (21.9%) has the highest clearance rate followed by arson (20.7%), burglary (12.9%), and auto theft (13.1%). In sum, only (46%) of violent crimes and (19.4 %) of property crimes result in the arrest of a suspect.

Evidence that the police are meeting their primary responsibility to effectively enforce the law by apprehending criminal suspects is simply missing. While clearance rates are largely unknown to the public, the police nonetheless must demonstrate that they can be trusted to effectively carry out their primary responsibility.

The role of the police then involves the dilemma between waging war against criminal offenders, using whatever means are necessary to subdue the enemy and exercising the reasoned restraint necessary to maintain the trust and confidence of the public (Bittner, 1970). The work of the police often vacillates between the tragically unpredictable and the stiflingly boring. Standing in the rain protecting construction workers on the job, or watching guard over a public park at midday is strikingly different from being suddenly summoned to an armed robbery in progress or a teenager threatening suicide in nearby middle school.

Most police activities are largely invisible carried out in plain view. The routine nature of maintaining order and public safety is so commonplace as to blend into the societal landscape. Yet, the public's expectation is that the police should be engaged in crime prevention and intervention, in the apprehension of criminal suspects and gathering evidence for successful prosecution.

It is the involvement of the police in the processing of crime scenes that is the central concern of this chapter. The public expects that the police will respond to a criminal event quickly, decisively, and convincingly; while maintaining their trust and confidence. The idea is that the offender has been arrested and will soon be convicted and sentenced.

Situational Factors

All crimes comprise a series of situations that flow into one another. The criminal event itself merges into an investigatory process, prosecutorial decision-making, plea bargaining negotiations, or possible jury deliberation and sentencing. The ebb and flow of criminal situations define and redefine themselves. That is, the investigatory process may focus on a particular suspect, which affects the gathering of evidence, eyewitness identification, obtaining a confession, and prosecutorial and judicial decision-making.

Situational factors, noted in the introductory chapter, shape the investigatory process. To Black (1976) the structure of the legal case – who does what to whom – drives the criminal justice response to it. Furthermore, the more invested the police and prosecutors are in the crime control versus due process model of criminal justice, the greater the effect of extra-legal factors on the outcome of the case (Packer, 1968).

As discussed in the introductory chapter, Herbert Packer (1968) has set forth two models to explain the functioning of law enforcement agencies across the country. These models – crime control and due process – embody strikingly different values that underlie law enforcement decision-making. Table 2.1. summarizes the key values of each model.

Table 2.1
PACKER'S CRIME CONTROL AND DUE PROCESS MODELS

Crime Control	*Due Process*
1. Efficiency	1. Reliability of fact finding
2. Speed	2. Equality in access to legal counsel
3. Informality	3. Skepticism
4. Uniformity	4. Morality and Utility
5. Finality	5. Legal Guilt
6. Presumption of Guilt	

When the crime control model takes precedence over the due process model, law enforcement agencies seek a quick, efficient, and final solution for the case. The ponderous skepticism of the due process model is thereby rejected. A process is set in motion that is vulnerable to psychologically induced biases that may well lead to a wrongful conviction.

Tunnel Vision

The urgency to close a criminal case sets in motion a series of investigatory processes. When possible, the victim is considered a prime source of information for the police. As soon as possible, eyewitnesses and other persons who may have information about the crime are also interviewed. The intent is to narrow the scope of the investigation and to identify a credible suspect. Once that suspect is identified and the police are convinced that he/she is "convictable," then the phenomenon of tunnel vision sharpens the investigation.

To Findley and Scott (2006) tunnel vision is a "well-recognized phenomenon in the criminal justice system." Tunnel vision is defined as:

> "that 'compendium of common heuristics and logical fallacies,' to which we are all susceptible, that lead actors in the criminal justice system . . . to focus on a suspect, select and filter the evidence that will 'build a case' for conviction while ignoring or suppressing evidence that points away from guilt." (Findley & Scott, 2006, p. 293)

Tunnel vision then drives the investigatory process, influencing police and prosecutorial perception of the situation, the "convictability" of the suspect, and strategy for securing a conviction. When we are faced with the need to make a decision without delay about an ambiguous matter, we may unwittingly invoke a series of related cognitive biases to assist us. These cognitive biases include: confirmation bias, hindsight bias, and outcome bias. Confirmation bias refers to the tendency to look for information that is consistent with our current perceptions of the situation, to validate what we believe to be true. Once a viable suspect has been identified, the police may seek out evidence that confirms the person's guilt. Tunnel vision shapes the handling of the victim's account of the crime and the ability to identify the offender. The kinds of questions asked to other witnesses or persons with some knowledge about the crime are affected by the need to fit testimonial evidence into a preconceived narrative of the guilt of the accused.

Hindsight Bias

Hindsight bias – "the 'knew-it-all-along effect' – operates as a means through which people project new knowledge – outcomes – into the past, without any awareness that the perception of the past has been tainted by the subsequent information"(Findley & Scott, 2006, p. 10). Our memories are not a detailed recording of what actually happened, what was said, or even the sociophysical context of the event. Instead our memories are reconstructions of past occurrences, a reassembly of the details of a myriad of past experiences, subject to emotional distortions and largely unwitting fabrications (Simon, 2012, pp. 92-95).

Given the limits of memory, caution is warranted in focusing on a particular suspect to the exclusion of all others. Findley and Scott (2006) suggest three ways that hindsight bias may lead the police to focus on an innocent person. First, information about the crime and the suspect is filtered through the prism of inevitability. The police increasingly believe that they have now and always had the "right one." Second, evidence is gathered, shaped and interpreted with the view that the suspect is guilty. Eyewitness, circumstantial, and even physical evidence may be assessed in a way that strengthens the conclusion that the suspect is convictable. For example, the memory of an eyewitness who identifies a criminal suspect or describes the circumstances surrounding a crime are malleable, subject to being altered by the person's interaction with the police. For example, a witness who is uncertain about identifying a suspect from a photo array, or a sequential series of photos may become more confident in their choice when praised by a police officer for their selection. The phrase "we thought you'd pick that guy" may well remove all doubt in the mind of a wavering witness. Certainty about the details of the crime-time of day, lighting of the scene, actions of the suspect-are also enhanced by the hindsight effect, however unwittingly, conveyed by police investigators. Third, when police and prosecutors become convinced that the suspect is guilty, they may well repeat their conclusion. Independent of the truth, the more an assertion is repeated; the more likely it is to be believed (Hertwig, Gigerenze & Hoffrage, 1997, p. 12).

Ratification of Error

Ronald Huff and his colleagues (1996) have identified a common error in judgment that compromises decision-making in formal organizations. Seemingly insignificant errors are often overlooked in the interest of efficiency. These minor errors are soon followed by additional errors intended to cover-up the initial flaws in judgment. Soon a web of errors is constructed, each ratifying those that preceded it. The intractable process of the *Ratification of Error* has been set in motion, too often ending in a wrongful conviction.

To Huff and colleagues (1986) the *Ratification of Error* commonly affects the processing of a criminal case. They observe:

> The criminal justice system, starting with the police investigation of an alleged crime and culminating in appellate courts, tends to ratify errors made at the lower levels of the system. The further the case progresses in the system, the less chance there is that the error will be discovered and corrected, unless it involves a basic issue of constitutional rights and due process. (p. 534)

Coherence Effect

It is a common psychological trait to want to make sense of our life experiences. We want our interpretation of reality to form a comprehensive, coherent whole. Things should fit together. Our experience of cognitive dissonance – being conscious of conflicting thoughts and ideas and their accompanying emotions – is distressing, resulting in the need to reduce its adverse effects.

Often, police investigators must deal with conflicting evidence. The reports of witnesses differ from one another. Victims may be unsure of the details of the crime, the description of the offender, and the circumstances surrounding the event. Faced with seemingly irreconcilable evidence, the investigatory process will be either suspended or a coherent narrative will be developed to identify a viable suspect.

The salience of some evidence is affirmed, other evidence is viewed as less credible. This process is known as the *Coherence Effect*. The *Coherence Effect* is based on the Gestalt psychological model founded by Max Werthemer (1944) who posited:

> The basic thesis of gestalt theory might be formulated thus: there are contexts in which what is happening in the whole cannot be deduced from the characteristics of the separate pieces, but conversely; what happens to a part of the whole is, in clear-cut cases, determined by the laws of the inner structure of its whole. (p. 84)

Put simply, the Coherence Effect then is often summarized as: *what goes together, must fit together* thereby generating an integrated narrative of the crime event. Simon (2012) points out: "The coherence effect is driven by a bidirectional process of reasoning: just as the facts guide the choice of the preferred conclusion, the emergence of that conclusion radiates backwards, and reshapes the facts to become more coherent with it" (p. 34). The suspect's identity becomes increasingly certain. Disparate evidence takes on a level of credibility that focuses the investigatory process. The coherence effect is closely aligned with *confirmatory bias* – the tendency to affirm one's judgment by excluding contradictory evidence. In short, a coherent narrative emerges that is confirmed by the selective attention to the evidence that supports it.

Escalation of Commitment

The need to form a coherent, convincing interpretation of the criminal event drives the investigatory process. To Lofquist (2001), wrongful convictions are often the "product of the normal, day-to-day routine operations of decision-makers acting free of conspiratorial intent or wrongdoing; the outcome was generated by the structures and routines in which actors act" (p. 192).

Sudnow's (1965) concept of "normal crime frameworks" supports Lofquist's argument that wrongful convictions are less the deliberate, premeditated actions of the agents of the criminal justice system and more the consequence of the structural arrangements of the acts in the criminal justice system. To Lofquist (2001) normal crime frameworks refer to the process by which "legal actors – the police, forensic experts, prosecutors, judges – adopt narrative frameworks into which particular crime scenarios are fitted more or less well" (p. 117). That is, normal crime frameworks "shape investigations, assessments of evidence, interpretations of legal rules and the entire range of decisions" (Lofquist, 2001, p. 177).

Eyewitness Misidentification

Paradoxically, eyewitness identification of a criminal suspect, while particularly compelling to a jury, is among the least reliable evidence. Gary Wells, a leading expert on the functioning of memory and eyewitness misidentification, notes that: "Here's a type of evidence that we rely on a lot, yet there is not a big foundation that it's reliable evidence other than the fact that we use it" (as cited in Jost, 2011, p. 855).

Approximately three in four wrongful convictions are the result of an eyewitness misidentification. Brandon Garrett (2011) provides an in-depth analysis of the first 250 DNA exonerations documented by the nation's first Innocence Project founded by Barry Scheck and Peter Neufeld at Yeshiva's Cardozo Law School. Garrett's study shows that 76 percent of the wrongful convictions involved eyewitness misidentification. Yet, testimonial evidence provided by witnesses is crucial to identifying, apprehending, and convicting offenders.

Methods of Eyewitness Identification

Eyewitness Description

Witnesses to criminal events, its victims, and others with information related to the crime are critically important to the investigatory process. Testimonial evidence, however, depends of the ability of the witnesses to recall what actually occurred at the time of the crime. The memories of the witnesses and victims often vary and are subject to decay over time. Memory of a traumatic event are often distorted by the surrounding circumstances – perception of danger, threat of physical injury, lighting, location, and race and age of the victim (Loftus, Doyle & Dysert, 2007; Loftus, 1979).

Witness and victim description of a crime are then dependent on memories often compromised by the event itself as well as the inherent flaws in the process of memory. As previously noted, memory is not a recording but a composite of the details of past occurrences blended with the details of other past experiences and distorted by the trauma of the current situation. Figure 2.1, provides the influences on memory of a criminal event.

Types of Eyewitness Identification

Lineups

Lineups are defined as: "a procedure in which a criminal suspect (or a picture of the suspect) is placed among other people (or picture of other people) and shown to a witness to see if the witness will identify the suspect as the culprit in question" (Wells & Olson, 2003, p. 279). Of course, the suspect may not be the actual criminal offender. There are

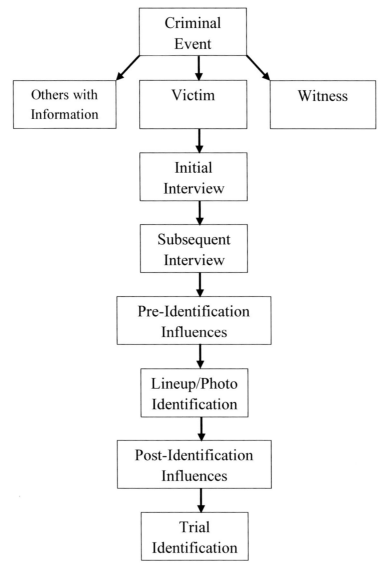

Figure 2.1. Influences of Memory of a Criminal Trial.

two kinds of lineups: simultaneous and sequential. A simultaneous lineup, most common used by the law enforcement agencies, permits witnesses to view all the members of the lineup at the same time. Sequential lineups permit the witness to view only one member of the lineup at a given time.

Factors Influencing the Outcome of the Lineup

Wells and Olson (2003) posit that two kinds of factors – estimator and system – influence the accuracy of witness identifications. Estimator factors involve the characteristics of the crime itself and other influences on its perception by the victim, other eyewitnesses, and persons with particular knowledge of the crime. System factors refer to how the case is processed by the agents of the criminal justice system.

Estimator Factors

Wells and Olson (2003) identify four categories of estimator factors: "(1) characteristics of the witness, (2) characteristics of the event, (3) characteristics of the testimony, and (4) abilities of the testimony evaluators to discriminate between accurate and inaccurate witness testimony." Characteristics of the witness found to influence the accuracy of their eyewitness testimony include: age and race differences between the suspect and the eyewitness. Young adults are better able to identify the actual offender, while children and the elderly are less able to do so. Cross-racial identifications are found to be less accurate than are intra-racial identifications. That is, eyewitnesses more accurately identify an offender of their own race than an offender of a different race. Characteristics of the event include: "the amount of time the culprit is in view, lighting conditions, whether the culprit wears a disguise, the distinctiveness of the culprit's appearance, the presence of absence of a weapon, and the timing of knowledge that one is witnessing a crime" (Wells & Olson, 2003, pp. 280-281). The setting of the crime and the obscurity of the offender affects the witness's ability to later recall details of the criminal event and its perpetrator. The use of a weapon in the commission of the crime tends to traumatize the victim and eyewitnesses, focusing their attention on the weapon itself rather than the offender. The potential for violence compromises the accuracy of subsequent eyewitness identification (as cited in Wells & Olson, 2003, p. 282).

Characteristics of the testimony involve two issues: (1) the certainty of the eyewitness, and (2) the accuracy of the information provided. A tenuous relationship exists between the witness's confidence in their statements and the validity of the information reported to the police. Wells and Bradford (1998, 1999) show that certainty of an eyewitness memory of an event is subject to manipulation. They find that persons who mistakenly identify a person as the true offender when given confirmatory feedback become more convinced of the accuracy of their identification. For example, subtle gestures, a nod, or pleasant facial express confirm the witness's judgment. The certainty-inflation effect is more pronounced among persons who identify an innocent person as the offender than those who identify the true perpetrator (Bradfield, Wells, & Olson, 2002). Lineup identifications are often influenced by the behaviors of the investigators as are the certainty and accuracy of the witness. Because the confidence of witnesses is malleable, the accuracy of their testimony should be viewed with caution.

Beyond the possible influence of the investigator conducting the lineup, the speed of the witness's decision affects the accuracy of the identification. Accurate eyewitness identifications are typically made more quickly than are misidentifications (Dunning & Perretta, 2002). The greater the number of lineup subjects, the more comparisons that are made among the subjects, and the greater the time for investigator influence, the less accurate is the identification (Wells & Olson, 2003, p. 284).

Finally, it is exceedingly difficult to assess the accuracy of witness statements. Simply put, eyewitness testimony tends to be accepted as accurate, particularly by jury members (as cited by Wells & Olson, 2003, p. 285).

System Factors

System factors refer to the manner in which the police seek to identify a possible criminal offender. This process depends on the ability of crime witnesses to provide information needed to single out a viable criminal suspect. Police rely on various methods of offender identification to assist in the process of witness identification. Lineups may include the suspect or only persons who did not commit the crime (fillers). If the lineup does not include the criminal suspect, then the witnesses must rely on their memory to construct a "most likely" offender. Wells and Olson (2003) point out that this relative judgment decision strategy prompts the witness "to select a person from the lineup who most resembles the eyewitness's memory of the culprit relative to the other lineup members" (p. 286). Culprit-absent lineups are far less reliable than when the culprit is actually in the lineup.

Wells and Olson (2003) have identified four categories of system variables related to the lineup process: instructions, content, presentation methods, and behavioral influences (p. 285). Instructions given to witnesses are vitally important to the accuracy of their identification. Witnesses who are told that the suspect "may or, may not be present" are far less likely to mistakenly identify the suspect. Steblay (1997) reports that witness misidentification is reduced by 41.6 percent when told that the suspect may not be in the lineup, compared to only 1.9 percent when they believed the suspect was actually in the lineup.

The content of the lineup – the inclusion of persons who did not commit the crime (fillers) – markedly affects the accuracy of the identification. Wells and Olson (2003) caution that: "Ideally, lineup fillers would be chosen so that an innocent suspect is not mistakenly identified merely from 'standing out,' and so a culprit does not escape identification merely from blending in" (p. 287). Studies of lineup content have shown mixed results. When witnesses have provided a description of a suspect to the police, the lineup may include fillers who closely resemble the description or persons who are strikingly different in appearance. Witnesses tend to mistakenly identify a suspect who most closely resembles their description of the culprit. However, the characteristics of the fillers do not affect the identification of the actual offender (Lindsay, Wells, & Rumpel, 1981). It is, of course, possible that the similarity in appearance between an innocent person and the offender may occur by chance alone, resulting in the misidentification of the offender (Wells & Olson, 2003, p. 287).

The method used to present the lineup participants to a witness also affects the likelihood of a false identification. Two forms of lineup presentations are typically used: *simultaneous and sequential.* Simultaneous lineup present the suspect and fillers to the witness at the same time. The witness then must rely on a relative-judgment decision to identify the suspect. That is, the witness must decide on an offender in comparison with the other possibilities in the lineup. In a sequential lineup, however, the members of the lineup are presented to the witness one at a time. The witness then must decide if the person is the offender. Sequential lineups rely on the witness's "absolute judgment" rather than a "relative judgment" that the person is the offender (Wells & Olson, 2003, p. 288). Sequential lineups are viewed as preferable to their simultaneous counterparts (Lindsay & Wells, 1985).

Finally, the behavior of the administrator of the lineup markedly affects the validity of the witness's identification of the suspect. If the lineup administrator knows the identity of the suspect, then cues may be given to the witness that the witness has made a correct identification. The verbal or nonverbal response to the witness's choice serves to alter the subsequent processing of the case. Witnesses innocent of any criminal liability typically want to cooperate and to seek approval for helping solve the crime. Appreciation by the police is reward enough for a victim or witness to a crime.

The dangers of unintentional witness-police complicity must be guarded against. The double-blind method of lineup administration is a highly recommended strategy to reduce the behavioral effects of the lineup administrator. Simply put, the double-blind method means that the person conducting the lineup does not know the identity of the suspect: therefore, s/he is unable to influence the witness's decision.

UNITED STATES SUPREME COURT DECISIONS AFFECTING EYEWITNESS IDENTIFICATIONS

Justice William Brennan (cited in Garrett, 2011) notes: "There is nothing more convincing than a live human being who takes the stand, points a finger at the defendant, and says 'That's the one!'" (p. 2). The United States Supreme Court in the landmark ruling *Manson v. Braithwaite,* 432 U.S. 98 (1977) held that "reliability is the linchpin" for the possible contamination of eyewitness identification. Yet, the question remains: how can reliability of an eyewitness' identification be determined? Eyewitness identifications may be compromised at various stages of the investigatory process. The police may have a suspect in mind when the initial witness interviews take place, and thereby influencing the witness's description of the suspect. During the lineup phase of the evidence gathering, the police, as we have seen, may inadvertently or otherwise, influence the identification of the suspect. Post-identification procedures are often subject to further suggestion by the police. Wells and Quinlivan's (2009) analysis of the eyewitness post-identification feedback effect concludes that:

> The post-identification feedback effect is robust and has profound forensic implications because the courts rely on witnesses' answers to these questions to make decisions about the reliability of the iden-

tification. The effect seems to occur because there is not an accessible memory trace formed about these retrospective judgments, thereby making witnesses rely on an inference process that responds to the feedback. (p. 1153)

Two questions were addressed by the Court in *Manson*. First, whether the process in obtaining the identification was "unnecessarily suggestive." Second, even if the procedures were suggestive, was the identification "reliable." That is, if suggestive procedures were used by the police, did they result in "a substantial likelihood of irreparable misidentification" (*Manson v. Braithwaite*, 432 U.S. 98, 97 (1977)). The Court in *Manson* followed the criteria for reliability set forth in *Neil v. Biggers*, 409 U.S. 199-200 (1972). In *Manson* the Court considered whether or not the Due Process Clause of the Fourteenth Amendment prohibits the inclusion of suggestive and unnecessary evidence in the absence of its reliability at trial. Table 2.2 summarizes the criteria for reliability established in *Manson v. Brathwaite*.

The Court ruled in *Manson* that an identification of a suspect made by a narcotics officer following an attempted narcotics buy from a single photo provided by a fellow police officer, while possibly suggestive, was nonetheless reliable, and thereby admissible in court.

Brandon Garrett (2011) provides a critical analysis of the criteria for reliability set forth in *Biggers* and *Manson*. Garrett finds that the five reliability factors identified in Manson are inadequate predictors of the ability of the witness to make an accurate identification. Rather, being able to recall the details of a criminal event and characteristics of the suspect are vitally important to a successful criminal investigation.

Garrett considers the effect of faulty memory and police suggestibility on the criteria for reliability set forth in *Manson*.[4] The *passage of time* criterion is certainly important, but if the police limit the number of identifications to those made soon after the crime, then a considerable number of suspects would be lost to the investigation. Central reliability factors identified in *Manson* – accuracy of the prior description of the criminal, the validity of the witness's initial recall of the suspect's physical characteristics, the witness's degree of attention, and the initial certainty of identification are not found to be independent measures of reliability. Rather, each of these factors is affected by the procedural methods used by the police, and their interaction with the witness

---

4. See Table 2.2–*Mason v. Braithwaite* Criteria for Reliability.

Table 2.2
MANSON V. BRATHWAITE 432 U.S. 98 (1977)
Criteria for Reliability

1. The opportunity to view
2. The degree of attention
3. The accuracy of the description
4. The witness' level of certainty
5. The time between the crime and the confrontation

(Garrett, 2011). Both estimator and system variables may compromise an eyewitness's identification independent of the guidance provided by the *Manson* reliability factors[5].

False Confessions

That anyone would falsely confess to committing a crime appears absurd. Yet, more than 25 percent of DNA exonerations reported by the Innocence Project in New York are found to involve the false confession of the accused. The National Registry for Exonerations at the University of Michigan finds that 18 percent of homicide exonerations are the result, in part, of false confessions. False confessions are the third leading cause of a wrongful conviction, following eyewitness misidentifications (75%) and flawed forensic evidence (50%) (Innocence Project, n.d.k).

The Reid Interrogation Technique

A defendant's confession is understandably compelling to the jury. Any attempt by the defendant to retract his confession is met with resistance by the prosecutor and the court. Police and prosecutors then find eyewitness testimony and confessions by the suspect to be particularly sought after forms of evidence. The *Reid Technique* is the principal method for interrogating a suspect in the United States.[6] Founded in 1947 by John E. Reid, a former Chicago police officer who became a polygraph expert, the Reid Technique is used by more than 18,000 police agencies across the United States alone and in Canada, Europe and Asia ("Company Information," n.d.). The process begins with an interview of the suspect to determine the extent of his criminal liability. Depending on the credibility of the evidence linking the suspect to the

---

5. See Chapter 6 for an additional discussion of *Manson* and *Biggers*.
6. See Table 2.3 on the Reid Technique.

crime, the interview may be relatively brief. Once the police are confident that the suspect is the true offender, then the Reid interrogation strategy is employed.

The Reid Technique is designed to progressively "breakdown" the suspect's denial of guilt and, ultimately, to secure his written confession. The setting for the interrogation should be small, private, and set apart from any interference. The room itself is sparsely furnished, without distractions of any kind. The intent is to create a controlled environment that focuses attention on the suspect. In the first phase of the interrogation, the suspect is unequivocally accused of the crime. The interrogators convey that they are convinced of the suspect's guilt and the evidence overwhelmingly supports their conclusion. The second phase builds on the theme of guilt and the active erosion of any attempt by the suspect to deny committing the crime. In the final stage of the interrogation, the investigators guide the suspect toward accepting the "truth" and confessing to the crime. This stage culminates in a confession, written and agreed to by the suspect. Table 2.3 summarizes the Reid Technique's nine-step process.[7]

Types of False Confessions

Kassin and Wrightman (1985) initially identified three types of false confessions: *voluntary, coerced-compliant,* and *coerced-internalized. Voluntary false confessions* typically involve innocent persons claiming they have committed highly publicized crimes to gain an identity, albeit negative, for their actions. Other reasons for a voluntary false confession include the need to resolve guilt from past behaviors, the protection of the actual perpetrator or a distorted sense of reality, common among persons with certain forms of mental illness (Kassin & Wrightman, 1985).

Coerced-compliant false confessions result from an intense interrogation of a suspect. To alleviate the unbearable stress from unrelenting demands for an admission of guilt, the suspect ultimately confesses to the crime. Short-term benefits for confessing may include: sleep, food, access to a phone, the chance to be released from custody, and for an addict access to their drug of choice (Gudjonsson, 2003). The desire for

---

7. For more information see: Buckley, J. P. (n.d.). The Reid Technique of interviewing and interrogation. Retrieved from http;//law.wisc.edufjr/clinicals/ip/wcjsc/files/buckley_chapter_on_reid_techniques.doc.

Table 2.3
REID TECHNIQUE - NINE STEP PROCESS

First Step-Direct Positive Confrontation	Involves directly confronting the suspect with a statement that it is known that he or she committed the crime. Often, the police lie and describe nonexistent evidence that points to the suspect as the offender.
Second Step-Theme Development	A theme is developed that minimizes the moral responsibility of the suspect. The interrogator may sympathize with the suspect, talk about possible leniency of the court, or provide an excuse for committing the crime. However, the evidence is reported to be overwhelming; denials are rejected.
Third Step-Handling Denials	Involves interrupting the suspect's denials of guilt.
Fourth Step-Overcoming Objections	Involves rejecting a suspect's excuses or explanations. Once the guilty suspect feels that objections are not getting him or her anywhere, he or she becomes quiet and shows signs of withdrawal from active participation. When the suspect becomes withdrawn, the interrogator acts quickly so as to not lose the psychological advantage.
Fifth Step-Procurement and Retention of the Suspect's Attention	To interrupt the withdrawal of the suspect, the interrogation becomes increasingly intense. Angry outburst and intimidation techniques are commonly directed toward the accused.
Sixth Step-Handling the Suspect's Passive Mood	Sympathetic appeals are made to the suspect. The emotional advantages of "telling the truth" are emphasized.
Seventh Step-Presenting an Alternative Question	Two alternative explanations for the commission of the crime are presented to the suspect, one less blameworthy than the other. While not directly stated, the implication is that the more morally defensible reason for the crime will result in a less severe sentence.

Continued on next page

Table 2.3 – *continued*

Eighth Step- Having the Suspect Orally Relate Various Details of the Offense	With only one interrogator in the room, the suspect is encouraged to talk about details of the crime, thereby providing evidence of his culpability.
Ninth Step-Converting the Oral Statement to a Written Statement	Following the suspect's admission of criminal liability, a written confession is quickly obtained. Some police agencies use video and/or audio recordings of the confession, while others rely only on a written version of the confession.

relief from an unbearable situation and the prospect of immediate comfort provide strong motivations for falsely confessing to a crime.

Internalized false confessions occur when memory of involvement in a criminal event is planted in the mind of a suspect. The interrogators create the suspect's distrust of his own memory. The suspect becomes increasing unsure of his possible involvement in the crime. The police interrogators, however, are convinced of the suspect's guilt. The suspect's dilemma is only resolved by confessing to the crime.

To Ofshe and Leo (1997) compliant false confessions should be separated into *stress-compliant* and *coerced-compliant*. And, persuaded false confessions should be considered as *coerced persuaded and non-coerced persuaded.* Even the term "coerced" has been replaced by "pressured" to more accurately describe the process of interrogating the suspect (as cited in Leo, 2010). While attempts have been made to refine Kassin and Wrightman's original typology, Leo (2010) concludes that: "It is important to understand that there are three conceptually distinct psychological processes at work in the production and elicitation of false confessions" (p. 200).

Persons Most Vulnerable to Falsely Confessing

Leading researchers in the field of false confessions cite two factors –the suspect's age and mental disorder–that predispose a suspect to falsely confessing to a crime (Kassin, Drizin, Griso, Gudjonsson, Leo, & Redlich, 2010). In a study of persons who were exonerated following falsely confessing, 44 percent were juveniles and 69 percent were mentally challenged (Gross, Jacoby, Matheson, Montgomery, & Patel, 2005). Drizin and Leo (2004) report that 35 percent of false confessions were made by persons 18 years of age or younger, and 55 percent of these persons were under the age of 15. Juveniles are developmentally unable to withstand an intense police scrutiny. Typically, they know less about their constitutional rights and the workings of the criminal justice system. Juveniles tend to be more easily intimidated by the interrogation process, more given to believe the benevolence of the police, and are susceptible to separation anxiety that may accompany being isolated from their parents.

Persons who are psychologically impaired are even more disadvantaged during a police interrogation. The disadvantages of youth are more pronounced for persons with emotional and intellectual limitations. Persons who are unable to reason effectively, to cope with a confusing and threatening situation, and to articulate a viable defense are prone to falsely confessing to a crime. As a consequence, the U. S. Supreme Court in *Atkins v. Virginia* (2002), recognizing the distinct possibility that intellectually challenged persons would falsely confess to a crime, ruled to exclude them from the death penalty.

INVESTIGATORY REFORMS

Eyewitness Identification-Lineups

The potential for flawed eyewitness identifications have long been recognized. The American Psychological Association's Law Society's review of the scientific literature on lineups and photo presentations of criminal suspects notes three themes: (1) "relative-judgment processes, (2) lineups-as-experiments analogy, and (3) confidence malleability" (Wells & Bradfield, 1998, p. 603). Relative-judgment processes refer to the tendency for a witness to compare suspects in a lineup and to choose the suspect who most closely resembles their memory of the criminal offender. Lineups-as-experiments means that police conduct lineups as if they were a scientific experiment. That is, they hypothesize that the suspect committed the crime and then design an experiment to test the hypothesis. The experiment may be a physical lineup or photo array of suspects, and may be presented to the witness simultaneously or sequentially. In addition, the interaction between the police and the suspect may also influence the witness's identification of a suspect. Verbal or nonverbal cues may be intentionally or unwittingly provided to the witness. These confounds of the experiment may markedly affect its outcome. Finally, confidence malleability means that the witness's confidence may change following their initial in the identification of the suspect. Interaction with the police and prosecutors may engender a cooperative spirit and desire to please them.

To counter the impact of these three themes running through the scientific literature on faulty eyewitness identification, The American Psychological Association proposed four rules to be followed by agents of the criminal justice system:

Rule 1: *The person who conducts the lineup or photospread should not be aware of which member of the lineup or photospread is the suspect.*

Rule 2: *Witnesses should be told explicitly that the person in question might not be in the lineup or photospread and therefore should not feel that they must make an identification. They should also be told that the person administering the lineup does not know which person is the suspect in the case.*

Rule 3: *The suspect should not stand out in the lineup or photospread as being different from the distracters based on the eyewitness's previous description of the culprit or based on other factors that would draw extra attention to the suspect.*

Rule 4: *A clear statement should be taken from the eyewitness at the time of the identification and prior to any feedback as to his or her confidence that the identified person is the actual culprit (Wells et al., 1998).*

More recently, Smalarz and Wells (2015) set forth strategies for conducting lineups that decrease process contamination and thereby increase the accuracy of witness identifications. Their proposals, largely in accord with the recommendations of the American Psychological Association, are: (1) to select the nonsuspects in the lineup who are similar in appearance to the suspect, (2) to instruct the witness that the suspect may not be in the lineup, (3) to reduce preidentification contamination, a video or at least an audio record of the witness's initial identification of the suspect should be made, and (4) a double-blind method should be used whereby the person conducting the lineup does not know who the suspect is (Smalarz & Wells, 2015, p.123).

The double-blind method serves to blunt the effects of common psychological bias inherent in any decision-making process. Decision-making by agents of the criminal justice system then is subject to the same psychological biases that affect us in everyday life. Confirmation bias, hindsight bias, tunnel vision markedly affects the processing of a criminal case. Specific training should be provided to police officers responsible for gathering evidence from suspects, victims, and witnesses. Awareness of common psychological biases in the processing information and forming conclusions may serve to guard against the pursuit of an innocent suspect.

Confessions–Recording the Interrogation

The process of interrogating a suspect takes place in an isolated, confined, and highly controlled environment. As a consequence the suspect is at a distinct disadvantage, making him more prone to falsely confessing to a crime. Transparency then is widely recognized as the key to reducing false confessions. Kassin and his colleagues (2010) recommend that: "custodial interviews and interrogations of felony suspects should be videotaped in their entirety and with a camera angle that focuses equally on the suspect and interrogator" (p. 25). Simultaneously videotaping the suspect and interrogator provides a more accurate depiction of the nuances of the interrogation process. Deceptive and intimidating tactics of the interrogators are recorded as are evasive and unconvincing responses of the suspect. Prosecutors and defense attorneys; judges and jurors are able to assess the voluntariness and reliability of the confession.

Interrogation Strategies

As we have discussed earlier, the Reid Technique–the most widely used interrogation strategy used in the United States–is largely confrontational and designed to elicit a confession from the person believed to have committed the crime. The use of the Reid Technique does result in a confession at a remarkably high rate, justifying law enforcement's decades'-long commitment to its use and resistance to abandon it. However, the voluntariness and reliability of the confessions elicited present a due process dilemma for the criminal justice system. The central question is: are confessions obtained during a high stress, confrontation interrogation given voluntarily with an under-standing of its legal consequences? The strikingly high number of wrongful convictions that result from false confessions signals the need to devise an alternative interrogation strategy.

PACE

In 1984, the United Kingdom passed legislation that established an alternative to a confrontational method of police interrogation. The Police and Criminal Evidence Act (PACE) required that suspect inter-views be audio recorded, suspects be represented by legal counsel, and detention before being charged be limited. In addition, police were for-bidden to lie to a suspect or to engage in deceitful tactics to elicit a confession.

The Police Criminal and Evidence Act prompted the need for fur-ther training of law enforcement officers responsible for interviewing criminal suspects. The PEACE method was developed to provide police officers with the detailed guidance necessary to carry out reli-able and legally defensible interviews. PEACE refers to *Planning* and *Preparation, Engage* and *Explain, Account, Closure,* and *Evaluate.* The *Prep-aration* and *Planning* is a critically important phase of the interview pro-cess. What is known about the crime and the possible involvement of the suspect is reviewed and the specific objectives of the interview are established. The sociocultural characteristics of the suspect are consid-ered, as are any physical or psychological disabilities. In addition, the physical location of the interview, equipment needed, and time that has elapsed between the suspect being taken into custody and the pos-sible criminal charge must be considered.

The purpose of the *Engage* and *Explain* phase of the interview is to establish a rapport with the suspect, to start a conversation about what the suspect may know about the crime. The focus is on the facts surrounding the criminal event, rather than culpability of the suspect. In short, the police want to know as much information as possible about the crime. The police are asking the suspect to explain what he knows about the crime to assist them in the investigation. A highly detailed written account of the interview is then prepared that covers the range of topics considered, the physical gestures of the suspect (i.e., signs of agreement or disagreement), and documented evidence of the suspect's criminal involvement.

During the *Accounting, Clarification,* and *Challenge* phase of the interview, active-listening is used to engage the suspect in the process of exploring detailed information about the crime itself. The suspect is prompted to answer questions about the sequence of events involved in the commission of the crime, the interaction among the culprit, victim, witnesses, and the possible reason for their presence at the scene of the crime. The questions are designed to give the interviewer control over the exchange with the suspect. Vague answers are challenged; clear and complete answers are the interviewer's objective.

In the *Closure* phase, the interviewer summarizes the suspect's recounting of the crime. The intent is to resolve any discrepancies between the intent of the suspect and the perceptions of the interviewer. A mutual understanding of the substance of the interview is essential to its meaningful closure.

The PEACE method of interviewing emphasizes an exploratory dialogue, rather than the confrontational approach of the Reid technique. The PEACE method then is designed to take into account the vulnerability of youth, the psychologically and emotionally compromised, and the disadvantages of racial and cultural minorities.

CONCLUSION

Wrongful convictions then are not aberrations. They do not inexplicably disrupt the administration of justice without warning only to fade from public view. Rather wrongful convictions emerge from the web of patterned, predictable investigatory processes that, for the most part, result in a defensible criminal justice outcome.

This chapter has considered the influences on the investigatory process that increase the likelihood of a wrongful conviction. Police are faced with a daunting task-to determine whether a crime has been committed, gather evidence, identify and apprehend a suspect, and present a convincing case to the prosecutor. Yet, the National Criminal Victimization survey (2015) reports that, excluding murder and manslaughter, considerably less than half of the felonies committed in the United States are reported to the police. The National Crime Victimization Survey finds that 46.5 percent of violent crimes and 34.6 percent of property crimes are reported to the police (Truman & Morgan, 2016). Further, the police report strikingly low rates of arrest for those crimes known to them (Federal Bureau of Investigation [FBI], 2016).

A sense of urgency and futility mark the efforts of the police. Public response to crime typically makes far more demands on the police than they can adequately meet. As a consequence police agencies tend to adopt the Herbert Packer's *Crime Control* model to expedite their investigatory efforts. Emphasis is placed on efficiency, finality, and the presumption of guilty in resolving a crime. Of less concern are the tenets of the *Due Process* model, which seeks to ensure the constitutional safeguards of the accused, skepticism about the evidence, and the presumption of the suspect's innocence.

This chapter reviews both estimator and systemic problems in the investigatory process. Estimator effects refer to the characteristics of the crime itself and the perceptions of its victims. Estimator effects lead to systemic problems. Inherent in the crime control model are systemic problems that may well compromise the investigatory process. Evidence provided by victims and eyewitnesses during interviews, the lineup and photo array identifications may be influenced by the methods of questioning and the manner of presentation to the witness. The systemic flaws in the processing of a criminal case will benefit from procedural and policy reforms.

We have also considered psychological biases, common to all of us when making an important decision. We would like to believe that our decision was correct, that it is the only one that made sense. Psychological biases that confirm our decision (*confirmation bias*); that in hindsight indicate that our choice was right from the very beginning (*hindsight bias*); and that all the credible evidence supports our conclusion (*tunnel vision*) unwittingly shape an investigator's decision-making. Once recognized, these psychological pitfalls in our decision-making can be consciously guarded against. Police training programs can specifically address these biases and provide the necessary psychological strategies to combat their effects.

A significant obstacle to reform is the autonomous, loosely organized, and largely fragmented array of criminal justice agencies across the country. Widespread adoption of procedural reform is typically met with skepticism at best and retrenchment at worst. Raising the specter of bias in the investigatory process may also be viewed as an attempt to undermine the integrity of the law enforcement community.

Nonetheless, the need to expeditiously confront criminal behavior should be balanced against ensuring the constitutional safeguards of the accused. A cautious and skeptical approach should be an integral part of the investigative process. To the extent that a balance is not struck, wrongful convictions may ensue. It is against this backdrop that we will next consider the prosecution of a criminal case.

Chapter 3

FORENSIC ANALYSIS

The forensic science system, encompassing both research and practice, has serious problems that can only be addressed by a national commitment to overhaul the current structure that supports the forensic science community in this country. This can only be done with effective leadership at the highest levels of both federal and state governments, pursuant to national standards.

– National Academy of Sciences, 2009

THE CASE OF CURTIS MCCARTY AND JOYCE GILCHRIST

In 1986, Curtis Edward McCarty was convicted of the 1982 murder of Pamela Willis. Eighteen-year-old Willis was found stabbed, nude, and strangled in an Oklahoma City home, where she was living with a friend. At the crime scene, hairs, a footprint, sperm and scrapings found under the victim's fingernails were collected by the police. McCarty soon became a suspect, because of his relationship with the victim. McCarty, however, was not arrested until 1985. Before his arrest, forensic scientist Joyce Gilchrist, an Oklahoma City Police chemist, compared hairs from the crime scene to McCarty's, finding that the hairs were not similar. Even after Gilchrist's findings, police continued to interview McCarty. Eventually, Gilchrist altered her notes and reversed her findings, now claiming that the hairs could have been McCarty's.

McCarty's trial began in March of 1986. The prosecution relied on Gilchrist's testimony. Based upon the hairs in evidence, Gilchrist claimed that McCarty "was in fact" at the crime scene. Gilchrist also found that, McCarty's blood type matched the sperm found on Willis's body (Innocence Project, n.d.j). McCarty was convicted and sentenced to death.

Two years after McCarty's conviction, the Oklahoma Supreme Court overturned his conviction because of improper forensic comments stated by Gilchrist. Gilchrist again testified for the state, explaining there was a match between the hairs. McCarty was convicted and again sentenced to death. Later in 1995, as a result of improper jury instructions in the second trial, an appellate court upheld McCarty's conviction but ordered a new sentencing hearing. In 1996, a new jury sentenced McCarty to his third death sentence.

In 2000, Gilchrist was brought under investigation for falsifying reports in other cases. McCarty's attorneys also discovered that Gilchrist's original notes had been changed. On appeal, Gilchrist was asked to reexamine the hair evidence, which she stated would be suitable for DNA testing. However, Gilchrist claimed the hairs were lost or destroyed. She was subsequently fired due to forensic fraud found in several of her cases, including those of Jeffrey Todd Pierce (Innocence Project, n.d.j) and Robert Miller (Innocence Project, 2007a) whom were also exonerated. Over her 20-year career, Gilchrist is stated to have testified in thousands of cases and was the lead forensic analyst in 23 cases resulting in a death sentence (Innocence Project, 2007a).

McCarty's attorneys were able to test the sperm recovered from the victim in 2002. The test indicated that the sperm did not match McCarty. In 2005, the Innocence Project secured a new trial for McCarty, after an evidentiary hearing ruled that Gilchrist's misconduct had contaminated McCarty's conviction. In 2007, other DNA evidence recovered from the victim's fingernails and a bloody footprint found on the victim's body were determined to have come from someone other than McCarty.

After 22 years of wrongful incarceration in Oklahoma prisons and jails, with more than 19 of those years spent on death row, Curtis McCarty was released from state custody on May 11, 2007. Barry Scheck, co-director of the Innocence Project, stated that, "This is by far one of the worst cases of law enforcement misconduct in the history of the American criminal justice system" (Innocence Project, 2007a). McCarty, an innocent person, was sentenced to death three times, in part, by a fraudulent analyst.

NOT A RARE PHENOMENON

Unfortunately, cases such as Joyce Gilchrist are not unique. There have been other infamous figures that have been known for forensic mishandling and fraud. For example, the testimony of Fred Zain, a police serologist, who spent 14 years in West Virginia and Texas, resulted in hundreds of convictions. In November of 1993, the West Virginia State's Supreme Court ordered a review of every case, where a current prisoner was serving time based on Zain's testimony (Hansen, 1994).

Lone analysts working at the state level are not the only culprits of forensic fraud. Multiple errors have also been found in the FBI's crime lab in Washington, D.C. In 2004, The Department of Justice's Office of the Inspector General identified multiple sources of errors in the FBI crime lab when conducting an investigation concerning the Brandon Mayfield case (OIG, 2006). Mayfield was a United States citizen, whose fingerprints the FBI claimed matched one of the fingerprints found on a bag containing detonators in the March 11, 2001 terrorist attack in Madrid, Spain. This error led to an innocent man being detained until the fingerprints were matched with the actual perpetrator (Cole, 2005; Gabel, 2014). Later in 2004, Stephen Cowans was exonerated after being wrongfully convicted of shooting a Boston police officer. After serving almost seven years in prison, it was discovered that the Boston Police Department crime lab misidentified the fingerprint as Cowans's (Cole, 2005; Saltzman & Daniel, 2004). Stephan Cowans became the first person to be convicted by fingerprint evidence and exonerated by DNA evidence in the state of Massachusetts (Cole, 2005). Among the more disturbing is the case of the five state troopers who pled guilty in New York for repeatedly planting fingerprints in criminal cases between 1992 and 1995 (Goldin, 1995; Perez-Pena, 1997; Westervelt & Humphrey, 2001).

Flawed testimony also contributes to several wrongful convictions. In April of 2015, *The Washington Post* reported that the Department of Justice and Federal Bureau of Investigation have acknowledged that almost every examiner in their forensic unit gave flawed testimony concerning hair comparisons (Spencer, 2015). At the state level, chemist Annie Dookhan in Massachusetts was found responsible for manipulating evidence to obtain false positives in more than 40,000 drug cases in which she provided flawed testimony (Ellement, 2015; Lavoie,

2013). Dookhan analyzed 500 samples per month, compared to an average 50 to 150 samples a month for a typical lab chemist. One of her supervisors reported that she tended to confirm drug substances without using a microscope (Peters, 2013), a clear violation of protocol. Her misconduct resulted in thousands of drug convictions over a nine- year period in Massachusetts.

Unreliability of expert evidence and testimony is not a new phenomenon. In one of the earliest studies concerning wrongful conviction, Borchard (1932) mentioned, "[t]he unreliability of so-called 'expert' evidence" is one of the common contributing factors leading to a wrongful conviction" (Borchard, 1932, p. xix). Nonetheless, there has been little research focusing on forensic science as a contributing cause to wrongful convictions (Cole & Thompson, 2013). The development of DNA testing in the mid-1980s further exposed the unreliability and inaccuracies of expert testimony (Cole & Thompson, 2013; Garrett & Neufeld, 2009). The undisputed accuracy of DNA evidence was used by two prominent attorneys Peter Neufeld and Berry Scheck to expose incidents of wrongful conviction (Cole & Thompson, 2013). Neufeld and Scheck seized the opportunity to establish the actual innocence of the wrongfully convicted. In 1992, they established the first Innocence Project at Yeshiva University. In 2000, the Innocence Project teamed up with the Center for Wrongful Convictions and formed the Innocence Network (Cole & Thompson, 2013; Godsey & Pulley, 2003).

According to recent estimates, from 1989-2012 in the United States, post-conviction DNA testing was the basis for 37 percent of wrongful convictions (Gross & Shaffer, 2012). The National Registry of Exonerations included 2,061 exonerees, 24 percent of these cases involved false or misleading forensic evidence.[1] On the other hand, according to the Innocence Project's first 325 DNA exonerations, unvalidated or improper forensic evidence was found in 47 percent of the cases (n.d.k).

---

1. As of July 10, 2017, for more information see: the National Registry of Exonerations. Retrieved from http://www.law.umich.edu/special/exoneration/Pages/detaillist. aspx?View={faf6eddb-5a68-4f8f-8a52-2c61f5bf9ea7}&SortField=F_x002f_ MFE&SortDir=Asc&FilterField1=F_x002f_MFE&FilterValue1=8_F%2FMFE.

FLAWED FORENSIC PROCEDURES

Insufficient Universal Standards
and Biased Interpretations

Interestingly enough, the development of forensic science has been described as a double-edged sword. It has exposed miscarriages of justice and has been the reason for these injustices (Cole & Thompson, 2013). A report published in 2009 by the National Academy of Sciences (NAS) announced that forensic analysis lack scientific validation (NAS, 2009). If the forensic sciences remain unvaildated, flawed forensic evidence will continue to be used to convict the innocent. Currently, there are several reasons for the perpetuation of flawed forensic science. The lack of universal standards for forensic laboratories around the country makes it difficult to compare findings across jurisdictions.

Forensic science includes an assortment of individuals, disciplines, laboratories, and practices with no single governing agency to establish universal standards for practice (Cole, 2014). Furthermore, some states do not require labs to be accredited, ensuring that the lab is monitored and reviewed (Gabel, 2014). Without an inspection and universal laboratory standards, differing practices, inconsistent procedures and the lack of accountability may well lead to wrongful convictions. The reputation of a forensic analyst and insufficient oversight of misconduct may also contribute to forensic misbehavior. The Dookhan case exemplifies how the desire for a reputation can lead to misconduct. For professional recognition, Annie Dookhan falsified or took shortcuts with testing to enhance her reputation as an exemplary forensic analyst (Murphy & Lavoie, 2012).

There have also been several instances where justice officials, instead of admitting wrongdoings and informing the appropriate participants of their wrongdoings, have hidden their misconduct. For example, in the 1990s the Department of Justice's Office of Inspector General examined cases processed by the FBI crime lab, which revealed sloppy work by examiners that produced unreliable forensic evidence (Bromwich, 1997). The investigation lasted nine years, but the information was only released to the prosecutors in the affected cases.

According to legal and constitutional obligations, the Department of Justice is not required to inform defendants about compromised evidence directly; even though this information could have led to an exoneration. For example, Donald E. Gates was imprisoned 28 years for the rape and murder of Catherine Schilling, a twenty-one-year-old college student. Gates maintained his innocence, but based on FBI agent Michael P. Malone's testimony on hair analysis he was found guilty. Prior to Gate's exoneration in 1997, Agent Malone was specifically targeted for his faulty work in an Office of Inspector General's report, revealing wrongdoings and improper practices within the FBI (Bromwich, 1997). The prosecutor withheld the Office of Inspector General's report and information concerning agent Malone's flawed analysis for 12 years (Hsu, 2012). Gates was exonerated in 2012 when this information became known to his defense team.

The location of the forensic crime lab and its relationship to law enforcement agencies may also affect the validity of its findings. Crime laboratories were developed in the 1920s in the United States as an adjunct to police departments (Giannelli, 2010). According to a survey in 1983 on crime labs conducted by Peterson and colleagues, approximately 80 percent of 300 crime laboratories in the United States were located within law enforcement and public safety agencies, and 57 percent of the laboratories would only examine evidence submitted by law enforcement officials (Giannelli, 2007a). In many locales both the police and prosecutor provide oversight for forensic labs (Hsu, 2012). This provides a convenient relationship between justice officials, both geographically and financially (Gabel, 2014). However, not all justice actors (e.g., prosecutors, law enforcement agencies, and defense) have equal access to forensic services. For example, a defense team typically does not receive the same cost-free access as prosecutors for crime lab services (Gabel, 2014). Furthermore, most states do not routinely fund indigent defendants with access to forensic experts. Although there is a strong argument that under *Ake v. Oklahoma (1985)* an indigent defendant should be entitled to forensic analyses as a matter of due process; however, courts routinely deny funds to cover the expenses (Garrett & Neufeld, 2009).

The lack of independent laboratories may result in misconduct, bias findings and is a great concern (Laurin, 2013). For example, the case of Fred Zain, the West Virginia state crime analyst who became widely known for his forensic misconduct (Chan, 1994). Zain routinely favored the prosecution and even after he left the state to take a position in the San Antonio crime laboratory, prosecutors from West Virginia would send him evidence to retest, assuming West Virginia serologists were incapable of reaching the "right" results (Giannelli, 2010). This is an example of motivational bias, in which there is a subconscious preference toward a specific result, Zain wanting the prosecutor to win (Giannelli, 2010).

Cognitive bias may also exist with police and prosecutors that affect the judgement of the forensic analysts. Cognitive bias refers to an individual's perception of their role in the criminal justice system. This group phenomenon means that a person's norms, attitudes and values are influenced by their socialization in an occupational setting (Singer, 1981). Therefore, a forensic scientist may view their role as being a part of the prosecution's team and not as an independent scientist (Giannelli, 2010). Again, their objective is to help the prosecutor win, is based on a misunderstanding of their role as an independent scientist. For example, the Inspector General Report on the Oklahoma City bombing, illustrates how the FBI laboratory's explosive unit "tilted [the evidence] in such a way as to incriminate the defendants" (Bromwich, 1997). In the end, the entanglement of science and law enforcement may result in different forms of bias leading to forensic misconduct and may ultimately lead to a wrongful conviction.

Little Oversight, Lack of Valid Forensic Techniques, Overclaiming, and the Courts

The 1983 survey of crime labs finds that government experts are rarely challenged (Giannelli, 2007a). Garrett and Neufeld (2009) analyses of 137 trial transcripts finds the most common testimony of forensic analysts includes serological analysis and microscopic hair comparison; however, bite marks, fingerprint comparisons, shoe prints, soil, DNA testing and fiber analysis were also included (p. 9). Roughly 60 percent of the forensic analysts provided invalid testimony. Defense counsel rarely cross-examined or obtained their own expert witness, and in the few cases where the expert's testimony was challenged, judges rarely provided relief (pp. 10–11). The failure to provide relief can be attributed to the legal system's inability to correct the problem of invalid testimony (NAS, 2009). The criminal justice system is ill-equipped to determine whether an expert's testimony is valid. Based on the varying terminologies used by expert witnesses and the absence of rigorous scientific methods, to judge expert testimony may result in the conviction of an innocent person.

In general, there has been little oversight in what forensic scientists can say during a trial (Garrett & Neufeld, 2009; NAS, 2009). Although there is no single ethical code that all criminalists follow, most forensic analysts in the United States follow a series of ethical codes based on the American Board of Criminalists ("ABC"), the American Academy of Forensic Sciences ("AAFS"), and the California Association of Criminalists ("CAC") (Garrett & Neufeld, 2009). However, ethical codes still do not provide guidelines concerning expert testimony. In sum, these professional entities are mainly concerned with ethical guidelines pertaining to general norms of conduct (Garrett & Neufeld, 2009). There have been far too many cases where experts have used convincing terms such as "certainty," "positively," "matched," or "beyond doubt" to support a guilty verdict. However, these terms, used to convince jurors, lack empirical support by peer-reviewed research. According to the NAS (2009) report, "[f]ew forensic science methods have developed adequate measures of the accuracy of inferences made by forensic scientists" (p. 184). The forensics community's inability to develop standard terminologies based on valid forensic methods may results in misleading testimony.

Currently, nuclear DNA analysis is the only forensic method able to link a specific individual to evidence found at a crime scene (Garrett & Neufeld, 2009). Because of misconceptions popularized by the media the public is often led to believe that forensic and expert testimony provides absolute proof of a person's guilt. As a result of the "CSI Effect," jurors tend to trust forensic experts (Nolan, 2007). This effect causes individuals to believe that science and experts are always right. In the 1990s, the Supreme Court adopted procedural safeguards to prevent introduction of unreliable forensic evidence to the jurors.[2] These more rigorous standards were developed to assist with the validity and reliability of forensic evidence. Yet, it is apparent from analyses of exonerations that "forensic junk science" is still being introduced to juries, even with the procedural safeguards in place. American courts continue to accept untested forensic techniques (Gable, 2014).

Until the availability of DNA evidence in 1989, forensic scientists drew from a multitude of disciplines to test a wide range of evidence. These disciplines provide "judgments of fingerprints, firearms examinations, toolmarks, bite marks, tire and shoe impressions, bloodstain pattern analysis, handwriting, hair, coatings such as paint and

---

2. See Chapter 4 for an additional discussion of *Daubert v. Merrell Dow*, Pharmaceuticals, Inc. 1993.

chemicals – including drugs and such materials as fibers, fluids, fire and explosive analysis, digital evidence, and serological analysis" (Kassin, Dror, & Kukucka, 2013, p. 43). However, analyses of non-DNA evidence do not permit an objective standard to link a specific individual to a crime. Instead, examiners can only determine a similarity between a specific individual and the forensic evidence (Kassin, Dror, & Kukucka, 2013). The criterion of "sufficiently similar" is very subjective. The Department of Justice and the FBI examiners, in the FBI Laboratory's Microscopic Hair Comparison Unit, overstated multiple forensic matches. The use of a subjective matching technique contributed to more than one-quarter of the 329 DNA exonerations beginning in 1989 (Hsu, 2015).

Subjectivity can also be found in other forensic techniques, such as fingerprint analysis, which is meant to provide a systematic method for identifying differences. The average fingerprint contains between 50 and 150 points of comparison (Gabel, 2014). However, considerable variation in the criteria to confirm a match is found across jurisdictions. The number of points needed for identification range from as few as eight points to 12 or more (Gabel, 2014). Yet, there is no agreed-upon number of points needed for a match by the scientific community. Variation also exists concerning voice analysis. Even though the National Academy of Science ("NAS"), in 1979, concluded that voice spectrograph is not supported by scientific data, some courts continue to permit its use as evidence in court (Garrett & Neufeld, 2009). Without having set standards or valid peer-reviewed research concerning forensic methods, these subjective-based forensic techniques may continue to result in wrongful convictions.

It is important to note that although DNA evidence provides a valid forensic technique, it is only found in a small number of crimes. For example, the leading cause of death for non-Hispanic black male teenagers is a drive-by shooting that result in a homicide (Miniño, 2010). Very rarely would blood from the shooter be found at the crime scene. As a result less valid forensic techniques may be used. Only 2 percent of new requests for forensic analyses are for DNA testing (Peterson & Hickman, 2005). Rape and murder, where DNA is more likely, account for 2 percent of all felony convictions (Durose & Langan, 2003). Therefore, the majority of felony convictions rely on other, less valid forensic techniques. Lastly, even in the small number of cases where DNA evidence is available, there is still a possibility of error in the analysis. Because the possibility of human error is always present, objective standards for forensic analyses and testimony are vitally important.

It appears that our system may not be well-situated to prevent forensic misconduct. Based on a survey conducted in 2002 by the Bureau of Justice Statistics, there are 351 public-funded forensic laboratories in the United States. Public-funded labs have grown exponentially, more than three times the number that existed in 1967 (Ginaelli, 2007). As the crime laboratories continue to grow it is important that reforms be developed to prevent the possibility of forensic error. Crime laboratories should be administratively separated from police departments. Universal accreditation standards and mandatory reporting of misconduct to all parties involved are essential, as are regulations governing appropriate valid forensic methods. In addition, reforms should address the use of incompetent or corrupt analysts and reduce unfounded testimony. Forensic misconduct undermines the administration of justice. It is necessary, therefore, to implement reforms that directly impact forensic analyses and their explanation to the jury.

HISTORY OF REFORMS

According to the National Academy of Sciences report, a uniformed forensic science community needs to be developed to implement reforms (NAS, 2009). Forensic reforms begun in 1967 after President Lyndon B. Johnson's Commission on Law Enforcement and the Administration of Justice recognized that there were deficiencies with expertise and equipment in police laboratories (Gabel, 2014; Melson, 2010). Later in 1973, during the Nixon administration, the Commission restated the same concerns. However, Congress appeared to remain silent about forensics practices until the advancement of DNA (Gabel, 2014). Differing views concerning DNA evidence lead to the establishment of standards governing admissibility set forth in *Daubert v. Merrell Dow Pharmaceuticals, Inc.*1993. Eventually legislation governing forensic laboratories followed the *Daubert* ruling (Gabel, 2014).

In 2004, the Justice for All Act was enacted, which provided federal funding under the Paul Coverdell Forensic Sciences Improvement Grant. To receive funding states would have to establish an independent state entity, which would review claims of laboratory misconduct or negligence (Justice for All, Pub.L. 108-405). A second bill required all 50 states to conduct an external investigation of forensic misconduct claims. By 2009 each state had received funds from the grant; (Nat'l Inst. Justice Fiscal Year 2009) however, many states have not fully complied with the grants requirements (Innocence Project, n.d.l).

Later in 2009, the National Research Council of the National Academies of Sciences ("NAS") published their report, which included a number of issues aside from mandating an external investigation requirement. The report discussed many of the aspects mentioned previously, including the absence of universal standards, adequate training, and accreditation (NAS, 2009). All of their recommendations could reduce a wrongful conviction.

JUNK SCIENCE WRIT

One state that appears to be taking action against junk science is Texas. On June 14th, 2013, Governor Rick Perry signed the Junk Science Writ or Senate Bill 344 into law. Since the enactment, at least three Texas cases have been overturned.[3] When new scientific evidence is found, the writ allows for a prisoner to challenge his conviction (Thomas, 2015). The writ may be filed even if a previous habeas corpus has been entered. This is important for several reasons. Usually once a prisoner files a writ of habeas corpus, known as the writ of last appeal, they are not granted any other appeals. However, the new Junk Science Writ allows for a prisoner to apply for a first time writ or another writ of habeas corpus based on new scientific research (Thomas, 2015). Hopefully other states will begin to follow suit.

INNOCENCE PROJECT RECOMMENDATIONS

The Innocence Project argues there are three areas of concern, which could reduce forensic misconduct and improve the overall quality of analyses. These include "research; assessment of validity and reliability, and quality assurance, accreditation and certification of laboratories and practitioners" (Innocence Project, n.d.l). These

---

3. For more information see: Thomas, S. (2015). Addressing wrongful convictions: An examination of Texas's new junk science writ and other measures for protecting the innocent. *Houston Law Review,* 52 (3), 1037–1066.

concerns were also mentioned in National Academy of Sciences 2009 report. The Innocence Project recommends that the community develop a national effort that focuses on expanding basic and applied research and assisting in the scientific credibility of examiners, methods and devices. Lastly, a national forensic standard should be created, which would govern practices for both public and private laboratories, as well as those independent experts who testify in a court setting. Noncompliance of the standards should include loss of accreditations, certification, and a possible closing of the forensic organization (Innocence Project, n.d.l).

CURRENT FORENSIC OVERSIGHT BOARDS

By 2011, there were 15 states[4] that provided forensic oversight, 13 states had created permanent review statutes, and in two others the attorney general provided forensic oversight (Norris, Bonventre, Redlich, & Acker, 2011). The commissions vary in scope of representation; in some states, the committee is mostly represented by law enforcement officials and prosecutor offices; others include defense attorneys, judiciary members, members of the medical community; and a few have representatives from academia (Norris et al., 2011). Illinois appears to represent the most comprehensive membership, which includes a total of fifteen representatives from a variety of state agencies including, "the state departments of agriculture, natural resources, public health, and transportation, as well as law enforcement representatives, attorneys, and forensic scientists" (Norris et al., 2011, p. 1327). Appointment of board members varies by state. For example, in New York, the Governor is responsible for appointing twelve of the 14 members (Goldstein, 2011). States also differ on how they implement their oversight. New York (Norris et al., 2011) and Texas (Goldstein, 2011) have two of the most comprehensive task forces for accreditation. Currently, there is still no national standard governing the field of forensics.

---

4. The 15 states include: Arizona (Attorney General), Arkansas, Illinois, Indiana, Maryland, Massachusetts, Minnesota, Missouri, Montana (Attorney General), New Mexico, New York, Rhode Island, Texas, Virginia, and Washington.

MISCONDUCT BY JUSTICE ACTORS

There have been several wrongful conviction cases where in both the opening statement and the closing argument the prosecutor misrepresented forensic evidence. For example, in the case of Jimmy Ray Bromgard, the Deputy County Attorney David Hoefer met with the forensic expert in advance and told the jury what to expect in the opening statement:

> . . . the experts at the State Lab out of Missoula will come and testify, and they will tell you that that hair has the same range of microscopic characteristics as that of the defendant, and they will tell you the percentage of the population that would have that kind of hair, first for the head hair, secondly for the pubic hair, and then for the two combined.[5]

This argument provides an example of the close relationship between the forensic analysts and the prosecutor, possibly sealing the fate of the defendant from the opening statement. Garrett and Neufeld (2009), in their review of 137 trial transcripts, also report several instances where a prosecutor exaggerated the forensic scientist testimony in the closing argument (p. 85). The "CSI Effect" already predisposes the jury to flawed forensic evidence. Even when the jury is aware of this effect, when a prosecutor further exaggerates the findings, a guilty verdict becomes more likely. Reforms should be created, which limit the wide latitude granted to prosecutors in addressing the jury.

The courts fail to correct miscarriages of justice when they do not question or hold forensic evidence to rigorous standards. The forensic community has failed to establish standards for the reliability and validity of their findings, and courts have yet to address this problem (NAS, 2009, p. 53). Also, courts have not provided relief to exonerees when flagrantly invalid forensic testimony led to their wrongful conviction (Garrett & Neufeld, 2009). Judges hold the key to setting standards and implementing reforms. If they are unwilling to provide relief for invalid forensic testimony, then reforms should be developed, which mandate relief for the wrongfully convicted.

---

5. Trial Transcripts, *State v. Jimmy Ray Bromgard*, No. 88108 (Minn. Dist. CT. Nov. 16, 1987), described by Garrett & Neufeld, 2009.

POLICY RECOMMENDATIONS

Universal Standards with Accreditation, Certification, and Terminology

Forensic science as a discipline is almost entirely self-regulated; however, the NAS (2009) report recommends mandatory accreditation and certification. Each lab should be either accredited by a professional organization or in the case of an individual analyst should be certified by a professional organization (Cole & Thompson, 2013). However, jurors and judges are typically not familiar with accreditation and certification standards and accept forensic expert testimony as reliable. Providing mandatory certification and accreditation would ensure a base level of educational attainment, expertise, and experience needed to provide reliable forensic testimony (Gabel, 2014).

In addition to accreditation and certification, there are no universal standards for forensic analyses that are accepted by the forensic science community. The forensic community should collaborate with academic researchers and forensic examiners, to more effectively use available resources to enhance the use of proper procedures and methodologies. Gabel (2014) explains that this partnership should mimic that of cancer researchers working with an oncologist. An oncologist administers treatment, the researcher records, analyzes, and continues to develop other methods to improve the original treatment. When the researcher publishes their findings in academic journals the medical community as a whole becomes aware of successes and failures of the treatment. Similarly, academic researchers would record all actions of the forensic examiner, analyze findings and outcomes, and then work to improve methodologies and procedures; eventually publishing their findings in peer-reviewed journals.

Developing unified standards will benefit both the forensic community and the criminal justice system. This collaborate effort will foster disclosure, ultimately leading to an enhanced adversarial scrutiny of evidence (Cole & Thompson, 2013; Krane et al., 2009; Mnookin et al., 2011; Risinger & Saks, 2003). Uniformity will help both with explaining what the results mean as well as providing a reference point for acceptable forensic methods.

A standardized language on what forensic results means may reduce the jury's susceptibility to inaccurate or misleading testimony and inform judges about forensic methodologies. Also, a standardized language could simplify the process of reviewing forensic reports (Cole & Thompson, 2013). The United States forensic community could use The International Organization for Standardization to assist in the development of uniform practices within the forensic community (Gabel, 2014). This international guide provides requirements for forensic testing as well as standards for reporting data.

Independent Oversight

Very few states provide independent oversight of forensic laboratories. New York and Texas are states that are leading the way with introducing a separate forensic science commission, which is not nestled in law enforcement or public safety agencies (Cole & Thompson, 2013). Independent oversight would assist with reducing the wide disparity in resources that are available to the defense counsel (Gabel, 2014). Instead, an independent scientific agency should be responsible for oversight of laboratories (Cole & Thompson, 2013). Furthermore, this would reduce motivational and cognitive bias, an inevitable consequence of forensic units, which is located within law enforcement agencies, or the office of the prosecutor.

Valid Forensic Techniques

Although it is clear that junk science has contributed to many miscarriages of justice, it is also important to consider the behavior of forensic analysts themselves. The primary function of the justice system is of course, to solve crime. To support this primary function, other disciplines, including forensic science, have been created. To the extent that a forensic technique assists in solving a crime continues unquestioned (Gabel, 2014). Crime labs and their forensic analysts downplay the importance of validating techniques. It was not until the advent of DNA evidence that law in forensic techniques became evident. However, the overall goal of solving crime is the overriding concern of the law enforcement community, including forensic scientists, and prosecutors.

Many of the scientific forensic methods lack the peer-reviewed research needed to establish basic validation. Although DNA evidence has been subjected to scientific evaluation, these same standards are absent for other forensic techniques. Validity standards are needed to ensure that each forensic method level of reliability is consistent with other validated measures (Gabel, 2014). The absence of reliable standards for forensic analyses may result in erroneous convictions.

In addition, education programs, trainings, or academic degrees should be developed for forensic personnel. As Cole and Thompson (2013) mention, "if forensic scientists are not reasoning statistically or if they are not thinking scientifically about how to validate their assumptions, they must be trained to do so" (p. 127). Education programs in general would serve to benefit lawyers and judges, as well as practitioners (Gabel, 2014). The National Academy of Sciences reports the absence of doctoral programs in forensic science (NAS, 2009, pp. 223-224). A forensic science education would improve the discipline immensely and possibly reduce the errors associated with forensic techniques or "expert" testimony.

CONCLUSION

The forensic sciences are continuing to evolve, and while criminal justice reforms are gaining acceptance, evidence of miscarriages of justice mount daily. Standards for the certification of experts, standardized terminology, or validation of forensics techniques are yet to be determined. Judges and juries are, therefore, ill-equipped to accurately assess the forensic evidence against the defendant (Gabel, 2014). Without a national standard or an independent agency governing the use of "standard terminology," states must develop reforms individually, causing forensic disparities across the country. The National Academy of Sciences report offers viable recommendations to assist states in the development of valid and reliable forensic techniques. Judge Cathleen Cochran summarizes the issue of forensic science perfectly: "the potential problem of relying on today's science in a criminal trial . . . is that tomorrow's science sometimes changes and, based upon that changed science, the former verdict may look inaccurate, if not downright ludicrous. But the convicted person is still imprisoned" (Tex. Crim. App., 2011).

PART II

Chapter 4

PROSECUTORIAL MISCONDUCT

There is no crueler tyranny than that which is perpetuated under the shield of law and in the name of justice.

– Charles de Montesquieu

THE CASE OF MICHAEL MORTON

The idyllic life of Michael Morton was shattered the day after his 32nd birthday. A supermarket manager with a wife, Christine, and a three-year-old son, Eric, Michael's life was unfolding in a very promising way. While he was disheartened that Christine neglected him on his birthday, he left an "I L Y" (I Love You) note for her before he left for work at 5:30 the next day. Later that morning Eric was found by a neighbor wandering around on his front lawn. When the neighbor brought him home, she found Christine in bed, beaten to death–a hunk of wood on the floor close by.

Soon thereafter the police interviewed Christine's mother who reported that Eric said that "Daddy was not home" when it happened, but a "monster" hurt his mother. Neighbors also reported to the police that a man parked a green van behind the Morton's residence who was later seen walking into the nearby woods. Surprisingly, Christine's credit card was discovered in San Antonio and a police officer there said he could identify the women who used it.

This evidence did not, however, deter the police and prosecutor from focusing on Michael as the most likely suspect. The prosecutor's case relied on the theory that Michael killed his wife because she refused to have sexual relations with him on the night of his birthday. At trial, no witnesses were called and no physical evidence was presented to the jury.

When the defense became aware that Sergeant Don Woods, the lead detective in the case, would not testify at trial, they were concerned that the discovery process was being compromised. The defense petitioned the trial judge to order the prosecution to make available Sergeant Woods investigative reports, including Eric's statement to his grandmother, information about the green van, and Christine's missing credit card. The prosecutor, Ken Anderson, did not comply with the trial judge's order to release the requested information. Further, at the time of the trial Ken Anderson told the judge that he did not have any evidence that would assist the defense. An innocent, young mother was murdered; closure was sought. The jury convicted Michael Morton of first degree murder and imposed a life sentence.

Michael Morton had served eight years in prison before the Innocence Project was able to request DNA testing of physical evidence from the crime scene. It took five additional years before the DNA testing of a bandanna found near the crime scene was granted. Present on the bandanna were the DNA of Christine and her murderer, later identified as Mark Norwood who victimized another person in the same manner. After serving more than 24 years in prison for a murder he did not commit, Michael was released and exonerated a few months later.

During the time Michael was in prison Ken Anderson, the prosecutor, became a judge and served on the bench for several years. Following Michael's exoneration, Ken Anderson "plead no contest to a court order to show cause for withholding exculpatory evidence" (Levs, 2013). As part of a plea agreement, Ken Anderson was sentenced to 10 days in jail (5 days were waived for good behavior), $500 fine, and 500 hours of community service. In addition, he agreed to vacate his judgeship, and surrender his license to practice law. Penalties for prosecutorial misconduct are exceedingly uncommon. The Innocence Project considers the Ken Anderson case "an extremely rare instance, and perhaps the first time, that a prosecutor has been criminally punished for failing to turn over exculpatory evidence."[1]

---

1. For more information on Michael Morton's case see: Innocence Project. (n.d.a). *All cases.* New York: Innocence Project. Retrieved from https://www.innocenceproject.org/all-cases/#exonerated-by-dna. And, Levs, J. (2013, December 4). Innocent man: How inmate Michael Morton lost 25 years of his life. CNN. Retrieved from http://www.cnn.com/2013/12/04/justice/exonerated-prisoner-update-michael-morton/index.html.

THE RESPONSIBILITY OF THE PROSECUTOR

Arguably the prosecutor is the most powerful agent of the criminal justice system. The prosecutor is responsible for reviewing the strength of the evidence – that is, the trustworthiness and reliability of the witnesses, results of forensic analysis, and credibility of any expert witnesses that may testify. The prosecutor decides whether to charge the suspect with a crime, to seek an indictment, and to "go forward" with the case. The prosecutor must decide if the evidence can be presented to potential jurors in a clear, concise, and compelling way. In short, the prosecutor must be convinced that the suspect is "convictable," and that the jury will find the defendant guilty.

Prosecutors across the United States are elected by the citizenry in their jurisdiction. Broadly speaking, the expectation is that the work of the prosecutor will result in the conviction of criminal offenders. Prosecutor's decisions, then, are driven by the need to maximize their conviction rate. As a consequence, about nine in 10 criminal cases are resolved by offering the defendant the opportunity to enter a guilty plea to a lesser charge and thereby avoid the possibility of a harsher sentence. Once a plea bargain is accepted by the court, the defendant forfeits the right to appeal the case. The prosecutor then has gained a final resolution to the criminal matter.

While rare, criminal cases that are tried present a considerable challenge for the prosecution. The actions of the prosecutor are subject to public scrutiny. The prosecutor is responsible for convincing the jury that the defendant is guilty "beyond reasonable doubt" for the crime. Media attention varies depending on the egregious nature of the crime – typically crimes involving innocent victims, or horrific methods fuel public fear and outrage are particularly newsworthy. As Donald Black (1976) has posited the structure of the legal case—*who does what to whom* – predicts its legal outcome. Cases involving victims of a higher status, who are more respectable and strangers to their assailants are of particular concern to the criminal justice system. Plea bargains are less likely to be struck; charges are likely to be elevated; and trial by jury is more likely to occur. Public attention is likely to be riveted on the actions of the prosecutor and the outcome of the case. Cast into a "must win" situation, the prosecutor's decision-making is vulnerable to breaches of ethical and professional conduct. Paradoxically, cases involving the greatest likelihood of public scrutiny-death penalty and other high profile cases-disproportionally lead to wrongful convictions (Gross, O'Brien, Hu, & Kennedy, 2014).

The integrity of the criminal justice system hinges, in large part, on the ethical behavior of the prosecutor. The prosecutor works in tandem with the police in framing the case against the suspect. Mutual self-interest underlies the relationship between the prosecutor and the police. Each depends on the integrity of the other to arrive at a just outcome of the case. The investigatory process flows into the prosecutor's decision-making assessment of the strength and reliability of the evidence, the criminal charge, the decision to offer a plea bargain or to try the case, and, if needed, the strategy for presenting the case to the jury.

AMERICAN BAR ASSOCIATION

Model Rules for Professional Conduct

The American Bar Association in their Model Rules for Professional Conduct outlines specific requirements for practice of law. Rule 3.8 entitled Special Responsibilities of a Prosecutor sets forth the expectations for the prosecution of a criminal case. Provisions of Rule 3.8 governing procedural requirements and constitutional rights are pertinent to our understanding of wrongful convictions. Procedural considerations include: (1) the prohibition to bring charges without probable cause, (2) ensuring that the accused is provided a preliminary hearing, and (3) the disclosure of any exculpatory evidence to the defense attorney(s). The prosecutor must also assist in providing the fundamental constitutional right to counsel for the defense. Table 4.1 summarizes key elements of the American Bar Association's Rules for Professional Conduct for Prosecutors.[2]

In addition, Rule 3.8 directs the prosecutor to become involved in the post-conviction process. If the prosecutor becomes aware of any evidence that would support the innocence of the convicted person, then prompt disclosure of the evidence must be made to the appropriate court or authority. Exculpatory evidence related to cases in the

---

2. For more information see: American Bar Association. (1983). *Model rules of professional conduct*. Retrieved from https://www.americanbar.org/groups/professional_responsibility/publications/model_rules_of_professional_conduct/rule_3_8_special_responsibilities_of_a_prosecutor.html.

Table 4.1

ABA MODEL RULES FOR PROFESSIONAL CONDUCT FOR PROSECUTORS

American Bar Association–Model Rules of Professional Conduct
Rule 3.8: Special Responsibilities of a Prosecutor

The prosecutor in a criminal case shall:

(a) refrain from prosecuting a charge that the prosecutor knows is not supported by probable cause;

(b) make reasonable efforts to assure that the accused has been advised of the right to, and the procedure for obtaining, counsel and has been given reasonable opportunity to obtain counsel;

(c) not seek to obtain from an unrepresented accused a waiver of important pretrial rights, such as the right to a preliminary hearing;

(d) make timely disclosure to the defense of all evidence or information known to the prosecutor that tends to negate the guilt of the accused or mitigates the offense, and, in connection with sentencing, disclose to the defense and to the tribunal all unprivileged mitigating information known to the prosecutor, except when the prosecutor is relieved of this responsibility by a protective order of the tribunal;

(e) not subpoena a lawyer in a grand jury or other criminal proceeding to present evidence about a past or present client unless the prosecutor reasonably believes:
  (1) the information sought is not protected from disclosure by any applicable privilege;
  (2) the evidence sought is essential to the successful completion of an ongoing investigation or prosecution; and
  (3) there is no other feasible alternative to obtain the information;

(f) except for statements that are necessary to inform the public of the nature and extent of the prosecutor's action and that serve a legitimate law enforcement purpose, refrain from making extrajudicial comments that have a substantial likelihood of heightening public condemnation of the accused and exercise reasonable care to prevent investigators, law enforcement personnel, employees or other persons assisting or associated with the prosecutor in a criminal case from making an extrajudicial statement that the prosecutor would be prohibited from making under Rule 3.6 or this Rule.

(g) When a prosecutor knows of new, credible and material evidence creating a reasonable likelihood that a convicted defendant did not commit an offense of which the defendant was convicted, the prosecutor shall:
  (1) promptly disclose that evidence to an appropriate court or authority, and
  (2) if the conviction was obtained in the prosecutor's jurisdiction,
     (i) promptly disclose that evidence to the defendant unless a court authorizes delay, and
     (ii) undertake further investigation, or make reasonable efforts to cause an investigation, to determine whether the defendant was convicted of an offense that the defendant did not commit.

Continued on next page

Table 4.1 – *continued*

(h) When a prosecutor knows of clear and convincing evidence establishing that a defendant in the prosecutor's jurisdiction was convicted of an offense that the defendant did not commit, the prosecutor shall seek to remedy the conviction.

prosecutor's jurisdiction must be provided to the defendant, and an appropriate investigation of a possible wrongful conviction be conducted. Further, prosecutors who are provided "clear and convincing" evidence of a convicted person's innocence must pursue a just remedy.

Yet, the clandestine nature of police investigations and prosecutorial decision-making tends to lessen compliance with externally imposed rules. In a sense there is a situational intersection between the investigative work of the police and the decision-making of the prosecutor. The procedural errors (e.g., faulty lineups and interrogation techniques) and psychological biases (e.g., tunnel vision, confirmation and hindsight biases, ratification of error, escalation of commitment that mar the investigatory process flow into prosecutorial decision-making.[3]

The work of the police and prosecutors is, for the most part, never made public. Only when the defendant is tried will the public be able to view the processes of identifying and apprehending the defendant, and gathering evidence intended to convict him. However, the prosecutor's decision-making process is not subject to public scrutiny. The evaluation of the witness/victim reports, physical evidence, and possible contributions of experts is held in confidence. The prosecutor also controls all charging decisions, selection of the evidence and strategy for its presentation in court, or alternately, objectives of plea negotiations.

Three conceptual formulations–organizational structure, subculture, and social situation–help us understand the police-prosecutor working environment. Organizational structure refers to the status hierarchy and individual responsibilities of the members of the organization. This formal arrangement of statuses affects the carrying out of policies and procedures within the organization. Police agencies typically have a paramilitary organization, which establishes a rigid chain of command

---

3. For a further discussion , See Chapter 2.

and specifies the duties of each member of the organization. While the office of the prosecutor is less rigidly organized, it nonetheless is structured to facilitate the flow of cases and to specify the responsibilities of each of the members of the office. Ultimately, the District Attorney is responsible for ensuring that the assistant prosecutors conduct criminal prosecutions in a fair, just, and constitutionally defensible manner.

Distinct subcultures also characterize police agencies and Offices of the District Attorney. Two subcultural values—secrecy and commitment to the conviction of criminal offender—are common among police and prosecutors. Once a viable suspect has been identified and apprehended, there is a concerted effort to bring the case to closure as expeditiously as possible. Any external interference is viewed as counterproductive and unwarranted. In an environment of inordinate demands on their time and resources, police and prosecutors value efficiency and shun scrutiny of their work.

Embedded in structural and subcultural influences on the actions of the police and prosecutors, is the criminal situation itself. The criminal situation refers to the complex interactions among the police, witnesses/victim, the suspect, the prosecutor, and possibly the defense attorney. Donald Black (1976) argues that the structure of the legal case—*who does what to whom*—shapes the investigatory process and subsequent investment of the prosecutor's time and resources in the case. As we have discussed in the introductory chapter, Black posits three hypotheses that bear on the social situation:

1. If the victim's social status is greater than the suspect, then there will be greater governmental investment of time and resources in the case.
2. If the victim's respectability is greater than the offender, then there will be greater governmental investment of time and resources in the case.
3. If the victim and offender are strangers, there will be greater governmental investment of time and resources in the case.

In sum, if low status persons who have criminal records, or who suffer from mental illness or addiction are suspected of victimizing a stranger who is of a higher status and respectable member of society, then the police and prosecutors are highly motivated to pursue a conviction.

Beyond the structure of the case, the perception of convictability influences each stage in the processing of a criminal case from its initial investigation through the series of decisions made by the prosecutor. The perception of convictability fuels the tunnel vision of the police and prosecutor. All other possible suspects are eliminated from consideration – the focus is on the only "convictable" suspect known to the police. In a sense, the perception of convictability results in a "self-fulfilling prophesy." Robert Merton (1948) notes that a self-fulfilling prophesy:

> in the beginning, a false definition of the situation evoking a new behavior which makes the original false conception come true. This specious validity of the self-fulfilling prophecy perpetuates a reign of error. For the prophet will cite the actual course of events as proof that he was right from the very beginning. (p. 195)

The perception of convictability may set in motion a series of law enforcement and prosecutorial decisions premised on the assumption that a jury would find the suspect guilty. The perception of convictability, then, justifies shaping the criminal justice process to ensure that the preconceived outcome of the case is achieved.

It is evident that a myriad of sociolegal, organizational, and perceptual factors form the context in which wrongful convictions become more likely. The enduring nature of the police-prosecutor nexus depends on a common understanding of the criminal justice process. It is their shared view of justice that may lead to common forms of governmental misconduct.

Definition of Prosecutorial Misconduct

Prosecutorial misconduct is defined as "any conduct by a prosecutor that violates a defendant's rights, regardless of whether that conduct was known or should have been known to be improper by the prosecutor, or whether the prosecutor intended to violate legal requirements" (Prosecutorial Oversight, 2016, p. 9).

Types of Prosecutorial Misconduct

A wide range of prosecutorial misconduct undermines the rights of a criminal defendant. Legal and constitutional rights are intended to protect a defendant against overzealous prosecution and to ensure fundamental fairness in the processing of a criminal case. Prosecutors must provide defense counsel with any evidence that would support the innocence of the defendant. Failure to provide exculpatory evidence is among the more common forms of prosecutorial misconduct. A related form of misconduct is the destroying or negligent processing of evidence, or introducing deceptive forensic evidence in a criminal case.

Prosecutorial misconduct also extends to the manipulation of testimonial evidence. Prosecutors may permit witnesses to testify when their statements are known to be false, or coerce defense witnesses not to testify at trial. Prosecutors may also exaggerate the strength of the evidence against the defendant to influence the jury, or to achieve an unfair plea bargain. Further, a prosecutor may manipulate the media to trigger public condemnation of the defendant.

Because more than nine in 10 criminal cases are resolved by a negotiated plea, prosecutors may charge the defendant with offenses not supported by probable cause to gain a bargaining advantage (Devers, 2011). Finally, the failure to disclose prosecutorial misconduct is itself a form negligent misconduct.

Scope of Prosecutorial Misconduct

Because of the hidden nature of prosecutorial work, it is exceedingly difficult to assess the extent of prosecutorial misconduct. The National Registry of Exonerations reports that 43 percent of wrongful convictions overall and 75% of homicide convictions involve governmental misconduct which included the actions of police or prosecutors, or both (National Registry of Exonerations, 2017; Center for Prosecutor Integrity, 2013).

The Veritas Institute, in conjunction with the Northern California Innocence Project, conducted a statewide study of prosecutorial misconduct occurring in California for the years 1997 through 2009. Their report, *Preventable Error: A Report on Prosecutorial Misconduct in California 1997-2009* is the most in-depth analysis of prosecutorial misconduct ever undertaken. After reviewing 4,000 state and federal appellate court rulings, media reports, and trial court decisions, 707 of the cases of prosecutorial misconduct were identified by the courts. However, in 78 percent (548 cases) the court ruled that the misconduct was harmless and did not compromise the fairness of the trial. In the remaining 22 percent of the cases (n=159), the court found that the misconduct did cause harm and resulted in the conviction and sentence to be set aside, a mistrial, or evidence to be excluded from further trial proceedings. However, only seven cases of prosecutorial misconduct resulted in any form of disciplinary action (Ridolfi & Possley, 2010, p. 11). Prosecutorial misconduct then is largely carried out with impunity, undeterred by legal or ethical sanctions.

Discovery

Brady v. Maryland (1963) is the landmark case concerning the right of the defendant to access exculpatory evidence at trial. In separate trials, John Brady and his companion Charles Boblit were each found guilty of first degree murder. During his trial, Brady testified that he was present during the murder, but that Boblit killed the victim. Brady's attorney argued that, while his client was guilty of first degree murder, he should be spared the death penalty. Prior to the trial Brady's attorney requested copies of all extra-judicial statements made by both defendants.

Boblit had admitted to the police that he actually committed the murder. However, the prosecutor withheld that statement from Brady's defense attorney prior to the trial. Boblit's statement that he actually carried out the murder became known to the defense only after Brady was sentenced to death and the sentence was affirmed by the Maryland Court of Appeals without prejudice.

Brady's appeal to the U.S. Supreme Court hinged on the denial of his 14th Amendment due process rights under the U.S. Constitution. While the U.S. Supreme Court did not find that Brady's due process rights were violated as to the trial court's finding of guilt, it did rule that the prosecutor's failure to provide evidence that would mitigate the death sentence was a violation of his due process rights. In sum, the U.S. Supreme Court ruled: "that the suppression by the prosecution of evidence favorable to an accused upon request violates due process where the evidence is material either to guilt or to punishment, irrespective of the good faith or bad faith of the prosecution" (*Brady v. Maryland,* 373 U.S. 83 (1963)). The Court did, however, uphold Brady's claim that his death sentence was imposed in a prejudicial manner.

Brady v. Maryland opened the door to greater scrutiny of the right of defense to exculpatory evidence. Central to the understanding of the *Brady* decision is the meaning of "material" evidence. In *United States v. Bagley,* 473 U. S. 667, 675 (1985), the Court held that evidence is material "if there is a reasonable probability that, had the evidence been disclosed to the defense, the result of the proceeding would have been different." More recently, in *Strickler v. Greene,* 527 U.S. 263, 281-82 (1999) the Court again ruled that materiality means that the failure to disclose the evidence is "so serious that there is a reasonable probability that the evidence would have produced a different verdict."

To establish materiality, the courts have relied on three considerations: "(1) the importance of the withheld evidence; (2) the strength of the prosecution case; and (3) other sources of evidence available to and used by the defense" (as cited in Cassidy, 2005, p. 74). Materiality then is a matter of judgment, initially made by the prosecutor and reviewed by the court. The stronger the prosecution's case against the defendant, the less likely other evidence will change the outcome of the case. If in the prosecutor's judgment the evidence is not likely to undermine the conviction of the defendant, then the withheld evidence will not be considered material, and therefore, not subject to disclosure. The burden of proof, then, is on the defense to show that the withheld evidence would alter the verdict of the jury (Medwed, 2010, p. 1541).

The benefits of Brady was further enunciated in *Giglio v. United States,* 405 U.S. (1972) which required the disclosure of any "promises, rewards, or inducements" made to informants for their testimony. In *Agurs v. United States,* 427 U.S. 97, 110-11(1976) the Court ruled that the prosecutor must disclose material evidence even if the defense does not request it. Due to the close police-prosecutor working relationship, prosecutors are held responsible for the disclosure of exculpatory evidence held by the police even if they did not know about it (Medwed, 2010, p. 1538; Cassidy, 2005, p. 74). In addition, the exculpatory evidence must be disclosed in a timely and continuous manner to assist the defense throughout the trial (Medwed, 2010, p. 1538; Cassidy, 2005, pp. 71-72). Prosecutors have wide discretion in their judgment of whether evidence rises to the level of "material." The question is:

would not disclosing evidence favorable to the defense result in a finding of "not guilty" by the jury?

The prosecutor may determine that the evidence is not credible, that jurors would not find it to be compelling, or would simply ignore it as not relevant. In a sense, prosecutors must see the evidence through the eyes of the jurors, and assess, as they would, its impact on their decision-making process. Dire consequence may follow from the prosecutor's failure to accurately peer into the future and decide, as would a trial jury, or appellate court justice.

The police and prosecutors are responsible for assessing evidence related to a criminal case. The lack of transparency of the process and control over the criminal justice decision-making underpin the police and prosecutor's largely unbridled discretionary powers. Justice depends on their exercise of sound legal, ethical and moral judgments.

Jailhouse Snitches

Alexandra Natapoff, a leading authority on jailhouse snitches, notes that "Criminal informants, or "snitches," play a prominent role in wrongful conviction phenomenon" (2006, p. 107). She defines "snitch" as "criminals who provide information in exchange for lenience for their own crimes or other benefits. Not included in this definition are informants who do not benefit from the information they provide" (Natapoff, 2007, p. 107). Daniel Medwed expands on the definition of informant to include: "any civilian who gives information to the police, such as jailhouse informants, criminal accomplices, and concerned citizens" (Medwed, 2012, p. 84). Informants expect to receive some form of benefit, either monetary or "immunity from prosecution" (Medwed, 2012, p. 84). In a sense, the informant sells their testimony to the government. Both parties benefit–the government gains a conviction and the informant criminal immunity, a reduction in sentence, or monetary compensation.

Despite the inherent flaws in the use of incentivized informants, the U.S. Supreme Court has upheld their use by the government. In *U.S. v. Hoffa*, 385 U.S. 293 (1966, pp. 310-312) the Court held that the use of compensated informants operating in secret is "not per se unconstitutional" and the truthfulness of their testimony would be scrutinized by cross-examination and by instructions to the jury. To the U.S. Supreme Court, existing procedural safeguards were in place to effectively uncover false testimony by an incentivized person. Overzealous prosecutors whose desire to convict the accused by any means available to them may be protected from accusations of ethical or legal breaches by the existing procedures intended to ensure the due process rights of the defendant.

Jailhouse snitches, persons who are incarcerated or who are placed in a cell near the defendant, are a particularly troublesome form of an informant. Jailhouse snitches are found to be particularly untrustworthy informants, driven almost exclusively to enhance their own ends. The Center on Wrongful Convictions at Northwestern University's School of Law conducted an in-depth analysis of the link between the use of jailhouse snitches and death row exonerations. The researchers reviewed 111 cases of death row exonerations from the reinstitution of the death penalty in the United States to the completion of the study in 2004. The findings show that in 45.9 percent of the death row exonerations, jailhouse snitches were instrumental in the imposition of the death penalty. The use of jailhouse snitches results in more wrongful convictions for capital crimes in the U.S. than any other cause. Eyewitness misidentification was the second leading cause of wrongful conviction in capital cases (25.2%), followed by false confessions (14.4%), and flawed scientific evidence (9.9%) (Warden, 2004). Similar findings are reported by Samuel Gross and his colleagues (2005) in their nationwide study of wrongful conviction of homicide defendants. Almost 1 in 2 of the wrongful convictions depended on a jailhouse snitch or informant who would benefit from their testimony (Gross, Jacoby, Matheson, Montgomery, & Patil, 2005).

In his study of the first 200 DNA exonerations, Brandon Garrett reports that 18 percent involved the testimony of incentive informants (Garrett, 2008). Jailhouse, other informants, or co-offenders provided testimony sufficiently convincing to the jury to convict an innocent defendant. More recently, The Innocence Project in New York finds "incentives to testify" were involved in 15 percent of the 342 current DNA exonerations (Innocence Project, 2016c).

Incentivized testimony permeates all levels of the criminal justice system (Natapoff, 2006, p. 112). Police rely heavily on informants to solve criminal cases. Prosecutors often depend on informant testimony to gain an advantage in a plea negotiation, or to convince a jury to find the defendant guilty. The mutual self-interests of the agents of the criminal justice system and the informant/snitch are weighed against the trustworthiness of the snitch's testimony. When a balance in these competing interests is not struck, a wrongful conviction may well ensue.

PROSECUTORIAL IMMUNITY

The wide discretionary powers of prosecutors should balance crime control initiatives with the due process rights of the accused. The responsibility for ethical prosecutorial decision-making is a central issue in misconduct cases. Misconduct may involve discovery violations, misrepresentation of the facts to the jury or media, or use of untrustworthy witnesses. The central question is: does the misconduct lie with an individual prosecutor, or does it reflect a pattern of behavior characteristic of a particular district attorney's office? If a culture of misconduct exists with a district attorney's office, then can individual prosecutors be held responsible for misconduct? Alternately, in the absence of evidence of a culture of misconduct, may individual prosecutors alone be held for breaches of ethics and constitutional safeguards?

In *Connick v. Thompson,* 131 S. Ct. 1350 (2011), the United States Supreme Court addressed the issue of responsibility for prosecutorial misconduct within a district attorney's office. John Thompson was erroneously identified as the perpetrator of an armed robbery and in an unrelated murder. Thompson was convicted of both crimes and condemned to death.

An assistant district attorney had deliberately withheld a forensic report, which excluded Thompson from involvement in both crimes. On his deathbed, the assistant district attorney told a colleague in the district attorney's office to release the lab report. The assistant district attorney ignored the request. Thompson served 18 years in prison and was within one month of execution before an investigator discovered the exculpatory forensic report. Thompson was subsequently exonerated of the armed robbery and acquitted of the murder (*Connick v. Thompson,* 131 S. Ct. 1355-57 (2011); Grometstein & Balboni, 2011/2012, p. 1259).

In a suit against the District Attorney and several assistant district attorneys, Thompson sought relief for the misconduct that led to his wrongful conviction and for narrowly escaping execution. The suit filed under Section 1983 claimed that the District Attorney's office violated *Brady v. Maryland* (1963) by not disclosing the forensics lab report at the time of Thompson's trial for armed robbery. It was alleged that the District Attorney, Harry Connick's was responsible for Brady violation for two reasons: (1) "for having unconstitutional policies in his office led to Brady violations; and (2) for "deliberate indifference" to a need to train his staff on avoiding such violations" (*Connick v. Thompson,* 131 S. Ct. 1355-57 (2011); Grometstein & Balboni, 2011/2012, p. 1259).

In *Connick v. Thompson, 131 S.* Ct. 1357-58 (2011), the United States Supreme Court, in a five to four decision, rejected the claim of "unconstitutional policies" in the District Attorney's office, and focused on the "deliberate indifference" to the need for training the staff members. Justice Thomas, writing the majority opinion, noted that the proof for his "deliberate indifference" hinged on Thompson's need to prove that: (1) "Connick, the policymaker for the district attorney's office, was deliberately indifferent to the need to train the prosecutors about their *Brady* disclosure obligation with respect to evidence of this type, and (2) the lack of training actually caused the *Brady* violation in this case" (*Connick v. Thompson,* 131 S. Ct. 1358 (2011); (Grometstein & Balboni, 2012, pp. 1261-62). Justice Thomas's majority opinion agreed with Connick's argument that "he was entitled to judgment as a matter of law because Thompson did not prove that he was on actual or constructive notice of, and therefore deliberately indifferent to, a need for more or different *Brady* training" (*Connick v. Thompson,* 131 S. Ct. 1357 (2011); Grometstein & Balboni, 2012, p. 1262).

The failure to disclose exculpatory evidence, while a violation of Brady, was viewed as "single incident" and did not constitute a pattern of "deliberate indifference." The District Attorney was found to have provided sufficient *Brady* training for his staff. Individual assistant prosecutors are to be held liable for their own misconduct.

In *Imbler v. Pachtman,* 424 U.S. 409 (1976), the United States Supreme Court considered the civil liabilities of the prosecutors. Following Paul Imbler's conviction for murder, new evidence was discovered that would have compromised the state's case. The prosecutor had knowingly introduced false testimony at trial and withheld evidence that would have significantly aided Imbler's defense. Imbler filed a suit for "loss of liberty" for the actions of the prosecution. The U.S. Supreme Court held that "A state prosecuting attorney who, as here, acted within the scope of his duties initiating and pursuing a criminal prosecution and in presenting the State's case, is absolutely immune from a civil suit for damages under Section 1983 for alleged deprivations of the accused's constitutional rights" (*Imbler v. Pachtman*, pp. 417-431). It should be noted that Section 1983 suits (42 U.S.C. Section 1983) provides in part for civil actions against agents of the government for violations of a person's constitutional rights. Section 1983 reads in part:

> any citizen of the United States or other person within the jurisdiction thereof to the deprivation of any rights, privileges, or immunities secured by the Constitution and laws, shall be liable to the party injured in an action at law, suit in equity, or other proper proceeding for redress. (U.S.C. Section 1983, 2010)

Nonetheless, the protection against civil suit of prosecutors afforded in *Imbler* (1976) was extended in *Van de Kamp et al. v. Goldstein*, 129 S. Ct. 855 (2009) to cover the misconduct involved in the administration of the District Attorney's office. Thomas Lee Goldstein was convicted of murder largely on the testimony of a jailhouse informant, known as Fink, who received a reduced prison sentence for his cooperation with the prosecution. District Attorney John Van de Kamp failed to inform the defense of the Fink's background as a repeat witness for the state in exchange for sentence reductions. Following his release from prison, Goldstein filed a suit alleging that Van de Kamp had failed to "properly train or supervise prosecutors or to establish an information system containing potential impeachment material about informants" (2009). The U.S. Supreme Court held in *Van de Kamp v. Goldstein*, 555 U.S. 335 (2009) that the District Attorney Goldstein was entitled to absolute immunity from civil claims involving his "supervision, training, and information-system management."

PROSECUTORIAL REFORMS

Law Professor Peter Joy (2006) argues that prosecutorial misconduct is a consequence of three institutional factors: (1) "vague ethics rules that provide ambiguous guidance to prosecutors; (2) vast discretionary authority with little or no transparency; and (3) inadequate remedies for prosecutorial misconduct" (p. 400). Reliance on ethical guidelines[4] to curb prosecutorial misconduct depends on the willingness of the prosecutor to accept them in their day-to-day decision-making.

---

4. See Table 4.1–Model for Professional Conduct for Prosecutors.

Oversight of the work of a prosecutor is virtually absent. Cases are processed as expeditiously as possible, evidence is assessed, charging decisions are made; for the vast majority plea bargains are negotiated, and the matter has been resolved. Strict observance of ethical rules of prosecutorial conduct is weighed against the institutional demands that measure success in terms of conviction rates and the avoidance of successful appellate review.

Fear of disciplinary action by a governmental entity or bar association rarely affects prosecutorial decision-making. Prosecutorial misconduct seldom includes elements of any criminal offense, making criminal prosecution exceedingly unlikely (Scheck, 2010). However, prosecutors are granted absolute immunity from any civil actions against them. Effective reforms must address the institutional context in which prosecutorial immunity is played out as well as the motives for engaging in a disregard for the American Bar Association's guidelines for professional conduct. The Center for Prosecutorial Integrity provides a comprehensive outline of policies designed "to assure prosecutor fulfillment of ethical principles" (Center for Prosecutor Integrity, 2014, p. 2). The Center's report follows the American Bar Association's Model Rules of Professional Conduct (1983). Particularly important for reducing wrongful convictions are the policy recommendations dealing with: (1) review boards and commissions, (2) District Attorney's office policies, (3) the adjudication of a criminal case, and (4) legal remedies for wrongful convictions.

Review Board Commissions

Prosecutors are admonished to remedy a conviction when they know of "clear and convincing evidence establishing that a defendant in the prosecutor's jurisdiction was convicted of an offense that the defendant did not commit" (ABA Rule 3.8). Innocence Commissions and Prosecution Review Boards are two reforms that address the reversal of a wrongful conviction. Innocence Commissions act independently to identify and reverse wrongful convictions.[5] Because of the ineffectiveness of existing disciplinary oversight of prosecutorial misconduct, the establishment of independent Prosecution Review Boards is recommended. The Prosecution Review Board would be composed of persons with particular expertise in the adjudication of a criminal case,

---

5. For more information on Innocence Commissions, see Chapter 9.

e.g., prosecutors, judges, and defense attorney. Following the scrutiny of appellate findings of misconduct, the Board would determine whether disciplinary action was warranted (Center for Prosecutor Integrity, 2014, p. 8).

District Attorney's Office Policies

Policy and Procedural Manuals

The American Bar Association recommends that prosecutor's offices institute "general policies to guide the exercise of prosecutorial discretion and procedures of the office." Similar guidelines should be developed "to determine whether criminal proceedings should be instituted" (ABA Model Rules 3-3 4 (c); Center for Prosecutor Integrity, 2014, p. 8). An office manual, which specifies the policies and procedures governing prosecutorial discretion and consequences for ethical or legal breaches, should be made available to the public, except in confidential matters. Making the office manual available to the public would significantly enhance the transparency of the District Attorney's office. The Center specifically recommends that the manual consider "compliance with Brady rules, plea bargaining procedures, and internal investigational and disciplinary measures for allegations of prosecutor misconduct" (Center for Prosecutor Integrity, 2014, p. 8).

Conviction Units

In addition, Conviction Units should be organized within the prosecutor's office "to review post-conviction claims of innocence in accordance with the state's Code of Criminal Procedure" (Center for Prosecutor Integrity, 2014, p. 9). These internal Conviction Units would be able to review decisions that led to the decision to "go forward" with the prosecution of innocent persons and the process of averting a "near miss."

Adjudication of a Criminal Case

Petitioning of Charging Decisions

Charging a person with a crime without probable cause, or over-charging in the absence of supporting evidence to gain a plea bargaining advantage is inconsistent with the American Bar Association Model Rules for Professional Conduct (Rule 3-3.9, and 3.9(1)). To counter these forms of prosecutorial misconduct, the Center recommends that the defendants have the "right to petition a court of competent jurisdiction to review the criminal charges lodged against him/her, and to have the benefit of an evidentiary hearing to determine if the facts reasonably support the crimes charged by the prosecutor. The court shall have the authority to modify, alter, reduce or eliminate the criminal charges" (Center for Prosecutor Integrity, 2014, p. 10).

Open-File Discovery

Open-file discovery refers to the ability of defense and prosecuting attorneys to review the files of each other. The timely disclosure of exculpatory evidence would forestall the prosecutor's pursuit of an unfounded conviction. Plea bargains would also be negotiated based on the actual strength of the prosecution's evidence. The open-file discovery recommendation is consistent with the American Bar Association guideline that prosecutors "should not intentionally fail to make timely disclosure to the defense, at the earliest feasible opportunity, of the existence of all evidence, or information which tends to negate the guilt of the accused or mitigate the offense charged or which would tend to reduce the punishment of the accused" (American Bar Association's Model Rule 3-3.1 (a)).

Witness and Jailhouse Informant Agreements

Jailhouse and other informants are compensated for their testimony against the defendant. Yet, the American Bar Association admonishes prosecutors "not to compensate a witness, other than an expert, for giving testimony" (American Bar Association's Model Rule 3-3.2(a)). The Center concurs with the Illinois's recommendations that prior to the trial the nature of the informant-prosecution relationship be disclosed to the defense. Specifically, the information to be disclosed includes:

1. the criminal history of the witness,
2. statements made by the accused to the in-custody informant,
3. any incentives that the witness has, will, or may receive in exchange for testimony,
4. whether and how often the witness has agreed to testify at prior criminal trials,
5. whether the witness has recanted his or her testimony, or made statements inconsistent with the testimony to be presented at trial (752 Ill. Comp. Stat. 5/115-21(c) (2003)).

The Justice Project: Jailhouse Snitch Testimony (2007) has set forth four specific recommendations to address the drawbacks of using jailhouse snitches and other compensated witnesses. The recommendations are:

1. **Written Pretrial Disclosure**–Prior to the trial, prosecutors should "make written disclosures regarding the circumstances of the cooperation agreements and any other information about the credibility of a jailhouse snitch."

2. **Pretrial Reliability Hearings**–The court would be responsible for determining "that the jailhouse snitch's testimony is sufficiently reliable to submit to the jury by considering all factors that bear on the credibility of the jailhouse snitch, based on all information made available through written pretrial disclosures."

3. **Corroboration**–To enhance transparency, "prosecutors should be required to disclose and present any information corroborating the witness' testimony."

4. **Cautionary Jury Instructions**–Juries should be provided the information needed to assess the credibility of testimony. Juries should be advised as to: "(1) explicit or implied inducements that the jailhouse snitch received, may receive, or will receive; (2) the prior criminal history of the informant; (3) evidence that he or she is a 'career informant' who has testified in other cases; and (4) any other factors that might tend to render the witness' testimony unreliable."[6]

---

6. For more information see: The Justice Project. (2007). *Jailhouse snitch testimony: A policy review.* Washington, D.C. Retrieved from http://www.pewtrusts.org/~/media/legacy/up-loadedfiles/wwwpewtrustsorg/reports/death_penalty_reform/jailhouse20snitch20testi-mony20policy20briefpdf.pdf.

Plea Bargaining Reform

Plea negotiations are central to the administration of criminal justice across the country. Defendants who invoke their right to a jury trial are a distinct minority and are often viewed as disruptive to the efficient functioning of the justice system. Except in high profile cases and those involving particularly heinous crimes, prosecutors make every effort to strike a plea bargain with the defense. The plea bargaining process then gives rise to misrepresenting the strength of the evidence to the defense to gain an advantage in the bargaining process. The American Bar Association cautions prosecutors to "not knowingly make false statements or representations as to fact or law in the course of plea discussions with defense counsel or the accused" (3-4.1(c), p. 12) and, "the prosecutor should disclose to the court any information in the prosecutor's files relevant to the sentence" (3-6.2).

The Center report cites the Department of Justice, Principles of Federal Prosecution (2002) suggestions for ensuring the integrity of the plea bargaining process. The Department of Justice's reforms include: (1) "end mandatory minimum sentences, (2) restore sentencing discretion to the judiciary, and (3) requires the prosecutor to present to the judge factors regarding the disposition of the case to justify each plea" (Center for Prosecutorial Integrity, 2014, p. 12).

Mandatory Judicial Reporting

Investigations into prosecutorial misconduct are rarely carried out and largely unknown to the public. A finding of "harmless error" most typically characterizes the outcome of any review of misdeeds of a prosecutor. Harmless error refers to "only the strength of the evidence, not on the egregiousness of the prosecutor's misconduct" (Center for Prosecutor Integrity, 2014, p. 13). If the "errors" of the prosecutor are found to be "harmless," then the matter is dismissed. Therefore, the Center for Prosecutorial Integrity (2014) recommends that states "should strengthen their judicial reporting to include *all* instances of violations of prosecutor ethics" (p. 13).

Legal Remedies for Wrongful Convictions

Given the totality of circumstances surrounding the prosecutor's misconduct, the Center recommends either case exoneration or sentence reduction. When the defendant's constitutional rights have been summarily ignored or the American Bar Association's ethical guidelines disregarded, the defendant's exoneration is warranted. However, the Center for Prosecutorial Integrity (2013, pp. 13-14) holds that cases that only involve minor ethical infractions, a sentence reduction may be appropriate.

Statute of Limitations

Statutes of Limitations on seeking redress for prosecutorial misconduct vary widely across the country. Nonetheless prosecutorial misconduct may occur at several stages of the processing of a criminal case. Defendants should not be prohibited from raising the issue of misconduct simply because it did not occur within the limited time frame covered by the state's statue. The Center for Prosecutorial Integrity (2014) recommends that: "Statutes of limitation concerning disciplinary proceedings should be eliminated, lengthened, or at least started at the time of discovery and not at the time of occurrence" (p. 15). [7]

Post-Exoneration Compensation

Monetary or other compensations for wrongfully incarcerating a person always falls short of justice. Yet, reparation for the failings of the criminal justice system must be provided to all wrongfully convicted persons. The Center concurs with Jessica R. Lonergan that states should provide monetary compensation for "time in prison, provide job training, and allow the wrongfully convicted to receive rehabilitative medical and psychological care" (Lonergan, 2008).

Peter Joy (2006) stresses clarification of ethical standard of prosecutorial behavior and increased accountability for their transgressions. Central to his recommendations is the need for greater prosecutorial transparency and establishing guidelines for the use of discretion. He further concurs with the recommendation of American Bar Association that each prosecutor's office develop a handbook that specifies policies for the use of discretion. Joy (2006, p. 421). He suggests that the American Bar Association conduct a nationwide "ground up review" of prosecutorial ethical violations of Model Rule 3.8. [8]

---

7. For further discussion of reforms see: Center for Prosecutor Integrity. (2014). *Roadmap for Prosecutorial Reform*. Posted at: http://www.prosecutorintegrity.org.
8. For a further discussion of compensation see Chapter 8.

Professional Integrity Programs

Attorney Barry Scheck, co-founder of the nation's first Innocent Project at Cardozo Law School in New York, provides a comprehensive analysis of the causes of Brady violations and the reasons for the failure of institutional and legal sanctions to curb prosecutorial misconduct. Scheck argues that: "Civil liability, state or bar disciplinary action, the stigma of appellate reversal, and the threat of criminal prosecution have failed to provide effective deterrence against Brady violations as well as other forms of misconduct" (Scheck, 2010, p. 2215).

Three leading causes of Brady violations, identified by Scheck, are:

(1) the Brady material was not in the prosecutor's file because the police did not provide it in written form to the prosecutor working on the case, 2) The Brady material was in the prosecution's file, or known to the prosecutor from an oral communication, but the prosecutor did not identify it as Brady material and, therefore, did not turn it over to the defense, and 3) The prosecutor did not turn over information to the defense that he or she knew or strongly suspected could be Brady material out of fear. (Scheck, 2010, p. 2216)

Administrative lapses between the police and prosecutors and within the prosecutor's offices result in Brady violations. Also, a prosecutor may fear reprisal from within the District Attorney's office for failure to disclose Brady material, or fear a reprimand from a judge, or simply fear of losing the case.

To Scheck, prosecutors themselves are central to reduction of Brady violations. Internal regulations, established within the prosecutor's office, are viewed as the most effective strategy for ensuring the disclosure of exculpatory evidence to the defense. Scheck recommends the establishment of Professional Integrity Programs within the office of the District Attorney to provide administrative guidelines and oversight for all matters relevant to the handling of potentially exculpatory evidence.

A Professional Integrity Program "refers to an office's quality assurance and compliance program" (Scheck, 2010, p. 2238). Scheck sets forth five principles that guide the functioning of such a program. First, checklist and disclosure conferences should be established and occur at the pretrial and post-arraignment phases of the processing of a criminal case. Scheck notes that the pretrial checklist and disclosures are crucial to uncovering *Brady* material, and left undetected may well alter the outcome of a criminal case. At the pre-trial stage a checklist of items to be disclosed to the defense would be created. The list would vary by the type of crime committed, e.g., drug offense, violent or property crime. In addition, any unique characteristics of the police units conducting the investigation would be considered when drawing up the checklist.

The post-indictment checklist and disclosure conference are designed to identify any *Brady* material that may have escaped detection during the pretrial phase. Consistency in the pretrial and post-indictment phases of the process is vitally important. To Scheck, consistency enhances efficiency and "enables the prosecutors' office to implement an effective error-tracking and data-gathering system" (Scheck, 2010, pp. 2242-43).

Second, the Professional Integrity Program should include procedures for "error tracking, data gathering" and the analysis of "near misses." While gathering data on all errors is important, it is an understanding of the "near misses," the "disclosures of *Brady* material that are made after the pretrial disclosure conferences" that are most crucial to the outcome of the case. Remedies may then be designed to address specific flaws in the processing of a criminal case (Scheck, 2010, pp. 2242-43).

Third, District Attorneys must provide their staff with a clear definition of *Brady* material. Each prosecutor must understand the kinds of exculpatory evidence and the procedure for its timely disclosure to the defense. Four, audits of cases involving reversals and harmless errors should be conducted. The "root cause" of the errors that resulted in the appellate court's reversal of the trial outcome must be understood and a decisive plan to remedy the defects in the process must be set in motion without delay. Likewise, harmless error cases should be carefully scrutinized to determine the flaws in the process before they become grounds for reversal. And, five, Scheck recommends that each District Attorney initiate a continuing education program to establish a "culture of integrity" for the entire staff. Acceptance of the values and procedures of the Professional Integrity Program by the prosecuting attorneys and their support staff is vital to the reduction of prosecutorial misconduct.

CONCLUSION

Prosecutorial misconduct is widespread, largely undetected, and rarely disciplined. The clandestine nature of prosecutorial decision-making and the unwillingness to reverse the consequences of common flaws fuel its continuance. The mutually dependent relationship between the police and prosecutors often obscures potentially exculpatory evidence and impedes its disclosure to the defense. Defense attorneys themselves may be compliant in the actions taken to quickly resolve a criminal case. Defense attorneys may work in tandem with the prosecutor to arrive at a plea bargain acceptable to the defendant and the court. Innocent clients, faced with lengthy prison sentences, or even the death penalty, may be encouraged by their own advocates to plead guilty to a lesser charge and accept a sentence reduction.

For some prosecutors, the assumption of guilt may justify any mishandling of potentially exculpatory evidence, overcharging the suspect in the absence of credible supporting evidence, and engaging in inflammatory remarks to the jury to gain a conviction. Believing that the defendant is eminently "convictable," the prosecutor may unwittingly become involved in a "self-fulfilling prophesy." As Scheck has argued prosecutorial misconduct is best countered by the prosecutors themselves. Ethical and legal self-regulation will guide their decision-making, significantly reducing the likelihood of a wrongful conviction.

Chapter 5

INEFFECTIVE ASSISTANCE OF COUNSEL

> In actuality, our criminal justice system is almost exclusively a system of plea bargaining, negotiated behind closed doors and with no judicial oversight. The outcome is very largely determined by the prosecutor alone.
>
> – Judge Jed S. Rakoff, 2014

THE CASE OF RON WILLIAMSON

The scene was horrific. Shattered glass was found at the entrance of the Debbie Carter's garage apartment; a small den was torn apart, and on the wall written in nail polish was: "Jim Smith next will die." On the kitchen table, scrawled in Catsup was – "Don't look fore us or ealse." The bedroom was torn apart – evidence of a violent attack. The bed was shoved against the door, blankets, night clothes, and stuffed animals were thrown around the room. Debbie Carter was found naked face down on the floor with a bloody washcloth shoved in her mouth. "Die" written with fingernail polish on her back along with the name "Duke Gram" in Catsup. An electrical cord and belt bucket with "Debbie" engraved on it was found under her body.

The night before her rape and murder, Debbie Carter was working as a waitress/bartender at the Coachlight Club in Ada, Oklahoma. She spent some time socializing with her friends who reported that Glen Gore insisted that she dance with him, only to have her storm off the dance floor to get away from him. Her friends knew that Debbie was afraid of him because of his violent temper. Later that evening she again was confronted by Glen Gore when she was attempting to leave the parking lot. After talking with him briefly, she shoved him away from her car and drove home. Glen Gore was the last person to see Debbie Carter alive.

The police initially interviewed several persons who were at the Coachlight Club the night before Debbie Carter's murder. Glen Gore was questioned by the police, but after giving a short statement, he was released. No physical evidence, e.g., hair, fingernail clippings, or skin scraping, was taken from him. Shortly after giving his statement to the police, Glen Gore mentioned to the police that the night before the murder he saw Ron Williamson bothering Debbie Carter at the Coachlight Club – no one at the club that night saw Ron Williamson there. Ron was well-known for his boisterous, attention getting behavior, so if he were there, it would have been widely known.

For the next four and a half years the murderer remained at large. In the small town of Ada, the residents became increasingly agitated, another young women had been murdered, they wanted "justice to be served" without delay.

Meanwhile Ron Williamson's life was in a tailspin. His promising career as a baseball player ended, as did his marriage to the former Miss Ada of Oklahoma. He was drinking heavily, getting into bar fights, and suffering from progressive psychological deterioration. He was arrested for passing worthless checks and held in a local jail. Terri Holland, held in the same jail for a similar offense, notified the police that she overheard Ron Williamson confess to murdering Debbie Carter. The police investigation quickly focused on Ron and Dennis Fritz, his bar-hopping friend, who was also known to frequent the Coachlight Club. Based on the scrawled message-"Don't look fore us or ealse"-found on the Debbie's kitchen table, the police believed there were two offenders involved in the crime.

To strengthen their case against Ron, the police reported that Ron had confided to them: "Okay, I had a dream about killing Debbie, was on her, had a cord around her neck, stabbed her, frequently pulled the rope tight around her neck" (Grisham, 2006). Ron immediately followed his comment with "I would never confess." The police, however, did view Ron's retelling his dream as a voluntary confession and, therefore, it constituted admissible evidence.

In 1988, about six years after the rape and murder of Debbie Carter the trials of Dennis Fritz and Ron Williamson began. Seventeen hairs, said to match both Dennis Fritz and Ron Williamson, were submitted as evidence at trial. Semen samples were also collected, but did not match either Dennis Fritz or Ron Williamson. Dennis Fritz was tried first, convicted of first-degree murder and sentenced to life imprisonment.

In a second trial, Terri Holland, a jailhouse snitch who allegedly overhead Ron Williamson confess to the murder of Debbie Carter, was a key witness for the state. Ron Williamson was also convicted of first degree murder, but was sentenced to death.

Ron Williamson was represented by a court-appointed lawyer whose trial preparation was minimal at best. The attorney failed to consider Ron's history of mental illness; the confession of Ricky Simmons, another suspect in the case, who confessed to the police that he killed Debbie Carter; and Glen Gore's refusal to testify at the trial because "he was serving a forty-year sentence on convictions for, among other things, burglary, kidnapping, shooting with intent to injure, and feloniously pointing a weapon all involving an attack on a young woman and her daughter" (*Williamson v. Reynolds*, 904 F. Supp. 1529 (E.D. Okla. 1995)). As a result of his unwillingness to testify at trial, the jury was unaware of Glen Gore's violent criminal history.

Further, Ron Williamson's defense attorney did not interview Tommy Glover who witnessed the argument between Glen Gore and Debbie Carter that ended with her shoving him away to escape from the Coachlight Club parking lot. The defense attorney's failure to conduct a diligent investigation of the witnesses and his lack of challenge to the validity of the state's forensic evidence resulted in Ron Williamson's conviction and sentence to death.

Eleven years after his conviction, Ron came within five days of execution before the Innocence Project in New York's motion was granted to have DNA tests conducted on the semen and hair samples collected at the crime scene. Both Ron Williamson and Dennis Fritz were excluded from any involvement in the crime. Glen Gore, however, was positively identified as the person who raped and murdered Debbie Carter.[1]

THE RIGHT TO ASSISTANCE OF COUNSEL

The Sixth Amendment to the United States Constitution provides, in part, that persons who are criminally prosecuted "shall enjoy the

---

1. For more information see: Grisham, J. (2006). *The innocent man: Murder in a small town.* New York: Doubleday. And, Williams v. Reynolds, 904 F. Supp. 1529 (F.D. Okla. 1995).

right . . . to have the Assistance of Counsel for his defense." The meaning of "Assistance of Counsel" has been variously interpreted by the courts and in the everyday practice of prosecuting criminal cases. The American Bar Association's Model Rules for Professional Conduct recommends that: "in all professional functions a lawyer should be competent, prompt and diligent. A lawyer should maintain communication with a client concerning the representation." With regard to competence, Model Rule 1.1 states: "Competent representation requires the legal knowledge, skill, thoroughness and preparation reasonably necessary for the representation." Competent legal representation is supported by Model Rule 1.3, which recommends that a lawyer "shall act with reasonable diligence and promptness in representing a client." Table 5.1, summarizes the model rules of professional conduct for defense attorneys[2].

The American Bar Association's Standards for Defense Functions specifically recommends guidelines for protecting the interests of criminal defendants. Rule 4-3.7(a) (f) states:

> Defense counsel should inform the client of his or her rights in the criminal process at the earliest opportunity, and timely plan and take necessary actions to vindicate such rights within the scope of the representation. For each matter, defense counsel should consider what procedural and investigative steps to take and motions to file, and not simply follow rote procedures learned from prior matters. Defense counsel should not be deterred from sensible action merely because counsel has not previously seen a tactic used, or because such action might incur criticism or disfavor. Before acting, defense counsel should discuss novel or unfamiliar matters or issues with colleagues or other experienced counsel, employing safeguards to protect confidentiality and avoid conflicts of interest. (ABA, 2015)

The American Bar Association further recommends that defense attorneys keep the defendant informed about the development of the case. In particular, Standard 4-6.2 (b) states that: "Defense counsel should keep the accused advised of developments arising out of plea discussions with the prosecutor." Standard 4-6.2(b) further notes that: "Defense counsel should promptly communicate and explain to the accused all significant plea proposals made by the prosecutor."

---

2. For more information see: American Bar Association. (2015). *Criminal justice standards for the defense function.* Retrieved from https://www.americanbar.org/groups/criminal_justice/standards/DefenseFunctionFourthEdition.html.

Table 5.1
AMERICAN BAR ASSOCIATION –
MODEL RULES OF PROFESSIONAL CONDUCT

American Bar Association – Model Rules of Professional Conduct *General Standards for Defense Attorneys*
Standard 4-1.9 (a) Defense counsel should act with reasonable diligence and promptness in representing a client.
Standard 4-1.8 (a) Defense counsel should not carry a workload that, by reason of its excessive size, interferes with the rendering of quality representation, endangers the client's interest in the speedy disposition of charges, or may lead to the breach of professional obligations. Defense counsel should not accept employment for the purpose of delaying trial.
Standard 4-3.7 (a) Many important rights of the accused can be protected and preserved only by prompt legal action. Defense counsel should inform the accused of his or her rights at the earliest opportunity and take all necessary action to vindicate such rights. (f) Defense counsel should consider all procedural and investigative steps to take and motions to file.
Standard 4-3.9 (a) Defense counsel should keep the client informed of the developments in the case and the progress of preparing the defense and should promptly comply with reasonable requests for information. (b) Defense counsel should explain the developments in the case to the extent reasonably necessary to permit the client to make informed decisions regarding the representation.
Standard 4-4.1 (a) Defense counsel should conduct a prompt investigation of the circumstance of the case and explore all avenues leading to facts relevant to the merits of the case and the penalty in the event of conviction. (b) The duty to investigate exists regardless of the accused's admissions or statements to defense counsel of facts constituting guilt or the accused stated desire to plead guilty. (c) The investigation should include efforts to secure information in the possession of the prosecutor and law enforcement authorities.
Standard 4-6.1 (b) Defense counsel may engage in plea discussions with the prosecutor. Under no circumstances should defense counsel recommend to the defendant acceptance of a plea unless appropriate investigation and study of the case has been completed, including an analysis of controlling law and the evidence likely to be included at trial.
Standard 4-6.2 (b) Defense counsel should keep the accused advised of developments arising out of plea discussions conducted with the prosecutor. Defense counsel should promptly communicate and explain to the accused all significant plea proposals made by the prosecutor.

Continued on next page

Table 5.1 – *continued*

(f) Defense counsel should not knowingly make false statements concerning the evidence in the course of plea discussions with the prosecutor.

(h) Defense counsel representing two or more clients in the same or related cases should not participate in any aggravated agreement as to guilt or nolo contendere pleas, unless each client consents after consultation, including disclosure of the existence and nature of all the claims or pleas involved.

(i) Defense counsel should not seek concessions favorable to one client by any agreement which is detrimental to the legitimate interests of a client in another case.

Standard 4-9.6 (b) If the defense counsel concludes that he or she did not provide effective assistance in an earlier phase of the case, defense counsel should explain this conclusion to the defendant and seek to withdraw from representation with an explanation to the court of the reason therefore.

The principle of fundamental fairness underlies the right of criminal defendants to be legally represented. Clarence Earl Gideon, an indigent defendant, was charged with felonious breaking and entering a poolroom in Florida. He asked the court for a lawyer to represent him at trial, but his request was denied. While serving a five-year sentence, Gideon drafted a handwritten Writ of Certiorari requesting the U.S. Supreme Court to review his case. In the 1963, landmark right to counsel case of *Gideon v. Wainwright*, 372 U.S. 335 the United State Supreme Court held: "The right of an indigent defendant in a criminal trial to have the assistance of counsel is a fundamental right essential to a fair trial and petitioner's trial and conviction without the assistance of counsel violated the Fourteenth Amendment." The Fourteenth Amendment states, in part, ". . . nor shall any state deprive any person of life, liberty, or property, without due process of law; nor deny any person within its jurisdiction the equal protection of the laws."

The Court in the Gideon decision extended the right to counsel provided by *Powell v. Alabama,* 287 U.S. 45 (1932) to include indigent defendants who are charged with any felony. Yet, indigent misdemeanant defendants would not be provided legal representation until the Court heard the case of *Argersinger v. Hamlin,* 407 U.S. 25 (1972). Jon Argersinger was denied legal representation for his trial on misdemeanor charge of carrying a concealed weapon, which carried a maximum sentence of six months and $1,000 dollar fine. He was convicted and sentenced to 90 days in jail. Florida Supreme Court upheld the lower court's ruling that Argersinger was not entitled to a defense attorney because the ruling in *Duncan v. Louisiana*, 391 U.S. 145 (1968) held the right that legal representation must only be provided "for non-petty offenses punishable by more than six months imprisonment." In Argersinger, the U.S. Supreme Court held that an indigent defendant who is charged with any crime that may involve the possibility of loss of freedom must be provided a defense attorney. The majority opinion concluded that:

> absent a valid waiver, a person may not be imprisoned even for lesser offenses unless he was represented by counsel at the trial. In simplest terms, this means that under no circumstances, in any court in the land, may anyone be imprisoned-however briefly-unless he was represented by, or waived his right to counsel. (*Argersinger v. Hamlin*, 407 U.S. 25 (1972))

The right to assistance of counsel in any criminal prosecution, provided by the Sixth Amendment, is interpreted to extend to all criminal defendants whose conviction may involve confinement in a prison or jail. However, the competence of the attorney and diligence exercised in representing the accused is not considered in the cases establishing the right to counsel.

EFFECTIVENESS OF THE ASSISTANCE OF COUNSEL

The U.S. Supreme Court has addressed the issue of the effectiveness of the assistance of counsel. In the 1984, the case of *Strickland v. Washington*, 466 U.S. 668 considered criteria for determining the parameters of ineffective assistance of counsel. David Washington was convicted in Florida of three capital murders. At the time of his trial, Washington told the judge that he had no prior criminal history, but his failure to be able to provide for his family caused him to resort to multiple burglaries that led to the murders. At the presentence hearing trial, Washington's defense attorney failed to introduce character witnesses, or arrange for a psychiatric examination. The judge commended Washington for his honesty and acceptance of responsibility, but nonetheless sentenced him to death *(Strickland v. Washington, 1984)*.

In *Strickland v. Washington*, 466 U.S. (1984), the Court reviewed Washington's claim of ineffective assistance of counsel that led to the

imposition of the death penalty. The Court held that to reverse a conviction or death sentence on the grounds of ineffective assistance of
counsel, the petitioner must show: "that counsel's performance was deficient and, second, the deficient performance prejudiced the defense
so as to deprive the defendant of a fair trial" *(U.S. Strickland v. Washington,* 1984). The Court further pointed out that the totality of circumstances must be taken into account when judging an attorney's
"reasonably effective assistance." For the representation by the defense
attorney to be considered below "an objective standard of reasonable-
ness," the Court held that:

> every effort be made to eliminate the distorting effects of hindsight, to
> reconstruct the circumstances of counsel's challenged conduct, and to
> evaluate the conduct from counsel's perspective at the time. A court
> must indulge a strong presumption that counsel's conduct falls within
> the wide range of reasonable professional assistance. (*U.S. Strickland v.
> Washington,* 1984)

Further, to show that the defense attorney's conduct prejudiced that
case, the Court held "that there is a reasonable probability that, but for
counsel's unprofessional errors, the result of the proceedings would
have been different. A reasonable probability is a probability sufficient
to undermine confidence in the outcome" (*U.S. Strickland v. Washington,*
1984). The Court concluded that Washington's attorney did not act un-
reasonable in arguing for the defense. However, the Court held that
even if the attorney did act unreasonably his conduct did not prejudice
the outcome of the case; thereby justifying the Court's refusal to over-
turn Washington's death sentence.

In *Strickland v. Washington,* the U.S. Supreme Court limited its decision to legal representation at trial. However, in *Missouri v. Frye,* 132 S.
Ct. 1399 (2012), the U.S. Supreme Court addressed the issue of ineffective assistance of counsel in plea bargained cases. Galen Frye was
facing his fourth conviction for driving with a revoked license, a felony
in the State of Missouri. The prosecutor presented two plea options to
Frye's defense attorney. Initially, the prosecutor offered a three-year
sentence with no probation, but a recommendation for a 10- day
"shock" jail sentence. The second plea offer would reduce the felony
conviction to a misdemeanor with three months in jail. Frye's attorney
was formally presented with each proposal with expiration dates

attached to each proposal. However, the attorney failed to notify Frye about either proposal. As a consequence, Galen Frye was convicted at trial and sentenced to a three-year prison sentence.

In *Missouri v. Frye,* 132 S. Ct. 1399 (2012), the U.S. Supreme Court considered two questions, First, "whether the constitutional right to counsel extends to the negotiation and consideration of plea offers that lapse or are rejected." The second question concerned: "what must a defendant demonstrate in order to show prejudice resulted from counsel's deficient performance." With regard to the first question, the Court noted "that as a general rule defense counsel has the duty to communicate formal offers from the prosecution to accept a plea on terms and conditions that may be favorable to the accused." In *Frye*'s case, the Court found that: "When defense counsel allowed the offer to expire without advising the defendant or allowing him to consider it, defense counsel did not render the effective assistance the Constitution requires."

The second question concerned the demonstration of prejudice resulting from the defense attorney's failings. The Court ruled that to show prejudice, the defendant "must demonstrate a reasonable probability the plea would have been entered without the prosecution canceling it or the trial court refusing to accept it, if they had the authority to exercise that discretion under state law." In the case of *Frye*, to establish prejudice he would be required "to show a reasonable probability that the end result of the criminal process would have been more favorable by reason of a plea to a lesser charge or a sentence of less prison time." Because the issue of prejudice involves Missouri state law governing the prosecution's right to cancel a plea offer or the trial court's right to refuse to accept it, the U.S. Supreme Court remanded the issue of prejudice to Missouri Court of Appeals. The U. S. Supreme Court did, however, conclude: "The Sixth Amendment right to effective assistance of counsel extends to the consideration of plea offers that lapse or are rejected and that right applies to all critical stages of the criminal proceedings."

In *Lafler v. Cooper,* 132 S. Ct. 1376 (2012) again considered the issue of ineffective assistance of counsel in the context of a plea negotiation. Anthony Cooper pointed a gun at the head of a woman, and, as she was running away, he shot her in the thigh and buttocks. The prosecutor offered a plea to intent to murder, which carried a 4-7-year prison sentence. Cooper's court appointed-attorney advised him to reject the offer on the grounds that the state would not be able to convict him for intent to kill since he shot the victim in areas that would not likely cause death. At the time of the trial, the prosecutor offered a plea bargain, but with a longer sentence. Again, Cooper's attorney recommended that he decline the offer and let the jury decide the case. The jury convicted Anthony Cooper on all charges; and a sentence of 15 to 30 years was imposed.

In their review of Cooper's claim of ineffective assistance of counsel, the U.S. Supreme Court accepted the stipulation of all parties that Cooper's court appointed counsel provided an inadequate defense. However, Cooper's claim of ineffective assistance of counsel required that he show:

> that but for the ineffective advice of counsel there is a reasonable probability that the plea offer would have been presented to the court, that the court would have accepted the terms, and that the conviction or sentence, or both, under the offer's terms would have been less severe than under the judgment and sentence imposed. (*Lafler v. Cooper,* 2012)

The Court then considered only the issue of prejudice to Cooper resulting from the unjustified advice of his attorney. The Court concluded:

> there is a reasonable probability he and the trial court would have accepted the guilty plea. In addition, as a result of not accepting the plea and being convicted at trial, respondent received a minimum sentence 3½ times greater than he would have received under the plea. The standard for ineffective assistance under *Strickland* has thus been satisfied. (*Lafler v. Cooper,* 2012)

Forms of Ineffective Assistance of Counsel

A wide range of defense attorney inadequacies underlie defendants' claims of ineffective assistance of counsel. Benner (2009) has identified specific obstacles to providing defensible legal representation:

1. Excessive attorney caseloads
2. Excessive defense investigator caseloads

3. Inability to interview prosecution witnesses
4. Failure of prosecutors to turn over favorable Brady evidence
5. Difficulty in obtaining DNA testing
6. Judicial pressure to expedite cases
7. County board pressure to keep costs down
8. Lack of independence

Benner's (2009) analysis of more than 2,500 assistance of counsel claims discovered that only 4 percent were supported by the court. In general, ineffective assistance of counsel claims result from the defense attorney's neglect to adequately investigate the circumstances of the case, including interviewing witnesses to the crime, and expert witnesses for the state.

Several obstacles to effective legal representation occur simultaneously, thereby undermining efforts to provide effective assistance of counsel. Similar findings are reported by the Innocence Project in New York City. Their review of their first 255 DNA exonerations cases shows about 27 percent of the defendants reported multiple defense attorney failings (West, 2010). The most common forms of ineffective assistance of counsel reported are: failure to present defense witnesses, failure to seek DNA or serology testing, failure to object to prosecutor's arguments or statements, failure to object to evidence or suppress evidence, and failure to interview or cross examine witnesses. Of the 54 cases involving claims of ineffective assistance of counsel, 81 percent were rejected by the court, 6 percent were considered harmless, and 13 percent were judged to be harmful to the outcome of the case (West, 2010, p. 3).

The Presumption of Guilt

A key element in the adversarial process is the presumption of innocence. The burden of proof is on the state to prove beyond a reasonable doubt that the defendant is criminally liable for an offense. The defense must simply convince one juror that a reasonable doubt does exist, and as a consequence, the defendant cannot be convicted of the crime. In everyday criminal proceedings, however, the agents of the criminal justice system do not presume the innocence of the accused, but rather his undeniable guilt. As we have seen in Chapters, 2 and 4, the close, largely clandestine, working relationship between the police and prosecutors underpins their belief that justice will only be served when the defendant either accepts a plea bargain, or is found guilty at trial. To the extent that the criminal control perspective takes precedence over the due process model of criminal sanctioning, the burden of the defense is increased (Packer, 1968).

For the most part, indigent criminal defendants are either represented by public defenders or court appointed attorneys. With limited time and few investigatory resources, the defense strategies of public defenders and court appointed attorneys are often compromised. Motions may neither be filed, witnesses interviewed, nor forensic evidence challenged. A vigorous defense premised on the presumption of innocence is less likely. Decisions of attorneys for the indigent may be driven by their intention to minimize the sanctions for their clients, rather than to pursue the presumption of their innocence.

To the extent that the defense attorneys accept the guilt of their defendant, they participate, albeit unwittingly, in a coordinated effort with the police and prosecutors to resolve the criminal case. The objective, then, of the criminal justice process is to bring final closure to the matter. Since most criminal defendants are represented by a public defender or court appointed attorney with limited resources, it is not surprising that more than nine in 10 criminal cases are plea bargained (Devers, 2011). The acceptance of a negotiated plea by the court and defendant, not only eliminates the uncertainty of a trial, but precludes an appeal by the defendant. In short, the case is closed. For a defendant who is guilty of a more serious offense, a plea bargained outcome is beneficial. For an innocent defendant, a carefully orchestrated plea offer is a crushing defeat – the presumption of innocence has been rejected.

Defense of the Indigent

Defense attorneys for the indigent occupy a unique position in the criminal justice system. They are responsible for protecting the constitutional rights of their clients while not impeding the flow of criminal cases through the judicial system. That is, they must try to strike a balance between acting in the best interest of the defendant and the process demands of an overburdened and underfunded criminal justice system. The defenders of the indigent are then caught between their professional responsibilities to their clients and the functional demands of the criminal justice system. In sum, then, attorneys for the indigent are confronted with two related problems to: 1) manage the systemic pressures to expedite the resolution of criminal cases), and 2) meet their professional responsibility to provide effective assistance of counsel to the defendant.

Systemic Pressures

Two central issues face public defenders and, to a lesser extent, court-appointed attorneys: (1) excessive caseload, and (2) lack of adequate funding. The American Bar Association Standards for the defense counsel states that: "Defense counsel should not carry a workload that, by reason of its excessive size, interferes with the rendering of quality representation, endangers the client's interest in the speedy disposition of charges, or may lead to the breach of professional obligations" (ABA Standards, 2015).

The American Bar Association's *Ten Principles of a Public Defense Delivery System* (2002) explicitly recommends that an attorney working full time should have: "no more than 150 noncapital felony defendants per year, or 400 nontraffic misdemeanor defendants, or 200 juvenile clients respectively." Limits on caseload should not be exceeded, and they may well be reduced depending on the legal complexities that arise and competing demands for the attorney's time and resources. Benner (2009) reports that in California (59%) of the public defenders offices represented more felony defendants than the recommended 150 attorney case limit, and attorneys in (75%) of the public defenders offices exceeded the 400 case limit for non-traffic misdemeanors. Excessive indigent defense attorney's caseload is the norm in the United States, rather than an occasional exception.

The Justice Policy Institute (2011) citing the Department of Justice-Census of Public Defense Offices reports that the attorney caseloads of 73 percent of county-based public defenders offices exceeded the national standard, and 23 percent of the public defenders' offices needed twice as many attorneys to meet the national standard. Only 12 percent of the public defenders offices that process more than 5,000 annually met that standard. Further, Farole and Langton (2010) have found that in 79 percent of state public defender systems the attorney caseloads exceeded the nationally recommended limit. Lefstein (2011) concludes that however well-meaning attorneys may be, excessive caseloads prohibit them from providing even a minimally adequate legal defense.

Unmanageable caseloads then underlie the inability of an attorney to comply with the American Bar Associates recommended principles of legal representation. Table 5.2 summarizes the ten principles of public defense delivery system.[3]

Professional Responsibility

Rule 4 of the American Bar Association's *Principles of Public Defense* (2002) states that: "Defense counsel is provided with sufficient time and a confidential space within which to meet with the client." Further, ABA's Rule 5 recommends that: "Defense counsel's workload is controlled to permit the rendering of quality representation." A burdensome caseload affects the attorney's legal and ethical responsibilities to the defendant. The consequences of an excessive caseload diminish the ability of the attorney to carry out other functions necessary for a minimally adequate defense. Time and resources devoted to individual clients are significantly reduced. Markedly compromised is the attorney's ability to consult with the defendant in any meaningful way, to investigate the circumstances of the crime, to interview witnesses, or to prepare a challenge for the state's expert witnesses.

Further, there is considerable judicial pressure to process criminal cases in a timely manner. Defense motions that disrupt the trial docket are discouraged. Public defenders are responsible for presenting more than eight in 10 criminal defendants (Devers, 2011). It is the expectation of the judiciary that public defenders, in particular, understand the importance of the uninterrupted flow of criminal cases. Any disruption in the process affects the work of the prosecutors and the police. It is in the long-term interest of attorneys for the indigent – `public defender and court-appointed lawyers–to elicit the aid of the defendant in resolving the criminal case. The constraints of an excessive caseload, limited resources, and judicial pressures motivate the defense attorney to convince the defendant to accept a negotiated plea. For the innocent person, the outcome is devastating.

---

3. For more information see, American Bar Association. (2002). *Ten principles of public defense delivery system.* Retrieved from https://www.americanbar.org/content/dam/aba/administrative/legal_aid_indigent.

Table 5.2
THE TEN PRINCIPLES OF PUBLIC DEFENSE DELIVERY SYSTEM

AMERICAN BAR ASSOCIATION
Ten Principles of
A Public Defense Delivery System

Principle One:

The defense function, including the selection, funding, and payment of defense counsel, is independent.

Principle Two:

Where the caseload is sufficiently high, the public defense delivery system consists of both a defender office and the active participation of the private bar.

Principle Three:

Clients are screened for eligibility, and defense counsel is assigned and notified of appointment, as soon as feasible after clients' arrest, detention, or request for counsel.

Principle Four:

Defense counsel is provided sufficient time and a confidential space within which to meet with the client.

Principle Five:

Defense counsel's workload is controlled to permit the rendering of quality representation.

Principle Six:

Defense counsel's ability, training, and experience match the complexity of the case.

Principle Seven:

The same attorney continuously represents the client until completion of the case.

Principle Eight:

There is parity between the defense counsel and the prosecution with respect to resources and defense counsel is included as an equal partner in the justice system.

Principle Nine:

Defense counsel is provided with and required to attend continuing legal education.

Principle Ten:

Defense counsel is supervised and systematically reviewed for quality and efficiency according to nationally and locally adopted standards.

In sum, then, the systemic obstacles to effective indigent representation–excessive workload and inadequate funding–impede an attorney's ability to fulfill professional responsibilities. Adherence to the American Bar Association's ten principles for public defense delivery is severely compromised. Excessive caseloads render it impossible to abide by principle four – time necessary to meet with the client – and principle five – the opportunity to provide quality representation. Limited financial and staffing resources undermine the parity between the prosecution and defense, and thereby upsetting the equity in legal representation (principle eight). Inadequate funding and caseload constraints also jeopardize efforts to meet an attorney's continuing education requirement (principle nine).

REFORMS FOR AN EFFECTIVE LEGAL DEFENSE

The American Bar Association's Ten Principles of Indigent Defense Delivery provide a framework for indigent defense reform. There is considerable overlap between systemic and personal responsibility reforms.

Systemic Reforms

The lack of funding for indigent defense representation undermines the fair and judicially defensible administration of justice. Publically supported defense is either provided by state legislatures or county of jurisdiction. Chronic underfunding reflects the lack of political support for indigent defense options. Tax dollars are typically viewed as more wisely spent on the apprehension and prosecution of the criminally accused than for their defense. Raising taxes to fund indigent defense attorneys or diverting monies from needed public services is politically indefensible. As a consequence, publically supported defense counsel must find innovative ways to provide even a modicum of legal representation.

A holistic approach has been proposed to remedy the lack of funding for indigent defense representation. The Holistic Defense model is premised on the understanding that the client's legal issues are typically enmeshed in an array of debilitating socioeconomic conditions. The Center for Holistic Defense, created by the public defender's office in Bronx, New York, posits that ". . . to be truly effective advocates for our clients, we as defenders must broaden the scope of our work to include the collateral consequences of criminal justice involvement as well as the underlying issues, both legal and non-legal, that have played a part in driving our clients into the criminal justice system in the first place" (The Center for Holistic Defense, n.d.).

Effective legal representation, then, depends on a comprehensive approach to the criminal case. The recognition that criminal behavior typically arises from adverse life circumstances influences the direction that plea negotiations may take and the conditions of a just outcome. Changes in the socioeconomic conditions of an indigent defendant's life may well reduce the likelihood of further criminal activity.

The four hallmarks of the Holistic Defense model are:

1. **Seamless access to services that meet clients' legal and social support:** *Issues related to the client's alleged involvement in criminal behavior, e.g., housing, child care, or funds for bail must be simultaneously considered.*

2. **Dynamic, interdisciplinary communication:** *The ability to effectively communicate across a variety of professions e.g., defense attorneys, prosecutors, social worker, and court administrators, is vital to meeting the complex needs of the client. This approach facilitates meeting the various legal and social needs of the client.*

3. **Advocates with an interdisciplinary skill set:** *The holistic team must include professionals who are able to address the collateral needs of the client, e.g., immigration issues, mental health, addiction, etc.*

4. **A robust understanding of, and connection to, the community served:** *Promoting pro-social interests and providing support for the client's reintegration into the community are vital to the success of a holistic approach to indigent legal defense (The Center for Holistic Defense, n.d.).*

For a publically supported defense attorney to achieve parity with the resources available to the prosecution, a cultural shift from an emphasis on the values of the crime control model to a balance with the values of the due process model. The crime control model emphases the values of efficiency, finality, and the presumption of guilt. Conversely, the values of the due process model advocate skepticism, deliberation, and the presumption of innocence (Packer, 1968). The perception of convictability of the accused is central to the adoption of either the crime control or due process model. The perception of convictability of the accused provides a justification for processing the case in an expeditious manner. The goal of expedience is shared by the police and prosecutors and, for varying reasons, by some publically supported defense counsel. Limited by an overburdened caseload and lack of staffing support for an adequate preparation of the case, defense attorneys for the indigent typically may engage in a negotiated plea arrangement with the prosecutor. In a sense the defense counsel become complicit in the efficient resolution of the case. The process of negotiating a plea may well be compromised—the legal interests of the defendant are traded to further the interests of the criminal justice system. As a consequence, innocent persons plead guilty rather than face the prospect of a lengthy prison sentence.

Plea bargaining is central to the administration of justice in the United States. Fewer than one in 10 federal or state criminal cases are actually tried, and in many cases a plea bargain is agreed on before the trial has ended (Devers, 2011, p. 1). Plea negotiations are conducted privately between the prosecutor and defense attorney. The process is largely unknown to the defendant who is simply advised of the prosecutor's charge and sentencing options in exchange for a guilty plea. If a plea bargain is not struck, then the defendant is informed that the prosecution will seek to convict for the most severe charge and for the imposition of the maximum possible sentence.

Reforms in the plea bargaining process are critical to providing effective indigent defense counsel. Transparency in plea negotiations is essential to achieving parity between the prosecutor and defense attorney for the indigent. Rather than a clandestine negotiation process, plea bargaining must become monitored by a third party to ensure that the constitutional rights of the defendant are protected. Barry Scheck (2013) advocates for a more active role of the judiciary in the processing of a criminal case. Scheck argues:

> When indigent defense funding is so inadequate that lawyers cannot even conduct investigations of cases on a regular basis, the executive branch accumulates too much unchecked power to prosecute and to influence the outcomes on grounds other than the merits, and, as a consequence, the judicial branch is denied its duty to decide cases independently. (Scheck, 2013)

Judges who are responsible for administering the work of publically supported defense attorneys should, in Scheck's (2013) view "create independent structures consistent with the Ten Principles to oversee how the system functions." He concludes: "In short, judges simply have to lead and be proactive, even forcing the defense to change its culture. . . . The enhancement of indigent defense is the linchpin reform that makes all other improvements in the criminal justice system achievable" (Scheck, 2013).

Personal Responsibility

System reforms pave the way for the adoption of greater personal responsibility by indigent defense attorneys. Efforts to affect greater parity between prosecutors and defense counsel will allow them to utilize the time and staffing resources needed to prepare an adequate defense for an indigent client. Greater parity will also be achieved by an increase in transparency in the plea bargaining process. As the plea bargaining becomes less driven by the value of expediency and presumption of guilt, a cultural shift will occur. Defense attorneys will begin to take a more active role in shaping the outcome of the negotiations. Recognition of the possibility of an innocent defendant, and the need to protect the constitutional rights of each client will alter the kinds of bargains that are negotiated. Freed from the constraints imposed by case overload, and inadequate funding for necessary investigatory preparation, effective assistance of counsel for indigent defendants will become more likely.

CONCLUSION

Ineffective assistance of counsel for indigent defendants is the result of legal and extra-legal factors. The legal standards for ineffective assistance of counsel at trial were initially defined in *Strickland v. Washington* and later broadened in *Missouri v. Frye* and *Lafler v. Cooper* to include pretrial stages in the processing of a criminal case.

Extra-legal factors – the systemic obstacles of case overload and lack of funding for indigent defense – are found to undermine the efforts of attorneys to adhere to the guidelines of American Bar Association's indigent defense delivery. The well-intentioned efforts of indigent defense advocates are weakened by the systemic drawbacks in the justice system. The American Bar Association recommendation for parity between the resources of the office of prosecutor and those available to publically supported indigent defense serves to guide effective reform measures.

Fundamental fairness is the linchpin of justice in the processing of a criminal case. Fundamental fairness should not be compromised by the inability of defendants to access their constitutionally mandated due process rights. Reforms intended to remedy the menace of ineffective assistance of counsel must not only consider the legal precedents that shape judicial decision-making, but the mundane, day-to-day context for the processing of a criminal case by agents of the criminal justice system: the police, prosecutors and defense attorneys. Effective reforms must consider the manner in which criminal cases are processed through the system. A re evaluation of the assumptions, decisions, and interests of the agents of criminal justice is central to any reform effort.

Chapter 6

INADEQUATE JURY INSTRUCTIONS

[I]t is better that ten guilty persons escape, than that one innocent suffer.

– Sir William Blackstone, 1765

THE CASE OF PAULA GRAY

On May 12, 1978, the bodies of Lawrence Lionberg and Carol Schmal were found in an abandoned townhouse, located in a mostly black neighborhood in Chicago known as Ford Heights. Both victims had been shot and Carol had been gang-raped. Based on a false tip, four African Americans, Verneal Jimerson, Dennis Williams, Kenneth Adams, Willie Rainge, and a mildly intellectually disabled 17-year-old Paula Gray, were brought in for questioning. After two days of being held without legal counsel, Gray confessed to taking part in the murders and in the process, incriminated the others. After a month, Gray recanted her story, claiming the police drugged her and told her what to say. Even with this information, the jury convicted Gray of murder and perjury. She was sentenced to 50 years. Because Williams and Rainge's lawyer had also represented Gray, whose testimony was used to convict both men, they claimed a conflict of interest and were granted a new trial. Prior to the new trial, the prosecutor offered to release Gray in exchange for her testimony against Williams and Rainge. As a result of her testimony and that of a jailhouse snitch, Williams and Rainge were convicted for a second time.

In 1996, DNA evidence exonerated all of the defendants. Later, the defense learned of a witness that had reported to the police that they had seen the real perpetrators. The police did not investigate the report. The case of Paula Gray exhibits many of the common contributing factors associated with a wrongful conviction[1]. Paula's age and her disability, contributed to her false confession. In the absence of jury instructions about false confessions, eyewitness identification, perjury and false accusation, and official misconduct, jury members may not know the problems associated with certain types of evidence, thereby increasing the risk of a wrongful conviction.

INTRODUCTION

Jurors are faced with a daunting task. Without a legal background, forensic or scientific expertise, or psychological training, they are entrusted with discerning the truth as it presumably emerges during the course of a trial. The adversarial process – a contest of opposing arguments–is intended to determine whether or not the defendant is guilty of a crime. The most compelling evidence is too often flawed, or deceptively wrong. Jurors tend to believe the testimony of eyewitnesses, particularly crime victims, the confession of the accused, expert witnesses, and perjured accounts implicating the defendant in the crime. These forms of evidence are among the leading causes of wrongful conviction.

In this chapter we explore the key issues confronting jurors as they attempt to arrive at a decision that is "beyond a reasonable doubt." For all criminal defendants, this decision is life altering, for the innocent defendant, it is a shattering experience. And for the jurors who wrongfully convicted the accused, it may be met with a haunting sense of dread and disbelief.

OVERVIEW OF THE JURY

The creation of the jury system has been debated by many historians (Donahue, 1999; Moschzisker, 1921). Although many have argued that the criminal jury system can be traced back to the thirteenth century (Donahue, 1999), the original system bears little resemblance to the jury system of today. The purpose of the jury initially was to guard against tyranny by the king (Graham, 2009). The right to a jury trial dates backs to the original Constitution, enacted in 1787 (Thomas,

---

1. For more information see: National Registry of Exonerations. Retrieved from https://www.law.umich.edu/special/exoneration/Pages/casedetail.aspx?caseid=3433.

2014). However, it was not until 1791, when the Bill of Rights was ratified to include criminal, civil, and grand jury protections (Thomas, 2014). The adoption of the Bill of Rights specified that "in all criminal prosecutions, the accused shall enjoy the right to a speedy and public trial, by an impartial jury" (U.S. Const. amend. VI). Jury services have continued to evolve with the changing conditions of our society.

Originally members of the jury were restricted to white males, who owned property. Now the right has been extended to minorities and women. Another two requirements, which has changed, is the jury size and the unanimous voting requirement. Initially, all juries had 12 members and a unanimous decision was required for a guilty verdict. However, the Supreme Court has become flexible with these two requirements. For example in *Williams v. Florida*, the Court stated that the 12-member jury was a "historical accident" and that a 6-member jury could provide meaningful deliberation. Due to this Supreme Court case, states vary in their appropriate size, ranging from 6 to 12 members (Siegel, Schmalleger, & Worrall, 2011). The second misconception concerning juries is the requirement for a unanimous decision. The Supreme Court has upheld both a Louisiana (e.g., *Johnson v. Louisiana*) and Oregon (e.g., *Apodaca v. Oregon*) state statute that a unanimous vote does not need to be reached. Now certain jurisdictions may or may not require a unanimous decision.[2] One possible issue that arises from not requiring a unanimous decision is that the jury members may succumb to the pressure of other jurors, thereby diminishing reliability (Siegel, Schmalleger, & Worrall, 2011).

According to Coleman (1919) a trial by jury is the corner-stone of our free society (p. 78). A jury system allows ordinary citizens to be a part of the administration of governmental affairs. The juror is considered the trier of facts in the adversarial system. In *Apprendi v. New Jersey* (2000), the U.S. Supreme Court emphasizes the importance of a jury trial and explains that jurors rather than judges are the ultimate fact-finders. What this means, is that jury members are responsible for making a determination after the adversarial system (i.e. defense and prosecutor) has presented their case. Although the *Apprendi* rule is of importance, it does nothing to protect an innocent individual from a wrongful conviction. It only grants a group of laypersons with the responsibility of arriving at a verdict; which can be a challenging task.

There are multiple challenges confronting a juror. At the outset,

---

2. For more information see: Siegel, Schmalleger, & Worrall, 2011, p. 354.

there is an unknown number of errors generated by the conventional investigative procedures leading up to a trial (Simon, 2012, p.146). These errors are not known to either the judge or jurors. Also, juries are composed of ordinary citizens who are often not familiar with adversarial proceedings. During the adversarial proceedings jurors may be exposed to extra-legal information, including pretrial-publicity and evidence deemed inadmissible by the court. Once exposed, they are often unable to evaluate and interpret this information (Dufraimont, 2008). Erroneous beliefs include the eyewitness's ability to accurately identify the suspect, how informants never lie under oath, how an expert's testimony is always reliable, and if errors do occur, the truth will be revealed through the adversarial cross-examination.

These common sense beliefs have caused innocent individuals to be convicted. Rarely is the jury guided on how to interpret the evidence. According to the National Registry of Exoneration (NRE) from 1989-2012, 82 percent of the 1050 exonerations were convicted at trial by juries (Gross & Schaffer, 2012). Governing standards concerning jury instructions are needed to assist these ordinary individuals to arrive at an accurate verdict.

THE ERROR RATE

Determining the possible error rate of a wrongful conviction is difficult. Spencer (2007) a statistics professor at Northwestern, examined 271 jury trials in four areas of Illinois. According to his findings, as many as one in eight juries have either convicted an innocent person or acquitted a guilty one. Exoneration data provides the only official rate of wrongful convictions. These data sources only include those that have been exonerated, but do not take into account innocent persons who remain in prison or who have not pursued their exoneration.

UNRELIABILITY OF SEEMINGLY RELIABLE EVIDENCE

Unreliable prosecution evidence is linked to a considerable number of wrongful convictions (Dufraimont, 2008). The prosecution evidence can include, mistaken witness identification, false or misleading forensic expert testimony, the use of perjury or false accusations (also known as using incentivized informants or jailhouse snitches) and a false confession. Without proper jury instructions about ways to interpret reliability and validity of the evidence, an unjust verdict may be reached.

EYEWITNESS IDENTIFICATION

Eyewitness identification is one of the most convincing pieces of evidence to jurors. Goldstein, Chance, and Schneller (1989) report that there are almost 80,000 suspects each year in the United States who are singled out by eyewitness identification. About four in 10 suspects are misidentified (Fradella, 2006). To a jury, eyewitness testimony is nonetheless, considered credible (Hoffheimer, 1989). The NRE reports that there have been 604 exonerations that were the result of an eyewitness misidentification.[3] According to the Innocence Project, eyewitness misidentification accounts for more than 70 percent of DNA exonerations (Innocence Project, 2017).

Eyewitness misidentification is the focus of considerable laboratory research, with most of it based on Wells (1978) development of system variables and estimator variables (Horry, Halford, Brewer, Milne, & Bull, 2014; Norris, Bonventre, Redlich, & Acker, 2011). System and estimator variable are used to explain eyewitnesses' reliability. System variables include any factor that can be controlled by the justice system (Horry et al., l 2014). For example, a particular response given by an officer to an eyewitness (i.e. "perfect", "great job", etc.). Estimator variables cannot be controlled by the justice system, for example, the presence of a weapon, proximity of the witness to the crime scene, lighting conditions and so forth. Some of the more common system and estimator variables contributing to a wrongful conviction will be discussed below.

System Variables

An important system variables, is post-identification feedback, which occurs when a lineup administrator may provide post-ident-

---

3. As of July 5, 2017, for more information see: National Registry of Exonerations. Retrieved from http://www.law.umich.edu/special/exoneration/Pages/detaillist. aspx?View={FAF6EDDB-5A68-4F8F-8A52-2C61F5BF9EA7}&FilterField1=MWID&Filt erValue1=8_MWID.

ification feedback by signaling unintentionally or intentionally to the eyewitness that they have identified the "right" suspect. The witness typically gains confidence, even though confidence does not mean the identification is accurate (Shell, 2013; Thompson, 2010). Instead, eyewitness accuracy is correlated with the amount of exposure, or how often the eyewitness viewed the suspect at the time of crime. The more frequently the suspect was observed, the more accurate the identification. However, if an eyewitness is shown photographs, or has viewed possible suspects in a lineup, the less the accurate the eyewitness identification (Deffenbacher, Bornstein, & Pernod, 2006). The frequency of viewing a suspect postidentification can instill false confidence, which can later misguide the jury.

Estimator Variables

Estimator variables are an inherent problem in our justice system that cannot be corrected by reforms or by the actions of justice officials. For example, nothing can change the fact that the presence of a weapon will decrease the accuracy of an eyewitness's identification, or that most robbery victims only see the culprit for a short period of time and a reform or a justice official cannot counter the flaws in cross-racial identifications, or how stress and trauma affects a person's memory. These estimator variables are associated with flawed eyewitness identification and yet, there is no procedure to fix these inherent problems (Thompson, 2009). Instead, an option would be that educational training for the jurors be mandated so they are aware of these inherent problems. Education will aid the jury in assessing the evidence and making unbiased decisions.

Estimator Variables–Cross-Racial Identification

Little research has focused on the ability of Asian, Native American, or Hispanic individuals to accurately identify criminal offenders or other races (Rizer III, 2003). Much of the literature considers only cross-racial identification between white and black individuals. Research has shown that cross-racial identification is extremely unreliable (Balko, 2013; Rizer III, 2003). Eyewitnesses are significantly better at identifying an offender of their own race compared to one of another race (Balko, 2013; Epstein, 2007; Loftus, Doyle, & Dysart,

2007). Socialization typically occurs among a person of the same race. Therefore, the unique features of a person of a different race are largely unfamiliar (Balko, 2013). Accurate identification cross-racially becomes extremely difficult.

Psychologists provide two explanations for inter-racial misidentification. First, different races have distinct features; therefore, a person cannot "encode" in their memory differing racial features, especially facial features. The second explanation is how more mistakes are made in cross-racial identification due to the fewer interactions and decreased attention paid to people of other race (Rizer III, 2003).

Estimator Variables—Trauma/Stress

Trauma and stress are other factors that affect memory. The levels of stress experienced in a situation can reduce the accuracy of a witness's testimony (Shell, 2013). According to Balko (2013) when low levels of stress are first perceived by the nervous system, a person's memory efficiency performs at its lowest level. Once the body experiences moderate levels of stress, the optimal level of memory efficiency is increased. However, as the stress increases, past the optimal point, memory efficiency deteriorates (pp. 1095-1096). The trauma associated with the presence of a weapon reduces the accuracy of eyewitness identification by approximately 10 percent (Shell, 2013).

Primary and Secondary Identification Error

There are two different sources of identification error, which may lead to a wrongful conviction. These may be a result of estimator or system variables. The first is primary identification, which stems from defects in the psychological processes, usually beginning with the original identification at the police station and aggravated by the investigative process (Hoffheimer, 1989). The second source of identification error occurs when the fact finder, usually a juror, erroneously evaluates the eyewitness identification evidence. Therefore, the primary identification error can cause the second identification error. Thus, the features of the adversary trial can contribute to the dangers of causing a secondary identification error. The courts have not begun to fully explain or focus on the difference between primary and secondary identification errors. Most opinions have accepted that primary identification is inevitable and therefore, has begun to examine features of the adversary process to reduce the prevalence of secondary identification (Hoffheimer, 1989). Much of the research on secondary identification, inherent in the adversary process, has been based on mock trials.

Previous Studies

Mock trials provide a starting point for understanding how the average layperson comes to a decision. Scholars have found two aspects, sympathy and eyewitness confidence, primarily affect the juror's decision. Often jurors sympathize with the eyewitness, causing them to overlook the accuracy and reliability with the identification (Hoffheimer, 1989; Loftus, 1979). Confidence has been found to be the most influential predictor of trial verdicts (Cutler, Penrod, & Dexter, 1990). For example, research on mock trials has found that level of confidence by the eyewitness outweighs the accuracy of the identification. However, confidence often results in an inaccurate identification (Lindsay, Wells, & O'Connor, 1989; Well & Murray, 1984). Nonetheless, the Supreme Court still uses confidence as a requirement for admissibility (*Neil v. Biggers*, 1972, pp. 199-200). This requirement by the Supreme Court may result in the jurors' misconception that confidence predicts accuracy.

Furthermore, many jurors are not aware of how an eyewitness's confidence may have changed over time. This phenomenon is known as confidence malleability, in which a person may become more or less confident in their original identification. Multiple factors affect faulty post-identification memory (e.g., with police or family members), post-identification feedback (from justice officials), and pretrial briefing (by justice officials) (Norris et al., 2011). Studies on mock-jurors conclude that jurors are ill-equipped when assessing accuracy and reliability of an eyewitness.

Jurors tend to hold beliefs that are not scientifically valid. In a survey of 1000 potential jurors located in the District of Columbia, there were several instances where lay beliefs conflicted with what research has found concerning eyewitness identification (Schmechel, O'Toole, Easterly, & Loftus, 2006). There are many lay beliefs found to conflict with scientific findings. The first concerns how jurors misunderstand memory in general. The survey found that approximately 68 percent of respondents thought the statement "I never forget a face" described memory at least "very well" or "fairly well." About 37 percent thought that the presence of a weapon increased a witness's memory and 39 percent of the potential jurors believed that a stressful event would increase the reliability of the witness's memory.

In addition, 83 percent of respondents incorrectly thought there was a correlation between confidence and accuracy. This belief results in an eyewitness's testimony appearing to be highly persuasive and can cause jurors to overlook other valid and reliable evidence (Dufraimont, 2008). The last misconception is cross-racial impairment. About 48 percent of the respondents thought cross-race or same-race identifications are equally reliable (Schmechel et al., 2006).[4] According to official exoneration data from 1989-2012, cross-racial misidentification was found in more than two-thirds of sexual assault exoneration, where the defendant was black. Of these black defendants, whom had been mistakenly identified, 72 percent had a white victim (Gross & Shaffer, 2012).[5] None of these beliefs is scientifically supported. Therefore, jurors need assistance with evaluating the frailties of eyewitness identification in criminal trials.

RELIABILITY AND VALIDITY OF EYEWITNESS IDENTIFICATION

Biggers and *Manson*

It is clear that both reliability and validity tests for admissibility are interpreted differently by judges and across judicial circuits. The *Manson* test provides guidance for judges when deciding to admit eyewitness testimony or a defendant's confession. It is important to note that the *Manson* test has also been called the *Manson* criteria, the *Biggers/Brathwaite* reliability test and the *Biggers/Manson* test. For the purpose of this book, we will use *Manson* test to explain the Court's criteria for evaluating the accuracy and reliability of an eyewitness's

4. For further discussion of survey findings see: Schmechel, R. S., O'Toole, T. P., Easterly, C. & Loftus, E. F. (2006). Beyond the Ken? Testing juror understands of eyewitness reliability evidence. *Jurimetrics Journal*, 46, 177-214.

5. For more information see: Gross, S., & Shaffer, M. (2012). *Exonerations in the United States, 1989-2012:1st report by the National Registry of Exonerations.* Retrieved from https://www.law.umich.edu/special/exoneration/Documents/exonerations_us_1989_2012_full_report.pdf

identification. In the Manson test, the U.S. Supreme Court created a two-pronged test to determine when eyewitness evidence should be excluded. The first prong determines whether the identification procedure was "unnecessarily suggestive." If the identification was not determined to be unnecessarily suggestive, the identification can be admitted into evidence. However, if the identification was found to be unnecessarily suggestive, a second test is used to determine whether the identification is still reliable (Wells & Quinlivan, 2008).

Following *Neil v. Biggers* (1972), which first recognized the need for jury instructions, the U.S. Supreme Court in *Manson v. Brathwaite* (1977) mandated five factors that the lower courts are to consider:

1. the opportunity of the witness to view the criminal at the time of the crime,
2. the witness' degree of attention,
3. the accuracy of the witness' prior description of the criminal,
4. the level of certainty demonstrated by the witness at the confrontation, and
5. the length of time between the crime and the confrontation (*Manson v. Brathwaite*, 1977).

The *Manson* test is used by most state and federal courts to determining whether eyewitness identification should be excluded (Mnookin, 2015). In sum, the *Manson* reliability test provides factors that should be examined when considering the "totality of the circumstances," used to regulate the accuracy of identification. Although this is a starting point for assisting with the admissibility of eyewitness testimony, there are several well-documented caveats associated with the *Manson* test.[6] One of the main problems is how *Biggers* and *Manson* were decided almost 40 years ago. Since then highly regarded empirical research indicates that these five factors, may not be the most valid and reliable method for jurors to evaluate eyewitness identification.

When we consider that all the cases of wrongful conviction resulting from eyewitness misidentification relied on the Manson test, it becomes obvious that the test does not prevent wrongful convictions. However, the test does point out the flaws in eyewitness identification and

---

6. For more information see: Thompson, S. G. (2010). Eyewitness identification and state courts as guardians against wrongful conviction. *Ohio State Journal of Criminal Law, 7,* 603- 635.

provides a starting point for the courts to reassess its reliability and validity.

Manson Test Reforms

Through the *Manson* test, the court system has attempted to expose eyewitness biases. However, current scientific findings have found several inherent problems with the assumptions used to determine reliability. Since the enactment of the *Manson* test, research has convinced some courts to expand or modify the five factors (Gardner & Anderson, 2016). New Jersey has led the way in addressing issues related to the admissibility of eyewitness identifications. In 2011, in the case of *State v. Henderson*, the New Jersey Supreme Court appointed a "special master" to conduct research on scientific findings concerning eyewitness identifications. The review based on the *Manson* test found a few assumptions to be false. The New Jersey Supreme Court held that the *Manson* test: "does not offer an adequate measure for reliability or sufficiently deter inappropriate police conduct. It also overstates the jury's inherent ability to evaluate evidence offered by eyewitnesses who honestly believe their testimony is accurate" (*State v. Henderson*, 2011). Based on these findings, the New Jersey Court established several procedures to be followed during the pretrial hearing to determine whether eyewitness identification should be admitted into evidence. These procedures are:

1. The defendant must introduce some evidence of suggestiveness to obtain a pretrial hearing, focusing on "system" variables rather than "estimator" variables. The defendant need not prove the higher burden of "impermissible" suggestiveness that is required under the current tests.
2. If suggestiveness is shown, the prosecution must offer evidence to prove the identification was reliable.
3. It remains the defendant's burden to prove the ultimate question: was there a "very substantial likelihood of irreparable misidentification"?
4. If identification evidence is admitted, the jury must be given instructions on the effect of "system" and "estimator" variables on the accuracy of an identification (Gardner & Anderson, 2016, citing *State v. Henderson*, 2011).

Moving Forward With the Outdated Manson Test

Empirical research has shown that the eyewitness's confidence does not correlate well with the accuracy of the identification. The characteristics observed and the circumstance surrounding the criminal event affect the degree of attention as well as the accuracy of the description. There are two safeguards, which can protect against the outdated *Manson* test. The first is skillful cross-examinations by the defense attorney. However, even with a skillful defense attorney, a "relation back" effect may occur where the eyewitness may insist that their mistaken identification was accurate (Tallent, 2011; *U.S. v. Mathis*, at 341). Ironically, defense attorneys' tenacious cross-examination may result in the jury becoming more convinced that the witness's misidentification is credible.

The second safeguard, the use of an expert witness, can explain the flaws in eyewitness identification and can assist the jury in evaluating eyewitness testimony. However, many judges do not allow expert testimony in court for fear that they may cause confusion among the jurors, citing Federal Rule 403 (Fed. R. Evid. 403; Tallent, 2011). For example, say an expert explains the misconceptions of eyewitness identification and how some of the factors in the *Manson* test conflicts with scientific finding. Later, a judge presents the *Manson* test and explains that the Supreme Court recommends its use for the jury to arrive at its verdict. Therefore, expert testimony concerning eyewitness identification is often excluded under the Federal Rule 403. Many states have recently begun to address the issues related to outdated jury instructions concerning eyewitness' testimony. The new proposed set of factors will be described in the following section on reforms.

NEW IDENTIFICATION MODELS

Telfaire Model

The *Telfaire Model*, developed after the *Biggers* and *Manson* Supreme Court decisions, is also used to aid the jury in assessing eyewitness testimony (Wise, Sartori, Magnussen, & Safer, 2014). In *United States v. Telfaire*, the U.S. Supreme Court specified five elements for jurors to consider when evaluating reports of eyewitnesses: (1) the ability of the witness to observe the perpetrator (i.e., length of observation, distance, lighting conditions), (2) whether there was a previous relationship with the defendant, if there is a history of animosity, and if there were any instructions given during observation, (3) circumstance of identification (i.e. length of time from crime to identification, witness degree of certainty), the jury is further informed that certainty does not mean accuracy, (4) consistency of identification, credibility of witness, and (5) the degree of eyewitness's attention to the crime. Currently, Connecticut[7] and New Hampshire[8] provide criminal jury instruction concerning eyewitness identification. However, Connecticut courts have never required that the model be given verbatim. Instead, it is used as an aid to make sure the jury is properly guided. Several other Federal Courts including the Third Circuit, Fourth Circuit, Sixth Circuit, Seventh Circuit, Eighth Circuit, and Tenth Circuit include some form of Telfaire- type instructions.[9]

The *Telfaire* instructions have been criticized for being difficult to comprehend. Although they were intended to assist with factors that influence the accuracy and reliability of an identification, they do not explain how these factors may affect both aspects of reliability and accuracy and nor do they explain how the jury should weigh the five factors when evaluating the identification (Cutler, 2009). While there is little scientific evidence that the *Telfaire* instructions have been effective with assisting jurors, it is still used in most jurisdictions.

REFORMS CONCERNING EYEWITNESS IDENTIFICATION

There are two different sources of identification error – primary and secondary – both need to be addressed to effectively reform the administration of justice. Primary errors occur when the witness(es) initially identifies the defendant. Reforms are needed to improve, police protocols and procedures that would aid in the eyewitness identification process (e.g. recording documentation of the identification process, use of a "blind" or "double-blind" administration, and use of a sequential presentation of photos and live individuals).

Secondary identification errors, those that are inherent in trial itself,

---

7. For more information see: Criminal Jury Instructions 2.6-4 identification of Defendant (2013) Retrieved from http://www.jud.ct.gov/ji/criminal/part2/2.6-4.htm.

8. See N. H. Criminal Jury Instructions 3.06 identification (1985). Retrieved from http://federalevidence.com/node/1382/.

9. For more information see: *Perry v. New Hampshire* impact: The role of eyewitness identification jury instruction (18 Jan 2012).Retrieved from http://federalevidence.com/node/1382/.

must also be considered. These reforms must focus on methods for instructing jurors about the most current scientific research on factors that influence eyewitness misidentification and ways to assess testimony of witnesses.

Federal Rules

Federal and state reforms can assist the jury with arriving at a just verdict. Through the enactment of the Federal Rules, both the executive and legislative branches of government have begun implementing reforms concerning eyewitness identification. Many of the federal regulations on eyewitness identification and expert testimony depend on the circuit and the judge hearing the case. If implemented, these reforms would reduce secondary misidentification, since an expert would inform the jurors about the possibility of a flawed identification.

In 1975, when the frailties of eyewitness reliability became more widely known, the Federal Rules of Evidence (FRE) was adopted. Three provisions of the FRE directly address admissibility of scientific research provided by expert witnesses (Schmechel et al., 2006). FRE 702 states that:

> If scientific, technical, or other specialized knowledge assist the trier of fact to understand the evidence or to determine a fact in issue, a witness qualified as an expert by knowledge, skill, experience, training, or education, may testify, thereto in the form of an opinion or otherwise, is (1) the testimony is based upon sufficient facts or data, (2) the testimony is the product of reliable principles and methods, and (3) the witness has applied the principles and methods reliably to the facts of the case (Fed. R. Evid. 702).

FRE 702 is important for several reasons. It provides a uniform standard for the admissibility of testimony. Further, FRE 702 represents an effort to prevent adversarial bias, while still functioning under the basic premise of the adversarial process. Adversarial bias occurs when the parties (i.e., defense and prosecutor) choose their own experts solely based on their particular views. Instead Rule 702 seeks to prevent this by using experts who show an "objectively verifiable basis for their testimony" (Bernstein, 2013). Research has shown that there are judges who disregard Rule 702 (e.g., Berstein, 2013; Schmechel et al., 2006); however, if the Supreme Court mandated its implementation this could considerably reduce wrongful convictions. This is a simple reform, already enacted, that only needs to be uniformly implemented.

Rule 704 also governs the admissibility of expert witnesses (Schmechel et al., 2006). This rule allows the expert to present testimony even if it touches on an ultimate issue, which will be decided by the fact-finder (i.e., jury or judge). And, the final provision, Rule 403, allows a federal judge wide discretionary power to reject and exclude any eyewitness identification expert testimony when its probity value is "substantially outweighed" by either confusion of the issues or prejudice (Schmechel et al., 2006). There is an exhaustive list of factors governing a federal judge's discretionary power (Tallent, 2011). Although there have been conflicting findings on whether circuits comport with the Rule 403, it is most often the primary justification for excluding expert testimony concerning eyewitness identification. The majority of circuits explain that under Federal Rule 403, expert testimony on eyewitness identification should not be admissible, because it confuses the jurors and diminishes their ability to determine a witness's credibility. Nonetheless there is evidence that as long as the expert employs "reliable scientific expertise," federal court should profit from their testimony (Tallent, 2011).

STATE REFORMS

Several other courts have also begun changing state rules governing eyewitness identification. Examples include:

Commonwealth v. Gomes, 470 Mass. 352 (2015): Juries must be instructed on the five "generally accepted" scientific findings concerning eyewitness evidence. These five findings include how (1) human memory is complex and does not function like a recording; (2) certainty by an eyewitness does not indicate accuracy; (3) stress can impact the accuracy; (4) information that witnesses receive during pre and post identification can influence memory and recollection; and (5) prior viewing of the same suspect during identification process may diminish the reliability of a later identification of the same suspect.

State v. Cabagbag, 277 P.3d 1027 (Hawaii 2012): The defense may request that jury instructions be given whenever identification evidence is central to the case. A separate list of cautionary factors that address the specific weaknesses of eyewitness testimony revealed by current studies must be included in the jury instructions (Gardner & Anderson, 2015). Further, a circuit court may provide instructions if they are deemed warranted in a particular case.

State v. Guilbert, 49 A.3d 705 (Conn. 2012): Any expert testimony concerning an eyewitness should be permitted, and that current jury instructions about evaluating expert testimony must be made more specific.

State v. Lawson, 291 P.3d 673 (Ore. 2012): The prosecution will have the burden to show that the identification was based on a permissible basis, if facts reveal that the identification might have resulted from suggestive factors. Even if the state satisfies the initial burden, a judge may still impose remedies, such as suppressing the evidence.

State v. Mitchell, 275 P.3d 905 (Kan.2012): Jurys should not be instructed to give weight to the expressed certainty based on a witness's identification.

Other states that have passed statutes in responses to eyewitness misidentification are Colorado, Georgia, Maryland, Illinois, Nevada, North Carolina, Ohio, Texas, Vermont, West Virginia, and Wisconsin (Innocence Project, n.d.e). The District of Columbia is another agency that has developed eyewitness identification reforms. Two states that are leading the way with reforms are North Carolina and Ohio. These statutes are more detailed. North Carolina's state statute requires that law enforcement officers follow specific policies. When the procedures are not followed, the statute provides legal remedies for the non-compliance of the law enforcement agent(s). North Carolina's statutes became effective in 2008 (Innocence project, n.d.h). The jury instructions in Ohio's statute include a provision that allows the jury to consider the repercussion of noncompliance with law enforcement agent(s). This will help with determining reliability of the eyewitness's identification. Ohio's statute became effective in 2010 (Innocence project, n.d.f). These other remaining states require that best practices be adopted for eyewitness identifications. Other states have at least recommended that best practices be further studied (Garrett, 2012). Following both New Jersey *Henderson* model and Massachusetts *Gomes*, judges and the juries can both be instructed on what factors affect the accuracy of an eyewitness testimony and what scientific research has found concerning reliability of eyewitness identification. Through the implementation of these cases, it is clear that courts are beginning to make changes to help prevent a secondary misidentification.

INNOCENCE PROJECT

Paul Cates, the Communication director for the Innocence Project (2011), has developed a list of several factors, which are shown to increase the risk of misidentification. These factors serve as a guide to develop specific jury instructions:

- Whether the lineup procedure was administered "double-blind," meaning that the officer who administers the lineup is unaware who the suspect is and the witness is told that the officer doesn't know.
- Whether the witness was told that the suspect may not be in the lineup and that they need not make a choice.
- Whether the police avoided providing the witness with feedback that would cause the witness to believe he or she selected the correct suspect. Similarly, whether the police recorded the witnesses' level of confidence at the time of the identification.
- Whether the witness had multiple opportunities to view the same person, which would make it more likely for the witness to choose this person as the suspect.
- Whether the witness was under a high level of stress.
- Whether a weapon was used, especially if the crime was of short duration.
- How much time the witness had to observe the event.
- How far the witness was from the perpetrator and what the lighting conditions were.
- Whether the witness possessed characteristics that would make it harder to make identification, such as age of the witness and influence of alcohol or drugs.
- Whether the perpetrator possessed characteristics that would make it harder to make identification. Was he or she wearing a disguise? Did the suspect have different facial features at the time of the identification?

- The length of time between the crime and identification.
- Whether the case involved cross-racial identification.[10]

SAFEGUARDS: EYEWITNESS MISIDENTIFICATION

There are several safeguards that address the frailties of eyewitness identification. According to Berman, Narby, and Cutlet (1995) there are four safeguards that protect defendants from mistaken eyewitness identification; however, three of the safeguards are rarely used. In *U.S. v. Wade* (1967), the U.S. Supreme Court ruled that an attorney could be present during post-indictment lineups. However, defense attorneys are not always present when their client is identified (as cited in Brigham & Wolfskeil, 1983). The identification process usually uses photos arrays rather than live lineups and in *United States v. Ash*, (1973) the Supreme Court ruled that a suspect is not entitled to counsel during a photo-identification. Also in *People v. MacDonald* (1984), the court permitted the admission of expert testimony by a psychologist to explain how certain factors may influence memory, concerning eyewitness identification. In practice, however, this appears to be an exception instead of a rule (as cited in Walters, 1985). Judges vary with the admissibility of expert testimony. Even when it is allowed, only a small percentage of suspects can afford this expensive safeguard (Wells, Small, Penrod, Malpass, Fulero, & Brimacombe, 1998). *U.S. v. Telfaire* (1972), held that judicial instructions concerning memory may be provided to the jury. Again this is hardly used (as cited in Waters, 1985). Finally, cross-examination is relied on for informing the jury about flaws in the evidence.

Cross-examination, granted by the Sixth Amendment, can assist jurors with detecting witnesses who are dishonest and those that are truthful. However, it does not assist the jury with determining who is being honest but are genuinely mistaken (Wells et al., 1998). Lawyers typically do not aggressively cross-examine witnesses, however, a wide range of tactics are used both by defense and prosecuting attorneys (Wren, 2011).

---

10. For more information see: Cates, P. (2011, August, 24). *New Jersey Supreme Court issues landmark decision mandating major changes in the way courts handle identification procedures.* New York: Innocence Project. Retrieved from http://www.innocenceproject.org/news-events-exonerations/press-releases-new-jerseysupreme-court-issues-landmark-decision-mandating-major-changes-in-the-way-courts-handle-identification-procedures.

There have been several wrongful conviction cases where a defense attorney fell asleep during the trial or did not actively represent his/her client. The case of Eddie Joe Lloyd provides a perfect example of how the safeguard cross-examination has failed innocent individuals. Eddie Lloyd was convicted of the 1984 murder of a sixteen-year- old girl in Detroit, Michigan. Lloyd suffered from mental illness and while receiving treatment in a hospital, he began to write to the police providing suggestions on how to solve different murders, including the murder of the sixteen-year-old girl. Police eventually convinced Lloyd to confess to the crime. Lloyd was under the assumption that if he confessed he would be able to help the police "smoke out" the real perpetrator. He was represented by a court-appointed attorney, eight days before the trial the lawyer withdrew and Lloyd was granted a new attorney. The new attorney did not meet with the pretrial attorney, he failed to cross-examine the police officer most directly involved in Lloyd's confession, and lastly, he did not call any witnesses for the defense [11](Innocence Project, n.d.d). The idea that the adversarial cross-examination will provide the jury with the truth is not accurate and can lead the jury to erroneously arrive at a guilty verdict.

The courts have begun to strengthen a defendant's right to a "complete and zealous" defense (Schmechel et al., 2006). Based on the due process clause of the Fourteenth Amendment and the Sixth Amendment, a complete and zealous defense includes the presentation of expert testimony concerning eyewitness identification. For example, the U.S. Supreme Court ruled in *Chambers v. Mississippi* (1973) that a defendant has a right to offer witness testimony on his or her behalf. An expert testimony can further educate the jurors, concerning reliability issues. There are, however, several problems with this trend. Many defendants that enter the justice system are unable to afford an expert and even if the option is granted, judges under Federal Rule 403 may reject and exclude any expert testimony pertaining to eyewitness identification (Fed. R. Evid. 403).

FALSE OR MISLEADING FORENSIC EXPERT TESTIMONY

Jury instructions are needed to counteract false or misleading forensic expert testimony. Law Professor Brandon Garrett's study of the first

---

11. For more information see: Innocence Project- Eddie Joe Lloyd's case. Retrieved from http://www.innocenceproject.org/cases-false-imprisonment/eddie-joe-lloyd.

200 DNA exonerations found that 57 percent of the exonerations involved convictions that were the result of false or misleading forensic evidence. According to the NRE, there are 496 exonerations, where the exoneree stated that false or misleading forensic evidence contributed to their wrongful conviction.[12] False or misleading forensic evidence includes any conviction that, "was based at least in part on forensic information that was (1) caused by errors in forensic testing, (2) based on unreliable or unproven methods, (3) expressed with exaggerated and misleading confidence, or (4) fraudulent" (National Registry of Exoneration, n.d.b).

Inadvertent forensic errors can arise from motivational and cognitive biases, lack of education, insufficient training, incompetence or sloppy procedures (Giannelli, 2007b). It is highly unlikely that jurors would know about these errors. To jurors, expert forensic testimony can be both compelling, yet misleading. For example, Chester Bauer was convicted of rape and aggravated assault in the state of Montana in 1983. During his trial, a lab analyst testified that the alleged hair found on the victim's bedding matched Bauer's hair. During the trial the analysts stated: "To have them both match, it would be the multiplication of both factors so approximately using that one out of 100, you come out with a number like one chance in 10,000" (Innocence Project, n.d.b). This analysis was not supported by empirical data. Further, it is invalid for an analyst to state that the consistency between the victim's hair and that of the accused is a rare or common event. The analyst also erred when testifying that blood found at the crime scene is only found in 7.5 percent of the population, but matched Bauer's blood type. Oddly enough the victim's blood also matched Bauer's.

When evidence from the perpetrator and the victim is mixed and the testing does not detect any blood group substance or enzymes that are foreign to the victim, then no potential donor can truly be excluded. This is known as masking. Masking occurs when there is possibility that the victim's blood group markers possibly "mask" the perpetrators. Because of "masking" a jury should be informed that 100% of the male population could be included. Stating that none could be excluded is misleading.[13]

---

12. As of July 5, 2017, for more information see: National Registry of Exonerations. Retrieved from http://www.law.umich.edu/special/exoneration/Pages/detaillist.aspx?View={FAF6EDDB-5A68-4F8F-8A52_2C61F5BF9EA7}&FilterField1=F_x002f_MFE&FilterValue1=8_F%2FMFE.

13. For more information see: Innocence Project-Chester Bauer case. Retrieved from http://www.innocenceproject.org/cases-false-imprisonment/chester-bauer.

Although one may assume that misleading or inaccurate testimony would not be admitted as evidence, the forensic sciences are plagued by the lack of universal accreditation standards, as well as not using a standard terminology. Forensic evidence is often misleading, especially when followed by terminology, such as, "identical," "positively," "match," "to the exclusion of all others" (Gabel, 2014). Only a few states require lab accreditation and often jurors are not aware of the differing accreditation requirements (Gabel, 2014). The lack of lab accreditation has led to "junk science" being admitted as evidence at trial.

The term "junk science" emerged during the advancement of DNA evidence in the late 1980s and early 1990s. Junk science was first popularized by Huber (1991), in *Galileo's Revenge: Junk Science in the Courtroom.* An average layperson is unlikely to be able to distinguish among junk, reliable, and valid science. Typically jurors rely on forensic experts to interpret the evidence presented in court. The "CSI Effect" can also impact the jury's decision-making (Thomas, 2015). Fictional television shows that use forensic evidence to solve crimes provides jurors with the unrealistic expectation that forensic evidence is essential and that it is unquestionably accurate.

REFORMS FOR EXPERTS AND EVIDENCE

American Bar Association

The American Bar Association has developed a list of seven factors that could be used to determine how expert testimony should be presented to the jury, as well as, whether to include jury instruction for evaluating expert scientific testimony. The seven factors include:

1. Whether the experts can identify and explain the theoretical and factual basis for any opinion given in their testimony and the reasoning upon which the opinion is based.
2. Whether the experts use clear and consistent terminology in presenting their opinions.
3. Whether the experts present their testimony in a manner that accurately and fairly conveys the significance of their conclusions, including any relevant limitations of the methodology used.

4. Whether the experts explain the reliability of evidence and fairly address problems with evidence including relevant evidence of laboratory error, contamination, or sample mishandling.
5. Whether the expert testimony of individuality or uniqueness is based on valid scientific research.
6. Whether the court should prohibit the parties from tendering witnesses as experts and should refrain from declaring witnesses to be experts in the presence of the jury.
7. Whether to include in jury instructions additional specific factors that might be especially important to a jury's ability to fairly assess the reliability of and weight to be given expert testimony on particular issues in the case (ABA, 2012).

SAFEGUARDS

Judges are the gatekeeper of evidence, responsible for determining which evidence should be admitted. Several Supreme Court cases in the 1900s significantly altered the role of the judge. *Daubert v. Merrell Dow Pharmaceuticals* (1993), *General Electric v. Joiner* (1996), and *Kumho Tire v. Carmichael* (1999) provided more detailed guidance on weighing the admissibility of scientific evidence. Judges now must base their decision on scientific validity, rather than only determining if there is acceptance among the professional community.

Previously, the courts used the "general acceptance" test established in *Frye v. United States* (1923) to determine the admissibility of scientific evidence. Evidence was thought to be admissible if it was accepted in the wider scientific community. Judges had a considerable amount of discretion for admitting scientific evidence, which led to an increase in the use of junk science in the courtroom (Thomas, 2015). Due to difficulty in applying the Frye test, the Supreme Court adopted a two-part test in the 1993 decision *Daubert v. Merrell Dow Pharmaceuticals*. *Daubert* held that the Federal Rules of Evidence (1975) superseded the Frye test and therefore, "scientific testimony must be both reliable and relevant: this entails a preliminary assessment of whether the reasoning or methodology underlying the testimony is scientifically valid and of whether that reasoning or methodology properly can be applied to the facts in issue" (as cited in, Thomas, 2015, p. 39).

Even with the guidance provided by the Supreme Court, most

judges lack a scientific background making it difficult for them to assess the validity of evidence. The *Judging Science* course offered at Duke Law School is one option that can help educate judges (Daftary-Kapus, Dumas, & Penrod, 2010). Other Law schools that provided courses that incorporate social scientific research and techniques are the University of Southern California, University of Illinois, University of Notre Dame, and Columbia University. These educational opportunities will make judges better able to evaluate scientific evidence and to clearly instruct the jurors.

PERJURY OR FALSE ACCUSATIONS

Perjury or false accusation, also referred to as a jailhouse snitch, or an incentivized informant compromise the juror's ability to assess the truthfulness of testimony (Dufraimont, 2008). A jailhouse informant is an inmate that comes forward, claiming to have heard a confession from a fellow inmate. These informants typically receive a sentence reduction for their testimony. According to the NRE, there have been 1162 exonerations where the exoneree cited perjury or false accusation as one of the contributing factors resulting in their wrongful conviction.[14] In U.S. capital cases, "snitches are the leading cause of wrongful convictions" (Warden, 2004). Snitches provide the prosecution with evidence, presumably "from the mouth of the defendant," which is particularly condemning.

The history of the snitch system dates back to common law. In England, snitches were called ubiquitous and even then their motives were deemed unholy (Warden, 2004). The Pilgrims brought the snitch system to the colonies (Warden, 2004; Zimmerman, 2001) and the first documented wrongful conviction in 1819, involved a snitch. The wrongful conviction involved two brothers, Jesse and Stephen Boorn. They were convicted of killing their brother-in-law in Manchester, Vermont. Before their execution, the brother-in-law was found alive in New Jersey.[15] While it has been almost 200 years since the first doc-

14. As of July 5, 2017, for more information see: National Registry of Exonerations. Retrieved from https://www.law.umich.edu/special/exoneration/Pages/detaillist.aspx?View={FAF6EDDB-5A68-4F8F-8A52-2C61F5BF9EA7}&FilterField1=P_x002f_FA&FilterValue1=8_P%2FFA.
15. For more information see: Bluhm Legal Clinic, Center on Wrongful Convictions. (n.d.a). *First Wrongful Conviction*. Retrieved from http://www.law.northwestern.edu/legal-clinic/wrongfulconvictions/exonerations/vt/boorn-brothers.html.

umented wrongful conviction, the use of informants/snitches continues in the American criminal justice system. One of America's most notorious informants, Leslie Vernon White, during a *60 Minutes* interview, joked about the slogans of the snitch system, where he said "If you can't do the time, just drop a dime," or "don't go to the pen, send a friend," and "Trouble? You better call 1-800-HETOLDME" (Scheck, Neufeld, & Dwyer, 2000).

Four of the most common problems with using an informant/snitch are (1) the reward system for compensation and the lack of truthfulness, (2) law enforcement agents are encouraged to use informants, (3) judicial protection for informants include confidentiality and even security, and (4) the use of informants maintains a systemic environment that values speed over accuracy (Zimmerman, 2001). A jailhouse informant's testimony can be highly persuasive but is invariably unreliable. Jailhouse snitches believe they have nothing to lose, but can advance their own interests (Dufraimont, 2008).

Compensation for their testimony can include outright immunity from the prosecution or a monetary reward. These rewards compete with the informant's obligation to tell the truth. As for the police and prosecutor, assessing reliability and credibility of an informant's statement can be a daunting task and might be something that they do not desire to do (Norris et al., 2011). Neither the police nor the prosecutor would want to discredit their witness, especially when the snitches testimony is needed for conviction. Therefore, both the criminal justice system (i.e., police and prosecutor) and the informant/snitch can benefit from the inculpatory information. It is evident then that jury instructions are needed to provide a perspective on incentivized testimony.

SAFEGUARDS

The Tenth Circuit Court decided two of the most notable cases concerning a snitch testimony known as Singleton I (*United States v. Singleton*, 1998) and Singleton II (*United States v. Singleton*, 1999). Singleton I, decided on July 1, 1998, held that the common practice of using rewards in exchange for a testimony by the federal prosecutor constitutes bribery of the witness. The panel of the United States Court of Appeals relied on Section 201 of the Title XVIII of the U.S. Code, which read:

> Whoever . . . directly or indirectly, corruptly gives, offers, or promises anything of value to any person, with intent to influence the testimony under oath or affirmation, such first mentioned person as a witness upon a trial, hearing, or other proceeding, before any court . . . shall be fined under this title or imprisoned for not more than two years, or both (As cited in the Justice Project, 2007; 18 U.S. C. § 201 (c) (2) (2007)).

The panel used the "whoever" to represent the federal prosecutors, and "anything of value" to include such things as sentence reductions. Almost two weeks later, the court granted a rehearing *en banc*.[16] Singleton II was decided on January 8, 1999. This decision reversed the previous ruling and specified the original assumed words (i.e., "whoever" & "anything of value"). The new ruling explained how the "whoever" could not be the sovereign government of the United States and the "thing of value" did not include benefits granted by the state. Meaning that even though prosecutors are agents of the United States government they are still able to grant rewards. Although Singleton I was reversed, the Tenth Circuit ruling illustrated the complexities of a snitch's testimony. Besides the Tenth Circuit ruling in the Singleton decisions, other federal courts of appeals have addressed the issue of informants. The Fifth Circuit (*United States v. Cervantes-Pacheo*, 1987), states that the trial court should give special cautionary instructions to the jury when assessing the credibility of a witness who has been compensated for their testimony (As cited in the Justice Project, 2007). Two other cases include:

United States v. Kaufman, 858 F.2d 994 (5th Cir. 1988), which held that whenever the government is giving an informant money, the jury must be made aware of this information and in *United States v. Cresta*, 825 F.2d 538, 541 (1st Cir. 1987) the court ruled that "when testimony is result of contingent fee arrangement the jury must be informed of the exact nature of the arrangement" (as cited in Gershman, 2007, p. 2006).

PROPOSED REFORMS

There are several recommended reforms that could assist the jury. A pretrial reliability hearing involves screening the informant prior to trial to determine whether the testimony is reliable and should be

---

16. *En banc* meaning, case heard before entire bench.

admitted as evidence. This is similar to assessing an expert testimony prior to consideration by the jury. If the testimony meets the threshold for reliability then a jury will be able to weigh the testimony. In addition, a juror should receive cautionary instructions that help assess the testimony of an incentivized informant (Norris et al., 2011). The instruction would at least highlight the potential dangers and provide proper cautions. Some of the factors to consider are:

1. explicit or implied inducements that the jailhouse snitch received, may receive, or will receive;
2. the prior criminal history of the informant;
3. evidence that he or she is a "career informant" who has testified in other criminal cases; and
4. any other factors that might tend to render the witness' testimony unreliable (The Justice Project, 2007, p. 2).

STATE REFORMS

There are several states that have reforms concerning criminal informants. These include:[17]

State v. Patterson, 886 A. 2d 777 (Conn. 2005): Special jury instructions need to be given when both an accomplices[18] and jailhouse snitches testimony is presented. CAL. PENAL CODE § 1127a (b) (Cal. 2004): The courts are required to instruct the jury on any in-custody informant testimony.

People v. Petschow, 119 P.3d 495, 504 (Colo. Ct. App.2004): Cautionary instructions will be given when there is no corroborating evidence that supports the testimony of an accomplice.

State v. Marallo, No. 1468-10-98 RdCr. (Vt. 2004): Instruction should be

---

17. For more information on state reforms see: The Justice Project. (2007). *Jailhouse snitch testimony: A policy review*. Washington, D.C. Retrieved from http://www.pewtrusts.org/~/media/legacy/uploadedfiles/wwwpewtrustsorg/reports/death_penalty_reform/Jailhouse20snitch20testimony20policy20briefpdf.pdf.
18. Accomplices or alleged co-participants pose some of the same unreliability issues. More states typically only address accomplice testimony; recently states have begun to include other types of informants. See Norris, et al. 2011 for more information.

used when a witness receives a plea agreement for testifying against a defendant who is being charged with participating in the same crime.

725 ILL. COMP. STAT. 5/115-21 (2003): Illinois courts hold pretrial hearings in capital cases in which a jailhouse snitches testimony is being entered as evidence. The courts will consider information provided by the prosecutor in a timely manner:

1. the complete criminal history of the informant;
2. any deal, promise, inducement, or benefit that the offering party has made or will make in the future to the informant;
3. the statements made by the accused;
4. the time and place of the statements, the time and place of their disclosure to law enforcement officials, and the names of all persons who were present when the statements were made;
5. whether at any time the informant recanted that testimony or statement and, if so, the time and place of the recantation, the nature of the recantation, and the names of the persons who were present at the recantation;
6. other cases in which the informant testified, provided that the existence of such testimony can be ascertained through reasonable inquiry and whether the informant received any promise, inducement, or benefit in exchange for or subsequent to that testimony or statement; and
7. any other information relevant to the informant's credibility(Sec. (c)).

State v. Spiller, No. 00-2897-CR, 2001 WL 1035213 (Wis. App. Sept. 11, 2001): The appellate court ruled that "[i]t is an error to deny a request for an accomplice instructions only in a case where the accomplice's testimony is totally uncorroborated" (para. 15).

Dodd v. State, 993 P2d 778 (Okla. Crim. App. 2000): Courts must give special instructions when jailhouse snitches testify; the special instructions require that the jury examines the testimony with special care taking into account specific factors. These factors include, whether the witness received anything of value in exchange for testimony, the informer's criminal history, any other case in which the informer testified, whether the informer ever changed his or her testimony, and any other evidence pertinent to the informer's credibility. The factors that will be included in the special instructions must be disclosed by the state at least ten days prior to the trial (para. 25).

State v. Grimes, 982 P.2d 1037 (Mont. 1999): Court must give cautionary instructions to the jury, if the informant testifies for a personal gain.

State v. James, No. 96-CA-17, 1998 WL 518135 (Ohio Ct. App. Mar.25, 1998): When there is no corroborating evidence based on an informant's testimony cautionary instructions are needed.

FALSE CONFESSIONS

A false confession poses an interesting dilemma for a jury. To a juror, a confession provides evidence of guilt and is among the most damaging, even though it can be unreliable. According to the NRE, there have been 242 exonerations where the exoneree cited false confessions as one of their contributing factors resulting in their wrongful conviction.[19] Through exoneration data the commonly held belief that an innocent person would not confess to a crime is debunked. The current exoneration data also exposes the widely-held belief that innocent people only confess when they are being tortured, which is not the case. Juries need instruction to assess the possibility that a confession is false.

Both the suspect's vulnerability and the coerciveness of the interrogation can lead to a false confession (Dufraimont, 2008). Juveniles and persons suffering from mental illness are found to be more vulnerable to falsely confessing to a crime. Coerciveness of an interrogation refers to the use of pressures, deceit and manipulation in order to cause a suspect to confess (Dufraimont, 2008). A police interrogation is designed to include stress, which can cause a suspect to feel isolated, hopeless, and nervous.

The Reid technique, the most widely used police interrogation strategy in the U.S., begins with a Behavior Analysis interview intended to determine if the suspect is lying. The interview may include polygraph

---

19. As of July 5, 2017, for more information see: National Registry of Exonerations. Retrieved from http://www.law.umich.edu/special/exoneration/Pages/detaillist.aspx?View={FAF6EDDB-5A68-4F8F-8A52-2C61F5BF9EA7}&FilterField1=FC&FilterValue1=8_FC.

testing and asking a series of unnerving questions such as, "With such a horrific crime, what kind of punishment should the offender get?" or "Is there is any reason your prints or hair would be found at the scene." The next phase of the interrogation, involves getting a suspect to confess. This again is done through a series of questions but it is followed up with some form of an offer or promise. This could include when an officer's states that they want to help the suspect or they will talk with the judge to ensure a particular sentence, as long as the suspect confesses. Finally, once the suspect agrees to confess, the officer would praise the suspect and then they would work together to develop a written confession (Starr, 2013).

As a result of Reid techniques or other interrogation practices, there are five factors that appear to cause a false confession:

- Real or perceived intimidation of the suspect by law enforcement
- Use of force by law enforcement during the interrogation, or perceived threat of force
- Compromised reasoning ability of the suspect, due to exhaustion, stress, hunger, substance use, and, in some cases, mental limitations, or limited education
- Devious interrogation techniques, such as untrue statements about the presence of incriminating evidence
- Fear, on the part of the suspect, that failure to confess will yield a harsher punishment (Innocence Project, 2015b).

Based upon these factors several states have enacted legislation that requires an electronic recording of the entire interrogation. By recording the entire process, a judge can determine if the confession was freely given. If the confession is not considered to be voluntary, then the judge may then determine that it should be suppressed. This will prevent the jurors from knowing about the confessions altogether. Since all states do not require that the entire interrogation be recorded, jurors need adequate instructions that explain the potential for a false confession.

REFORMS

Several states have enacted legislation mandating video recording of the entire interrogation process to prevent false confessions. These states include: Connecticut, Illinois, Maine, Maryland, Michigan, Missouri, Montana, Nebraska, New Mexico, North Carolina, Ohio, Oregon, Vermont, Wisconsin, and the District of Columbia (Innocence Project, 2015b). However, in states that do not require electronic recording, the jury must decide the merits of the confession. Jurors then need to be provided informed cautionary jury instructions or hear from an expert witness about the risk factors of providing a false confession. In addition, the jury should be advised to carefully consider other evidence that may link the defendant to the crime.

SAFEGUARDS

Two safeguards designed to prevent the admission of a false confession are the defendant's pretrial motion to suppress evidence obtained in violation of their constitutional rights and second, the use of expert testimony at trial. An expert is able to explain to both the judge and jury the psychological factors that can contribute to a false confession. This is very important because jurors and justice officials at each stage of the criminal process, place considerable weight on a confession (Leo & Liu, 2009). It appears that the confession, even when false often leads to a conviction.

JURY INSTRUCTIONS

Jury instructions are authoritative and efficient. A benefit of jury instructions is that an expert is not needed to explain the instructions. Instead the instructions provide a uniformed standard that is applicable in cases. Instructions are important because jurors are tasked with handling unreliable evidence, identifying lies, overcoming biases, having to ignore inadmissible evidence, and acknowledging any prejudice that they might harbor (Simon, 2012, p.145). Furthermore, jurors as ordinary citizens are likely to be unaware of the potential problems associated with a wrongful conviction, including eyewitness identification, false confessions, incentivized informants, faulty forensic evidence and expert testimony. Because of these problems jury instructions are needed to assist with evidentiary regulations.

There are, of course, many complex judicial decisions when giving jury instructions. Many times juries are guided on how to interpret and apply the law. For justice to be achieved jurors have to be able to comprehend the instructions provided by the judge. Therefore, jury instruction must be understood; however, jury instructions are often a mix of legal terms and complex sentences intended for lawyers (Marder, 2006). The comprehension of judicial instruction by jurors tends to be low (Haney & Lynch, 1994; Hastie, Penrod, & Pennington, 1983; Severance & Loftus, 1982).The inability to comprehend instructions leads a juror to rely on their own interpretation of evidence, concerning reliability and validity. In addition, a trial judge reads the instructions prior to jury deliberation, but jurors are not always allowed to take notes, nor are they given a written copy detailing the instructions. The instructions read by the judge could take hours to complete. For example, in the case of Michael Jackson the jury instructions spanned 98 pages (Marder, 2006).

To improve jury comprehension standard jury instructions may be rewritten to use simple terms, have shorter sentences, and replace all complex abstract terms with concrete words. Several studies have found a few suggestions that can help with comprehension. Elwork, Alfini, and Sales (1982), found that when standard jury instructions were rewritten with these suggestions, mock jurors' comprehension improved from 51 percent to 80 percent (as cited in Daftary-Kapus et al., 2010). To reduce the possibility of distorting the new instructions, a flowchart or decision trees may be used. Visual depictions also improve the presentation of instructions to the jury. In a comprehensive review of jury decisions over a 45-year period, Devine, Clayton, Dunford, Seying, and Pryce (2000) identify several reforms that enhance juror's comprehension:

> (a) using court-appointed experts, (b) pre-instructing jurors, (c) providing jurors with written copies of judicial instructions, (d) revising/simplifying judicial instructions, (e) allowing jurors to take notes and/or ask questions during the trial, (f) having judges and/or attorneys provide summary comments on the evidence, and (g) using verdicts forms that include interrogation. (p. 712)

Also included in jury instructions are scientific findings concerning eyewitness identification, valid and invalid forensic science techniques, and reliability concerns with the use of an informer. Faulty jury instructions may also lead to an incorrect verdict (London & Nunez, 2000).

When inadmissible evidence is entered, a judge may either strike the information, by providing instructions to disregard the information, or may declare a mistrial. To assist the jurors, the judge may explain why the evidence is unfair or irrelevant to the parties involved (Daftary-Kapus et al., 2010). The jury should be provided with a clear rationale when inadmissible evidence is discovered.

There are a few states that have begun taking action to make jury instructions more easily understood. California has undertaken an extensive effort to rewrite both civil and criminal instructions. On September 1, 2003 as a results of 19 legal organizations, as well as hundreds of individual lawyers the California Plain Language Civil Jury Instructions took effect (Marder, 2006). Later on January 1, 2006 the new plain-language criminal instructions were implemented (Judicial Council of California, 2015). The plain-language criminal instructions includes using active voice, or simple words, avoiding any legal jargon, double negatives, and provides examples from everyday life (Marder, 2006). Several other states have revised their jury instructions. States that attempted to simplify civil jury instructions include: Hawaii, Iowa, Michigan, Oregon, Pennsylvania, and Wisconsin (Marder, 2006).

Arizona has taken a different approach to revising their jury. Jurors are allowed to submit written questions for witnesses to clarify points of concern. In addition, a more constructive approach, the 1896 *Allen* charge has been instituted. Originally when a jury could not reach an agreement, a judge would deliver an *Allen* charge, which reminds the jurors that it's their duty to reach a verdict (Smith, 2012). This directive can cause confusion when the jurors are conflicted by their sense of what is right in a case (Marder, 2006). To alleviate the confusion, an Arizona judge-jury dialogue takes place to determine if there is any additional information that could assist with the verdict. This approach is consistent with an "active" model of jurors. The active model moves the jury away from strictly adhering to the adversarial practice, and encourages an active involvement between the jury and the judge. This prevents juror passivity by allowing its members to ask questions to improve their ability to comprehend the admitted evidence (Hans, 2002). Active participation is one way to assist laypeople with understanding complex matters presented at a trial.

CONCLUSION

It is apparent that jurors may be misled by flawed evidence admitted at trial. There are several variables – estimator and system–that can explain the jury's confusion. Estimator variables refer to the characteristics of the eyewitness and the circumstances surrounding the crime, while system variables are inherent in the actions of the agents of the criminal justice system itself. Both sets of variables should be addressed by criminal justice reforms, in the judge's instructions to the jury, or by the testimony of expert witnesses.

Many states have now begun to examine how jury instructions may prevent miscarriages of justice. Judges are providing an instruction focused approach to juries that incorporates scientific findings on eyewitness misidentification, forensic and expert testimony, the unreliability of incentivized informants, and practices that result in false confessions (Dufraimont, 2008). Reforms that emphasize skepticism and the protection of the constitutional rights of the suspect during the processing of a criminal case by the police and prosecutors are also vital to the reduction of wrongful convictions. Because human error is inevitable, reforms that specifically address both estimator and system errors are critical to criminal justice outcomes.

PART III

Chapter 7

POST-CONVICTION REVIEW

The image that comes to mind is an assembly line or a conveyor belt down which moves an endless stream of cases, never stopping, carrying the cases to workers who stand at fixed stations and who perform on each case as it comes by the small but essential operation that brings it one step close to being a finished product, or, to exchange the metaphor for the reality, a closed file.

– Packer (1968, p. 159)

THE CASE OF NATHAN BROWN

In 1997, a 40-year-old white woman was attacked outside of her apartment complex. She was able to fend off her assailant by hitting him with her high heels. The victim then told the police that she had been attacked by a black man, with no shirt. She believed that her attacker did not live in the apartment complex; however, a security guard for the apartment directed police to Nathan Brown. He was one of the few black individuals that resided in the apartment complex. He had been questioned earlier concerning a Peeping Tom incident. The officers conducted a one-on-one "show-up." This practice involved bringing a single suspect – Brown – to the victim, so she could identify the perpetrator. This identification practice is highly suggestive and led to the victim identifying Brown as her assailant.

Three months later Brown's case went to trial. The police never found the victim's purse that was stolen or the bike that the victim said her assailant escaped on. Brown was convicted in less than a day. Four relatives testified that Brown was at home during the attack. Brown was nonetheless convicted of attempted aggravated rape and sentenced to 25 years in prison without the possibility of parole. Throughout Brown maintained his innocence, and in 2002, he contacted the Innocence Project who was able to test DNA evidence from the victim's dress. The DNA test excluded Brown who had served nearly 17 years for a crime he did not commit.[1]

SAFEGUARDS AND DUE PROCESS OF LAW

Theoretically, the American criminal justice system protects the rights of the accused by providing safeguards established in the Bill of Rights. The United States Supreme Court has held that the Bill of Rights governing criminal procedures in federal courts are so crucial to a fair trial that based on the due process clause of the Fourteenth Amendment they are also applicable to criminal proceedings at the state level (Salassi, 1996). Judicial post-conviction remedies and/or reviews provide particularly important safeguards for the wrongfully convicted. Judicial post-conviction remedies are founded on the principle of due process. Put simply, due process means that laws need to be applied equally and fairly to all citizens accused of a crime, derived from Chapter 39 of the Magna Carta, which states that "No freeman shall be arrested, or detained in prison, or deprived of freehold, or outlawed, or banished, or in any way molested; and we will not set forth against him, nor send against him, unless by the lawful judgement of his peers and [or] by the law of his land" (King John, 1215). In present day, the due process of law is found in the Fifth and Fourteenth Amendment of the U.S. Constitution, and is the only command mentioned twice in the Constitution, which holds that "no person shall be deprived of life, liberty, or property without due process of law" (U.S. Const. amends. V & XIV).

POST-CONVICTION DIFFICULTLY WITH CLAIMS OF INNOCENCE

Post-convictions reviews and constitutional safeguards should benefit all defendants including the wrongfully convicted. In general,

---

1. For more information on Nathan's Brown case see: Innocence Project. (n.d.g) *Nathan Brown.* Retrieved from http://www.innocenceproject.org/cases/nathan-brown/.
And, Possley, M. (2014). *Nathan Brown.* Retrieved from https://www.law.umich.edu/special/exoneration/pages/casedetail.aspx?caseid=4457.

there are several possible reasons why post-conviction reviews are not always granted for claims of innocence. Specifically, an understanding of Herbert Packer's crime control and due process models can help explain why adherence to a certain part of the model can cause obstacles to pursue an exoneration. In addition, Donald's Black's (1976) innovative work, the Behavior of Law, predicts the likelihood of a wrongful conviction and the difficulties faced in the pursuit of an exoneration.

Further, the game-like nature of the adversarial system itself assumes that if procedures were followed by all parties, there should not be a wrong outcome (i.e., wrongful conviction). This could be why the appellate system appears to only review the trial procedures and not claims of innocence. Even when an appeal is available, the restrictive nature of these appeals can make post-conviction relief difficult.

PACKER'S CRIME CONTROL VERSUS DUE PROCESS

In 1968 Herbert Packer wrote *The Limits of the Criminal Sanction,* which explained the daily operations of the justice system based on two different philosophical orientations: the due process and the crime control models. The models are based on the competing goals of the justice system, which is the need to enforce the law while maintaining social order (i.e., crime control model) and the need to protect individuals from the possibility of injustices (i.e., due process model).

The crime control model emphasizes speed and efficiency, "routine, stereotyped procedures"(Packer, 1968), where weak cases are dropped by the prosecutor and the rest of the cases follow the assembly line process explained by Packer, until a conviction, a closed file, is reached with few instances of post-conviction relief. Post-conviction relief is similar to an appeal but it attacks a conviction. Meaning that the convicted person's rights were violated during the trial. It is often entered after an appeal has been unsuccessful or anytime there is new evidence that has been discovered that the court should consider. And, it is the only option available when a plea was entered, since the right to appeal is waived as a result of the plea agreement. It is governed by state and federal laws; however, each state has its own laws concerning relief.

Based on the crime control model, there would be few instances of post-conviction relief, since it's assumed that the police have apprehended the correct person, respected the person's rights throughout the arrest process and have provided sufficient evidence for the prosecutor to go forward with the case. The assumption is that the person is truly guilty of "something" since they have moved through the criminal justice assembly line. The crime control model also finds mistakes to be acceptable as long as they do not affect the goal of repressing crime. Therefore, convicting the innocent is an acceptable risk in the pursuit of crime control. The limited use of post-conviction relief and appeals might also be the result of the frequent use of plea deals. This bargaining tool is supported by the crime control model, since it assists with the speed and efficiency of achieving a closed file. Plea bargaining restricts the innocent from certain courses of action when fighting for their freedom.

The due process model on the other hand, supports slowing the process down, making sure the accused are afforded their due process rights. Convictions become more difficult because of the obstacles the justice actors encounter to close a case. During the time of Packer's writings, there were several Supreme Court decisions under the Warren Court that expanded the rights of the accused, establishing more safeguards concerning one's due process rights (i.e., *Gideon v. Wainwright* (1963), *Miranda v. Arizona* (1966), and *Katz v. United States* (1967)). Despite these safeguards afforded by the due process model, in actual practice the criminal justice system appears to be dominated by the goals of the crime control model, emphasizing the importance of conviction, speed, and efficiency over protecting the rights of the accused. This is inferred from several current practices found within the justice system, including the implementation of the PATRIOT ACT, the use of plea bargaining, and the promotional and reward structure for justice officials. If not a wrongful conviction, all of these have contributed to at least a wrongful detainment.

PATRIOT ACT

The USA PATRIOT Act (2001) provided for wide discretion to aggressively control criminal activity, including profiling, wiretapping, and undercover sting operations. These strategies are often inconsistent with individual civil liberties. For example, Attorney Brandon Mayfield, a resident of Oregon, was wrongly accused of being involved in the 2004 Madrid bombing based on mistaken fingerprint identification. The FBI without a warrant entered Mayfield's home, copied computer drives, seized DNA samples, and took roughly 335 digital photographs. Attorney General Gonzales acknowledged that the PATRIOT Act supported the search. Mayfield spent two weeks in custody, the first week in lockdown in a federal prison, before the error was discovered (Sarasohn, 2005). The extent of other citizens having their rights violated or being wrongfully detained and searched is unknown. The secrecy of national security letters (NSL) mandates that recipients agree to a "gag" order (Albanese, 2008). A gag order is not a warrant nor is it signed by a court; rather it is a letter mandating that certain information be provided to the federal government and that the arrangement be kept secret from all other individuals. More recently, the USA FREEDOM Act of 2015 modified the PATRIOT Act to deal with the publics' demand for protection of their civil liberties and protection against unwarranted investigations.

PLEAS

In the United States, plea bargaining is a common practice. According to Siegel and Worrall, (2015) roughly 90 percent of criminal convictions are a result of a plea bargain (p. 389). Plea bargaining has become such a regular and needed practice that even the Supreme Court of Justice has referred to it as an "essential component of the administration of justice" (*Brady v. United States*, 397 U.S. 742 (1970)). The due process model emphasizes the importance of a formal fact-finding process, which includes the right to confront witnesses and cross-examine accusers (Sixth Amendment), the right to a jury trial (Sixth Amendment), the right to counsel – if unrepresented (Sixth Amendment), and the right against self-incrimination (Fifth Amendment). These individual rights are no longer provided once a plea is entered. Furthermore, if the convicted person pled guilty or accepted a plea then they are no longer eligible for many post-conviction remedies and appeals. These restrictions make over 90 percent of convicted individuals ineligible for possible post-conviction relief.

It is commonly assumed that an innocent person would not take a plea deal but this assumption is unfounded. For example, Brian Banks took a plea deal that sent him to prison and labeled him as sex offender for a crime that the victim admitted, years later, never happened. Brian was a high school football athlete that had committed to play at Southern California when a female classmate told her parents and authorities that she had been raped by Brain. He was 16 years old when he was tried as an adult. He was sentenced to six years after accepting a plea deal. In total he served five years and two months in prison and five years on parole, and had to register as a sex offender once released. Russel D. Covey (2011) summed up the innocence problem associated with plea bargaining when he stated: "When the deal is good enough, it is rational to refuse to roll the dice, regardless of whether one believes the evidence established guilt beyond a reasonable doubt and regardless of whether one is factually innocent" (p. 450). The vulnerability and fear of a draconian sentence can cause a defendant to admit guilt even though they had nothing to do with the crime.

EMPIRICAL SUPPORT THAT THE INNOCENT ADMIT GUILT

Dervan and Edkins (2013) report that college participants, falsely admitted guilt in return for a perceived benefit. The researchers created an experiment that mirrored what is found in a criminal trial when a plea deal is offered. They examined what is known as the innocent defendant's dilemma. This is when an innocent person says they are guilty and accepts a deal because of the possible repercussions that might arise if they were to be tried.

The participants believed that they were involved in a study that examined individual versus group problem-solving performances. One by one, the participants would gather in a room with another student, who was a part of the research staff but was thought to be another student by the student participant group. They were asked to collectively solve the first logic problem together and then told to answer the next questions on their own. The undercover research participant followed different scripts to cause a response from some of the student participants. Once finished, the research staff proctoring the logic test stated that an issue had arisen and then separated the students. The student participants individually were told that it was clear that they cheated during the experiment. Because of their cheating they were first offered what the researchers claimed was the "plea." This is where students could admit there guilt and as a punishment would lose their compensation, a reward for being a participant in the experiment. They were also offered two alternative options, depending on the group, if the plea was rejected. In about half of the cases– known as the "harsh sentencing condition" the researcher stated if they did not accept the plea the researcher would bring the matter to Academic Review Board (ARB). To make this similar to a jury, they explained that the ARB was a group of ten or twelve faculty/staff members that would review the case. Making the experiment more similar to a criminal trial, the researcher stated that ARB found between 80-90 percent of the students guilty. Next, the participants were told the consequences of a possible conviction. In the other half of the cases, known as the "lenient sentencing condition," the same information was provided concerning the ARB; however, the penalties were less severe. Although not precisely equivalent to the criminal justice process, the researchers attempted to recreate the innocence dilemma; they found that more than half of the student participants falsely admitted guilt for the benefit of either a lenient or harsh sentence (p.34-37). It is clear, then, that innocent individuals do admit guilt when they perceive a benefit for doing so (Gregory, Mowen & Linder, 1984; Russano, Meissner, Narchet & Kassin, 2005).

Personal accounts reported by the Innocence Project and news outlets provide insight into the reasons why the wrongfully convicted plead guilty. For example, Michael Marshall, who in order to avoid a harsher sentence, purposely accepted a plea deal for a robbery that he did not commit. Marshall stated in a letter that "I plead guilty out of being scared" (Innocence Project, n.d.i). By accepting a plea, a person does not have to fear the unknown. Think about it, knowing you are innocent but the justice system continues to build a case against you is very frightening. It naturally makes sense that someone would rather know the outcome by admitting guilt than by taking their chances by going to trial.

To Blume and Helm (2014) our justice system contributes to the innocent accepting a plea deal. First, for our justice system to run efficiently the majority of defendants must plead guilty. Since plea bargains are a normal function, prosecutors and defense attorneys strongly encourage the defendant to accept a deal. Furthermore, because of the possibility of a severe sentence innocent defendants may take a plea bargain out of fear. Blume and Helm (2014) also argue that the current plea system is, in part, an unregulated industry (p. 7). Fear of punishment and the unmonitored plea system can increase the likelihood of a wrongful conviction. If the crime control model continues to emphasize speed and efficiency, then plea deals will continue to dominate criminal adjudications. No longer should innocent individuals who accept a plea out of fear or because pleas are a normal function of justice system be barred from the appellate process.

REWARDS AND INCENTIVES

Monetary rewards or incentives given to law enforcement officers and prosecutors based upon conviction rates, individual promotions or departmental goals may well undermine the constitutional rights of the accused. During colonial America the Sheriff, the most important agent of law enforcement, was paid based on the number of persons arrested (Siegel & Worrall, 2013). This payment based solely on arrest rates was later replaced to reduce unwarranted arrests. Even though this practice was replaced, police departments and prosecutorial offices still use monetary incentives.

An incentive either individually or departmentally may play a role in how an officer handles a reported crime. For example, when an officer unfounds or defounds a case. Unfounding occurs when a police officer rejects a person's claim that he or she was a victim of a criminal act. Defounding is when an officer believes that a crime took place but is not as serious as described by the victim or witness. An officer may unfound or defound complaints to align with a supervisor's goal of convincing the community that crime rates are decreasing. It may also be done for personal gain. For example, in Chicago for more than 20 years detectives unfound 21 percent of serious crimes that were reported. According to the FBI, in comparison to other larger departments less than 2 percent of cases were unfounded. By unfounding victim's complaints more cases are closed, which attributes to detectives receiving a higher rating, resulting in faster promotions (Karmen, 2016; "Chicago Police," 1983). Unfounding or defounding cases suggest that speed and efficiency are rewarded by a department and can contribute to an individual's promotion. As long as the community feels that crime is on the decline this practice may continue to occur.

Again, these practices are supported by the crime control model.

A similar practice based upon incentives is when prosecutors grant bonuses for convictions. According to Joy and Mcmunigal (2011) trusting a prosecutor to seek justice can become convoluted when a prosecutor is motivated by either monetary reward or preferential treatment (para. 1). Police and prosecutors may select cases based upon the ease of a conviction and to increase their financial or career interests. If our justice system continues to reward convictions, more innocent individuals will be convicted for personal gain. Bonuses and rewards can only compromise the integrity behind the justice system.

Monetary and promotional incentives are consistent with the crime control model. Claims of innocence hamper the speedy and efficient model, which may be overlooked when an incentive is being jeopardized. If emphasis is placed on the crime control model, then post-conviction remedies and claims of innocence will play a limited role in the exoneration process.

BLACK'S BEHAVIOR OF LAW

Donald Black's (1976) work on the Behavior of Law provides a way to understand how the legal processing of a case can be influenced by the criminal situation. He defines law as governmental social control (i.e., the more involvement of the justice actors, the greater the governmental social control). Although laws are written down, Black explains that these laws are not put into effect the same way as they are written.

Black provides 29 propositions, three of them as mentioned in the introduction are important for the understanding of a wrongful conviction.[2] These include relative status (i.e., the higher status of the victim compared to offender, the greater governmental social control), respectability (i.e. the greater the respectability of victim in comparison to the offender the greater the government control), and relational distance of the offender and victim (i.e., the greater the relational distance between victim and offender, the greater the governmental social control). These three propositions argue that the structure of a legal case the – *who does what to whom* – will affect the behavior of law. We can predict the extent of involvement with the justice actors (i.e.,

---

2. See Chapter 1 for an additional discussion of Black's propositions.

time, effort, and resources) based upon the characteristics of the suspect and the victim. These propositions are inversely related. Meaning that as status of the victim decreases, so does the governmental social control. Therefore, based on Black's predictive models concerning governmental social control, less time, energy and resources would be expanded by justice agents if the offender was considered a higher status than the victim.

Because these propositions explain the investment of the criminal justice system in securing a conviction, they can also be used to understand the obstacles encountered in the exoneration process. For example, it would only make sense that the same efforts by the justice actors used to obtain a conviction would be used to deny and avoid post-conviction judicial relief. The greater government social control would not end after conviction but would naturally continue until all legal remedies were exhausted.

Packer's crime control model clearly states that it supports the presumption of guilt (Packer, 1968) and Black explains how certain defendants are more convictable.[3] Presumption of guilt and the convictability imply that justice actors make assumptions that guide their decisions. In sum, Packer's crime control model and Black's social structure of a legal case may help explain the likelihood for a conviction and the justice system's review of innocence claims.

Both Packer and Black's theoretical formulations help us understand both miscarriages of justice and obstacles to post-conviction judicial relief and exonerations. Black's structure of a legal case explains how some defendants are more convictable than others and the time and resources devoted to each case. Packer's crime control model provides us with a systematic method for understanding criminal justice decision-making. Our justice system does not strictly adhere to Constitutional and procedural safeguards. Simply put, if a "convictable" suspect is identified, then a conviction is typically sought in a speedy and efficient manner.

The Nathan Brown case discussed at the beginning of the chapter provides an example for how Black's structure of a legal case drives the expenditures of the government and how devotion to the crime control model can lead to a wrongful conviction. Although innocent, Nathan Brown was perceived to be convictable, based on the relative statues of the victim – an older white female and the accused – a young, black

---

3. See Chapter 1 for an additional discussion of both Packer's models and Black's theory.

male living in the same apartment complex. His respectability appeared to be tainted because of being questioned for a Peeping Tom incident. The relational distance between the victim and accused (i.e., they were strangers) may also have contributed to the perception of his "convictability." Once the victim identified Brown, the police ceased to gather additional evidence and simply forwarded the case to the prosecution. For example, if the police had questioned the feasibility of Brown riding his bike back to his apartment, showering, and changing into his pajamas prior to their arrival, then they may have been more skeptical about their conclusion.

Furthermore, the attack happened on August 7, 1997 and Brown's trial began November 19, 1997. It took one day to convict Brown but nearly 17 years to prove his innocence. The brief time to convict highlights many elements of the crime control model, namely, speed, efficiency, finality and even the presumption of guilt by the justice system, until a conviction was reached. Vanessa Potkin, an attorney with the Innocence Project, stated it perfectly when she told the *Time- Picayune*: "A lot went wrong in this case. A crime happened, and there was a rush to judgment. No one stopped and scrutinized on any side. People just didn't hear his screams that he was innocent" (As cited in Innocent Project, 2014). For years Brown's appeal for post-conviction relief were denied. He had reached out to attorneys, clinics, judges, and legal scholars (Innocence Project, 2014). Packer's crime control model and Black's social structure of a legal case provide a context for understanding the justice system's response to Brown's claims of innocence.

ORGANIZATIONAL REASONS FOR POST-CONVICTION DIFFICULTIES

According to Siegel and Worrall (2013), there are roughly 14 million individuals arrested each year, of these, one million are convicted of felony charges in state and federal courts, and 1.5 million juveniles are handled by juvenile courts. Aside from the arrest and court population there are more than seven million people under some form of correctional supervision, roughly two million in jail and in prison. The other five million convicted individuals are either on parole or probation. The cost to run the state and local criminal and civil justice system is $215 billion. Therefore, each time a post-conviction review is granted, this further adds stress onto the overburdened system and may increase the overall cost of the criminal justice apparatus.

The goal of an organization is to have all pieces work together, collectively, to achieve an overall goal of justice. A post-conviction review essentially reviews the failures of the system. Individuals make up this system and if individuals in the organization are monitoring, investigating, and potentially accusing wrongdoers or wrongful actions within their own organization, this may threaten the collective nature of the organization. Success of an organization depends on its ability to work together. Again, this could explain why claims of innocence and judicial post-conviction reviews are rarely granted.

Individual fear of reporting a possible injustice may also be associated with the lack of post-conviction reviews. These individuals are often ostracized by other members of the organization (Miceli & Near, 1992). For example, Frank Serpico, was a New York City police officer, who reported widespread police corruption in the mid-1960s. His complaints were often ignored, and because of his persistent crusade he was shot in the face during a drug bust, where fellow officers left him for dead (Comer & Vega, 2011, p. 33). A post-conviction review brought on the justice system could open "Pandora's Box" causing fear among individuals and possibly leading to unexpected problems for the individual or department as a whole.

JUDICIAL REVIEW FOR THE WRONGLY CONVICTED

A judicial review is an important mechanism used to address and remedy violations of our constitutional rights. There are many types of judicial reviews. The focus here is on post-conviction judicial reviews. There are several types of post-conviction relief to challenge a conviction. These can be the "last resort" for a convicted person. Two common mechanisms used by the wrongfully convicted are either an appeal or a post-conviction motion. When challenging a federal conviction, a direct appeal precedes a post-conviction motion. With an appeal the court is limited to only inspecting the trial record. In some states, however, post-conviction motions would be filed prior to an appeal. Motions challenge the errors that occurred during a trial or sentencing hearing. They can also be used to raise new issues and new facts, such as when a defendant decides to withdraw their plea. These are motions that have reshaped habeas corpus for prisoners.

Habeas corpus "that you have the body" was a practice that was found in English common law. Mainly, it used to ensure that the detention of a prisoner is valid. It is commonly used as a post-conviction remedy for state and federal prisoners to question the legality of the judicial proceeding that resulted in their detention. Originally, the writ only applied to prisoners convicted of federal crimes, but in 1867 Congress extended the writ to state prisoners.

In most states, if you were convicted of a crime in a federal court, you can challenge your conviction or sentence using motion 2255. The motion is filed after a direct appeal becomes final. Unlike the direct appeal, this motion relies upon facts that were not a part of the court record. New facts can include: prosecutorial misconduct (i.e., Brady violations), ineffective assistance of counsel, proof of actual innocence or any other mitigating evidence that could reduce the sentence. Congress adopted section 2255 to supersede the current habeas corpus post-conviction remedy. It was enacted mainly for procedural reasons, to divert federal prisoner's petitions into the district where the prisoner was originally sentenced, instead of the district of their confinement. Prior to enactment, habeas corpus proceedings occurred in the district of the confinement, resulting in areas with federal prisons to handle an excessive number of habeas cases. Furthermore, if the motion was granted it caused witnesses and experts to have to travel to the federal prison location instead of where the original trial took place. Now motion 2255 spreads collateral proceedings evenly over the federal court system (Bergmann, 2010). Interestingly enough, even though motion 2255 did provide protections that paralleled the habeas corpus writ, the Supreme Court stated that it was in fact distinct. Motion 2255 does not take on the full identity of habeas, meaning that a convicted person, should the motion fail, will still have habeas protection. The motion needs to be filed within a year after a person's conviction has become final. Figure 7.1 provides the typical progression of motion 2255.

A person will still have habeas protection if motion 2255 fails from 2241 motion. This is the true habeas corpus, a direct descendant from the Judiciary Act of 1789. If a federal prisoner is eligible for a 2255 motion and loses the motion or fails to file the motion, then 2241 motion for habeas is filed. A benefit to this motion is that technical deadlines for filing do not exist.

Another available motion is 2254. This motion is the statute that

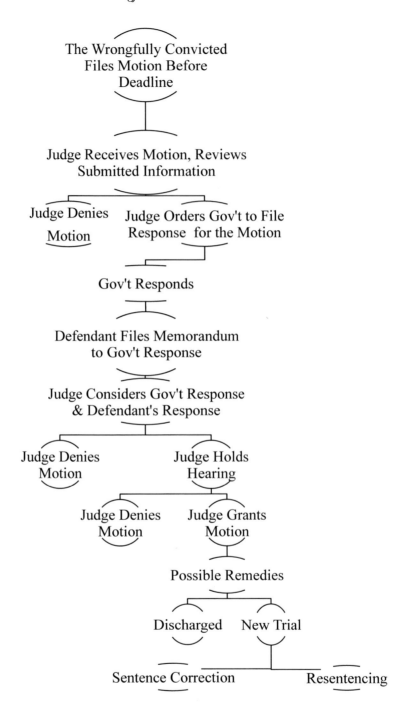

Figure 7.1 Progression of Motion 2255

governs convictions that occurred in a state court but the challenge occurs in a federal court. Unlike 2255 motion, 2254 motion is itself habeas corpus. This motion asks a federal judge to review possible violations of constitutional rights that led to an unjust sentence. This motion tends to have strict demands and time limits.

There are many barriers that a wrongfully convicted person encounters when filing a post-conviction petition or an appeal. One issue concerning relief is how appeals and motions tend to be subjected to strict time limits. An issue that only affects post-conviction litigation is how the Constitution does not guarantee counsel or investigate post-conviction petitions (King, 2013). Furthermore, according to King and Hoffman (2011), of all the post-conviction petitions filed by noncapital prisoners in federal habeas proceeding, roughly half are dismissed without merit review (p. 78).

In addition, the defendant must consider the procedural options available to him or her. The defendant cannot file a direct appeal and a 2255 motion at the same time. If he or she does, the district court will dismiss the 2255 motion. For notice of appeal, this is time sensitive and normally needs to occur 14 days after the verdict is entered.

A problem arises when certain post-conviction issues like ineffective assistance of counsel or evidence of witness tampering is what the defendant believes to be the strongest evidence that his due process rights were compromised. Normally these types of issues are rarely effective in a direct appeal. In most cases if the defendant loses, the issue could not be raised in a 2255 motion. Therefore, the defendant needs to choose whether to skip the direct appeal and pursue the motion 2255 only. It's important to note though, that if there are other issues aside from your strongest issue, these issues must rise to the level of constitutional error, if they do not, they cannot be raised in a 2255 motion. For example, this would include- improperly impaneled juries, prejudicial remarks during statement and arguments, and faulty jury instructions. Additionally, the defendant needs to satisfy the "cause and prejudice" test, which explains why the issues mentioned in the 2255 motion were not raised on direct appeal. This is a difficult test to satisfy.

The most common form of a post-conviction relief is a direct appeal prior to a habeas writ. An innocent person who has been convicted in a criminal trial, as a result of entering a guilty plea or a finding of guilt, may challenge their sentence or conviction. A direct appeal examines the court file, transcripts, and sentence. A direct appeal may result in an order for a new trial, an order vacating the current sentence with a remand for a new sentencing hearing, reversal of a conviction or a sentence correction.

REMEDIES THAT BENEFIT THE WRONGFULLY ACCUSED

There are several traditional judicial remedies available to a convicted person claiming innocence. These motions may or may not aid the wrongfully convicted. Mainly, they fail the wrongfully convicted because judicial review is limited to enforcing rules of procedure (King, 2014). Therefore, new evidence of innocence typically cannot be entered without a viable procedural claim. Below are examples of some of these traditional remedies including motion for a new trial, new scientific methods or discoveries, and witness recantation and perjury.

Motion for a New Trial

When newly discovered evidence is discovered after a conviction, the convicted person can file a motion for a new trial. Evidence can include but is not limited to new scientific methods or discoveries (i.e., DNA, fingerprint, footprint or hair analysis), witness recantations, evidence of another's guilt, undisclosed testimony and evidence correcting an injustice when a defendant's constitutional rights were violated (i.e., *United States v. Fuentes*[4]). One problem is that new evidence appears to surface with investigative assistance (i.e., Innocence Projects, private investigator, etc.) but it is often not found until long after the trial. This can pose a problem for the wrongfully convicted, especially when states have time restrictions, known as the sunset provision, for filing claims of innocence based on new evidence. Furthermore, states are reluctant to enact legislation concerning new scientific methods, making the motion for a new trial difficult to obtain. In addition, judges may be skeptical of a witness recantation or evidence of another's guilt causing motions to be denied. Several of these considerations are discussed below, explaining some of the difficulties that arise when an innocent person prepares to file a motion for a new trial.

---

4. *United States v. Fuentes*, 988F. Supp. 861 (ED Pa. 1997) No. 2:12-CR-50-DBH (D. Me 2013). A judge granted new trial when defense learned of racist comments during trial, referring to the defendants as "guilty wetbacks," two Mexican restaurant owners convicted of harboring undocumented aliens for profit.

New Scientific Methods or Discoveries

Evidence of innocence based on new scientific method or discovery is often rejected because it does not point to an error that occurred during trial, which is needed for a procedural claim. Currently only California and Texas grant motions for a new trial when experts recant or when new scientific advances undermines the previous evidence used in trial (Fox, 2017).

According to Rule 33 of the Federal Rules of Criminal Procedure, a motion for a new trial based on newly discovered evidence must be filed within three years after a guilty finding. This strict time limit poses problems for overturning a wrongful conviction. For example, imagine if a person is wrongfully convicted and a cellphone video or a CCTV recording is found one day past the three-year time restriction, showing someone else committing the crime, the innocent person could not obtain post-conviction relief. It's clear that new science can take decades to emerge. This is based on the 2009 National Academy of Science report. Again, the time limit would bar individuals from obtaining a new trial.

Another problem associated with Rule 33 is that judges, detectives, and even forensic experts can be slow to embrace new scientific methods. A leading arson expert Richard Roby, president and director of Combustion Science and Engineering, has testified in several arson cases. In the case of Michael Ledford of Virginia, whom Roby firmly believes could not have been present at the scene of the fire that killed his son. Roby states that "It's amazing to think how long it takes for basic science to be accepted . . . I lose sleep over this every week" (Rigby, 2013). Ledford is serving a 50-year sentence. Junk science may still prevail causing difficulties for relief to be granted.

Witness Recantations and Perjury

Prior to the 1900s a wrongfully convicted individual did not have any judicial remedies for cases of perjury, such as witness recantation that surfaced post-conviction. Near the beginning of the century perjury was common and affected half of all criminal cases (Repka, 1986). There have even been cases where defendants have been convicted of murdering individuals who have later been found alive. As seen in the first possible wrongful conviction in the United States was the 1812 case of the Boorn brothers from Manchester, Vermont. The two brothers were accused of murdering their brother-in- law, Russell Colvin who was later found to be alive. The National Registry of Exonerations (NRE) further provides shocking evidence of cases that never actually occurred. Currently there have been 478 cases where the NRE found no crimes occurred.[5-6] Recently, a woman from Maine filed a false report of a sexual assault that she claimed occurred in the broad daylight in Portland. This caused panic among the community. Other high-profile cases over the last few years have included an alleged gang-rape of a woman at the University of Virginia, and the case of Katherine Clifton who made false allegations concerning stalking and a rape by her college professor. Although these recent cases of false reporting have not led to the wrongful conviction of an individual, they illustrated the importance of judicial remedies, on the chance that false testimony is used to convict an innocent individual.

Originally, the court appeared to lack the power to grant relief for perjured testimony. For example, there are several technical writs including coram nobis and even the writ of habeas corpus, which have provided little assistance for frustrated defendants seeking remedies for perjured testimony. The writ coram nobis, aims to correct errors of fact that would have resulted in a different judgement, had they been known prior to the conviction. However, most courts rejected the writ when applying it to an offender's recantation (Repka, 1986). The writ of habeas corpus, on the other hand, is issued only if the state officials "knowingly" allowed for the use of the perjured testimony (Repka, 1986). A uniform rule has become widely accepted, allowing for a new trial as a result of recanted testimony (Repka, 1986). Initially, two uniformed tests were used to evaluate newly discovered evidence to assess a motion for a new trial, the Berry Test and the Seventh Circuit *case- Larrison v. United States* to determine if a new trial shall be granted. The Berry test grants a new trial if:

---

5. As of October 9, 2015, for more information see: National Registry of Exonerations. Retrieved from http://www.law.umich.edu/special/exoneration/Pages/detaillist.aspx? View={FAF6EDDB-5A68-4F8F-8A52-2C61F5BF9EA7}&FilterField1=Group&FilterValue1=NC.

6. *A no crime is defined as a case where the exoneree was convicted of a crime that did not result, possible because of fabrication, an accident, or when a suicide was mistaken for a murder.* For more information see the National Registry of Exonerations. Retrieved from http://www.law.umich.edu/special/exoneration/Pages/about.aspx.

1. Evidence has to come to knowledge since the trial;
2. the evidence could not have been discovered before trial by the exercise of due diligence;
3. the evidence is material and would probably result in a different verdict;
4. that evidence is not cumulative only;
5. the affidavit of the witness himself should be produced; and
6. the evidence is not impeaching (*Berry v. State* 10 GA, 511 (1851)).

Courts have continued to apply the Berry test today (Brennan, 2008). Since 1851, the only change in the Berry test is the requirement that the evidence will likely change the result and the dropping of the fifth requirement – "*that the affidavit of the witness himself should be produced.*" Courts additionally vary in using a five-pronged test or a four-pronged test, combining the "material" and "cumulative" requirement into one prong:

1. The evidence is discovered subsequent to the trial;
2. the evidence could not have been discovered before trial by the exercise of due diligence;
3. the evidence is material;
4. the evidence will probably change the results if a new trial is granted; and
5. the evidence is not merely cumulative or impeaching (*Berry v. State* 10 GA, 511 (1851) as cited in Repka, 1986, p. 1439).

Overall the elements afforded by the Berry test are almost uniformly applied by the circuits (Brennan, 2008).

The Larrison test provides three requirements that must be met for a new trial to be granted:

1. The court is reasonably well satisfied that the testimony given by a material witness is false;
2. the jury might have reached a different conclusion with such testimony; and
3. the party seeking the new trial was taken by surprise when the false testimony was given and was unable to meet it or did not know of its falsity until after trial (*Larrison v. United States* 24 F.2d 82 (7th Cir. 1928), as cited in Repka, 1986 p. 1439).

The Larrison test was developed with witness recantations in mind, whereas, the Berry test was not (Armbrust, 2008). The verb usage also differs between the tests. For example, the words used to prove that the new evidence either *might* (Larrison test) or *probably* (Berry test) result in a different verdict. In practice, as Armbrust (2008) notes, it makes little difference which test is used on the outcome of the case.

Perjured testimonies,' resulting in a recantation, is routinely denied because the courts find recantations to be highly unlikely (Armbrust, 2008, p. 82). For example, California only had two motions for new trials granted of the basis of a recantation prior to 1966 (Repka, 1986). Even years later, with the first DNA exoneration of Gary Dotsun in 1989, a victim's recantation and the wrongly convicted defendant's persistent claim of innocence were not enough to order a new trial. Without the presence of DNA, there is a possibility that Dotson may have never been exonerated. More recently, in the state of Virginia, the *Daily Press* reports that according to experts a recantation is not sufficient to grant a new trial (Speed, 2014). A recanting witness might be the innocent defendant's only way to prove their innocence. The infrequent motion for new trials based on recanting or perjured testimony will result in a further injustice for those whom have been wrongfully convicted.

SUNSET PROVISIONS AND POST-CONVICTION DNA TESTING

Sunset provisions limit or establish absolute deadlines for submission of post-conviction DNA evidence. While all 50 states have post-conviction DNA testing statutes; there is variation in eligibility to apply, standards for granting an application, and the limitations on the ability of testing. For example, some states place the burden on the wrongfully convicted person to prove that the DNA will implicate the true perpetrator. Juveniles are included in all but five states (Tepfer & Nirider, 2012). Other states have laws that do not permit access to DNA when the convicted person either confessed or pled guilty to the crime. According to the Innocence Project, 27 percent of the first 325 DNA exonerations involved individuals who have falsely confessed to a crime.[7] Some states restrict post-conviction testing for certain offenses

---

7. For more information see: Innocence Project. (n.d.k). The causes of wrongful conviction. New York: Innocence Project. Retrieved from http://www.innocenceproject.org/causes-wrongful-conviction.

(National Conference of State Legislatures, 2013) or exclude those that did not request testing during trial (District Attorney's Office for the *Third Judicial District v. Osborne*, 2009). In several states, an appeal option is not provided when testing is denied (Gabel & Wilkinson, 2008). These varying statutes can significantly hinder claims of innocence.

In 2004, the Justice for All Act (JFAA) extended the statute of limitation for crimes where the suspect was identified by DNA evidence. The Act provides post-conviction relief by mandating that biological evidence be preserved. However, universal standards have not been established, leaving states to determine if a motion for a new trial will be granted based upon post-conviction DNA relief.

According to the National Conference of State Legislatures (2013), application for post-conviction DNA laws are based on the seriousness of the offense or the length of the prison sentence. In 20 states, anyone convicted can apply for testing, whereas in 17 states only felony convictions can apply. The standards for approving testing are also governed by state laws. These laws provide guidance for judicial officials. Just under half the states (24) require that there is "reasonable probability" that the applicant is, in fact, innocent. Other states such as New Hampshire and Virginia require that there be "clear and convincing" evidence of innocence. Several states, Colorado, Massachusetts, New Mexico, South Carolina, and Texas require "preponderance of the evidence" that the convicted person is innocent.

Other states prohibit an appeal when the applicant was previously denied a petition for testing. Once DNA testing is granted, a number of states fail to require prompt proceedings (Innocence Project, 2015a). One example is the case of Joseph Sledge, who was released, based on a witness's recantation and newly discovered DNA evidence after multiple failed attempts for a new trial. In 1978, Joseph Sledge was wrongfully convicted of the murder and sexual assault of Josephine Davis and her daughter Aileen Davis. Sledge had escaped from White Lake Prison Camp where he was serving time for a larceny conviction that occurred four years prior. His escape occurred a day before the murders, from a prison camp close to the crime scene. Based upon his escape, two jailhouse informants, and DNA evidence, Sledge was convicted. Sledge maintained his innocence and filed several post-conviction motions, all were denied without a hearing until 2003 when his request for DNA testing was finally granted. However, the testing did not begin until five years later (Sneha, 2015). Joseph Sledge was finally released in January of 2015, after serving 37 years in prison.

Although states have begun to remove time restriction and qualification for post-conviction review, the standards for relief can still be challenging. King (2014) explains that in order for a new trial to be granted, the newly discovered evidence must be convincing enough for a judge to believe that a retrial would end in an acquittal. Skepticism may exist about the newly acquired evidence, especially if the judge believes that the defendant received proper representation of counsel and was recently convicted (p. 2). The proof needed to prove innocence can be difficult to obtain, given the procedural restrictions, judicial skepticism, and differing standards for post-conviction.

IMPORTANCE OF DNA FOR
POST-CONVICTION REVIEW

Post-conviction DNA testing dilemmas highlight the appellate system's limits in sorting the innocent from the guilty. The National Registry of Exonerations and various Innocence Projects, document hundreds of cases where post-conviction DNA testing proved that an innocent person was wrongfully convicted. Law professor Brandon Garrett (2008) examined the appellate histories of the first 200 post-conviction DNA exoneration cases, including cases of rape, murder and rape-murder. Of the 200 cases, 133 of the cases produced a written appellate opinion, but only 14 percent won a reversal from their appeal. Thus, 86 percent of the courts failed to recognize the defendant's innocence and grant relief. Garrett examined a matched comparison group that shared the same characteristics as the 200 proven innocent cases. The match comparison showed that the two groups had the same reversal rate of 14 percent. Appeals appear to be a limited option for the innocent.

Garretts' analysis also examined the common contributing factors (i.e. eyewitness misidentification, flawed forensic science, false confessions, and jailhouse snitch/informant testimony) and how the courts repeatedly failed to recognize flawed evidence that resulted in a wrongful conviction. In 79 percent of Garrett's cases where eyewitnesses offered mistaken identification, none of these cases were reversed based on a direct challenge either to the reliability or admissibility of the eyewitness evidence. Flawed forensic science was found in 57 percent of the first 200 DNA exoneration cases, and of these, only 32 percent were challenged. Nineteen of the twenty-five forensic based claims were also rejected by the courts. As for false confession, another common contributing factor, of the 200 DNA exonerations, 16 percent had falsely confessed. However, none of the innocent individuals was granted relief or was able to have the confession suppressed. Again similar findings were found with jailhouse snitch or perjured testimony cases. None of the challenges were successful.

INNOCENCE COMMISSIONS

In 2006, North Carolina Innocence Inquiry Commission (the NCIC) was created to serve as an independent commission with the capacity to provide relief for the wrongfully convicted.[8] Modeled after the British Criminal Case Review Commissions, the NCIC investigates claims of actual innocence. Its members consist of a three-judge panel; however, they are separate from the judicial branch (King, 2014). In order to vacate the conviction, the petitioner has to prove his or her claim of innocence "by clear and convincing evidence."

Innocence commissions have several advantages over the court-based appellate procedures. Innocence claims are brought to the court without procedural barriers, such as time restrictions, or the need to claim a legal, constitutional or procedural error at trial. Defendants who have pled guilty at trial can also seek relief (Wolitz, 2010).

Traditional post-conviction review procedures are not able to directly address claims of innocence. The adversarial nature of the justice system provides that the judge serves as a referee, only interfering when breaches of the rules occur between the prosecutor and defense. The outcome–winning–depends on the skills of the prosecutor and the defense team. Based on this model, defendants can only challenge whether or not the trial was administered fairly. If the procedural rules were followed by both sides, then the outcome was considered to be fair, even though an innocent person was convicted (Woltiz, 2010). Instead, innocence commissions focus on whether a wrong outcome did in fact result independent of the procedural fairness.

---

8. For more information see: North Carolina Innocence Inquiry Commission. (2016). *NC Innocence Inquiry Commission case statistics.* Retrieved from http://www.innocencecommission-nc.gov/about.html.

CURRENT REFORMS AND PRACTICES

In general, DNA statutes first adopted in New York in 1994 have had a significant impact on establishing the actual innocence of the wrongfully convicted. However, states do vary in granting DNA testing. And, more states have expanded post-conviction relief based on new evidence establishing innocence (Norris, Bonventre, Redlich, & Acker, 2011). Nonetheless, state statutes may bar certain defendants and require varying standards for the burden of proof for a claim of innocence. The standards include, "a showing of probable innocence, clear and convincing evidence of innocence, "affirmative" proof, or evidence that "unquestionably" establishes innocence" (King, 2014, p. 12). Other states, notably Virginia use a special innocence remedies or a "writ of actual innocence" to assist exoneration based on non-DNA evidence. A similar practice is used in Utah, Maryland and Washington D.C. (King, 2014).

Wisconsin provides a mechanism for a convicted defendant to file a post-conviction motion in the circuit court before taking the case to the court of appeals (WIS. STAT. § 809.30(2)(h) (2013-2014)). After final judgement and sentencing, the defendant files a Notice of Intent to Pursue Post-Conviction Relief. This is different from several other states that require the defendant to file a notice of appeal within a specified time frame. In Wisconsin, this motion provides a defendant with a copy of the trial transcript and assignment of new post-conviction and appellate counsel. The counsel has 60 days after the transcripts are filed to determine issues with arguable merit either for appellate review or for post-conviction review. If issues are identified in the trial court record, then the counsel would file a notice of appeal. If other post-conviction issues are found that would be deemed meritless on appeal, the counsel can file a post-conviction motion in the circuit court. If the circuit court denies the post-conviction relief, the defendant can then still file a notice of appeal. Wisconsin provides a means for introducing new evidence into the direct appeal process that is not found in other states.

There are several states that have formed a commission to study the problem of post-conviction review. These states include: California, Connecticut, Florida, Illinois, Louisiana, New York, North Carolina, Oklahoma, Pennsylvania, Texas, Virginia, and Wisconsin. These commissions have resulted in changes with law-enforcements procedures and various legislative reforms (Innocence Project, 2007b; Ostendorff, 2011; Wolitz, 2010). As the problem of innocence in our justice system continues to gain attention, hopefully other states will begin to examine the problem and implement various reforms to prevent injustices.

CONCLUSION

Several obstacles confront the wrongfully convicted when they seek an exoneration. Our appellate system is designed to provide a safety net for convicted innocents. However, there are several considerations that weaken its ability to reverse a wrongful conviction. Adherence to a crime control model at the expense of ensuring the due process rights of the accused diminishes the justice system's ability to filter out innocent defendants. In addition, the influence of the structure of the legal case – *who does what to whom* – on its legal outcome further undermines the credibility of the justice system.

The appellate system itself is limited to the review of trial procedures, rather than claims of innocence. Available judicial remedies tend not to directly benefit the wrongfully convicted. However, organizations outside the justice system – Innocence Projects and Commissions–are significantly advancing efforts for criminal justice reform and providing advocacy for the wrongfully convicted. As these organizations continue to be developed and as more states reevaluate their post-conviction remedies and appellate reviews, options will widen for the exoneration of the convicted innocents.

Chapter 8

COMPENSATION AND THE
REENTRY PROCESS

> We hold these Truths to be self-evident, that all Men are created equal,
> that they are endowed by their Creator with certain unalienable Rights,
> that among these are Life, Liberty, and the Pursuit of Happiness.
>
> – The Declaration of Independence

THE CASE OF DREW WHITLEY

In 1989, Drew Whitley of Pennsylvania was convicted of murder. He spent 18 years in prison before DNA evidence exonerated him in 2006. Whitley lives in one of the few states that does not grant compensation or offer reentry assistance following a wrongful conviction. His only option to receive a financial award was to file a federal complaint, arguing that the city of Philadelphia owed him because of police and prosecutorial misconduct. Although the judge believed the police officers were negligent in their investigation, their behavior did not constitute intentional misconduct. Whitley lost all hope for compensation. He survives on his $700 a month social security check and by cleaning local meat shops in exchange for food. His apartment cost roughly half of his social security check. Aside from his financial struggles, he explains that, "Every time somebody walks up the hallway steps, I look out the peephole, because I think they might be coming to get me . . . [and]I wake up with nightmares that I'm still locked up" (De Melker, 2014).

THE NEED FOR ACTION

A wrongful conviction violates our unalienable rights, provided by the constitution. These convictions do not discriminate on the basis of gender or color. Men, women, and even children of all races have been unjustly deprived of their freedoms. Our justice system, then has a responsibility to compensate the wrongful convicted and assist in their reentry into society.

Since June 23, 2017, The National Registry of Exonerations (NRE) has documented 2,049 wrongful convictions. On average, it took over ten years before these individuals were exonerated. For The Innocence Project exonerees, the average is higher, about 14 years before innocence is proven through post-conviction DNA testing (n.d.a).

A wrongful conviction causes the person to be separated from family and friends, missing functions. These include celebrations or even a funeral. Either way, they are barred from taking part in life's joys and sorrows. Dependent upon age, a wrongful conviction can prevent a person from pursuing an education or, in most circumstances, from establishing oneself professionally. The simple enjoyment of participating in the ever-changing society is withheld from these individuals.

Even after release, the innocent person can face several hardships, compounded by the lack of proper assistance for reentry. As the Innocent Project argues, when a state fails to compensate the wrongfully convicted persons, this "adds insult to injury" (n.d.c). Compensation has a duel benefit, which acknowledges the wrongs of the conviction and helps ease the process of reentering society. Reentry services can address the impact of the wrongful incarceration and can provide tools that are needed to become productive members in a community.

AVENUES FOR RELIEF

There are several avenues for relief afforded to the wrongfully convicted. One option is to present a private bill to the state legislature asking for an exception. The next option is to file a civil rights lawsuit under U.S.C. § 1983, alleging official misconduct, which resulted in a constitutional civil rights violation. A final option is to obtain compensation from a common law tort suits or relief (Trivelli, 2016, p. 258). A private bill requires the innocent person to lobby for compensation from their state legislature. The private bill seeks money from the state treasury to remedy the miscarriage of justice. Even if the bill passes, the financial amount varies (Mostaghel, 2011). According to Norris (2012) only 9 percent of exonerees from the Innocence Project have received compensation though private bills (p. 353). The second avenue, a civil rights lawsuit, offers the wrongly convicted person a chance to sue the justice actors responsible for their wrongful conviction. The justice actors are normally immune from a civil suit unless a claim is made concerning a constitutional rights violation. For example, these claims include but not limited to: coerced confessions, fabrication of evidence, false arrest and imprisonment, ineffective assistance of counsel, malicious prosecutor, retaliatory prosecution, suggestive eyewitness identification procedures, improper forensics, phony expert testimony, and suppression of exculpatory evidence. Each of these potential claims poses a particular legal difficulty because of the high burden of proof needed to prove the justice actor erred. As a result these cases can be difficult to win (Bernhard, 2009).

Prior to filing a civil suit several requirements need to be satisfied, which continues to delay the compensation process. Often civil rights lawsuits or private bill options require a long legal and/or political battle. Even when claims are successful, compensation may not be provided until years later (Avery, 2009; Slifer, 2014). A common law tort is another avenue available to the wrongfully convicted. While these suits can be brought in both a state and federal court they are difficult to win (Mostaghel, 2011).

A tort is a civil wrong committed against an individual. The level of proof needed to prevail is preponderance of evidence. Put simply, a tort intends to restore the victim to his or her previous state prior to the wrongful act. This can be achieved through compensation damages. These damages include, but are not limited to: lost wages, loss of financial support, medical expenses, property damage, loss of consortium and other noneconomic damages such as pain, suffering, and emotional distress (Trivelli, 2016). Both noneconomic and economic losses are factored into the compensation and can be tangible and/or intangible. Tangible losses typically include loss of property. Intangible losses refer to deterioration of the "quality of life,", loss of reputation and any quantifiable amount that highlights aid and affection from relationships. Some damages relevant to the wrongfully convicted include: education denial, emotional distress, grief, humiliation, loss of earning and earning potential, physical and mental medical expenses and treatment, aggravation of symptoms of both mental and physical conditions that the wrongfully convicted person had prior to his or her incarceration, loss of investments, loss of business, loss of parental rights, and the loss of enjoyment of life (Trivelli, 2016). This list is not exhaustive and there are many other possibilities an innocent person could pursue.

Currently, the District of Columbia, 32 states and the federal government have direct compensation statutes. Even then, scholars argue that the compensation awards granted by the statutes are mediocre and are not consistently provided. These statutes should include more of a comprehensive and holistic approach, aside from compensation (Innocence Project, n.d.c; Trivelli, 2016, p. 258). The ideal comprehensive and holistic approach would include monetary assistance as well as noneconomic assistance, such as counseling, career services, physical or mental healthcare, educational opportunities, and other available resources to help with reentry or any other personal challenges that the innocent person is encountering.

HEALTH IMPACT OF A WRONGFUL CONVICTION

There are many health risks associated with a lengthy incarceration. These health risks are not limited to those, whom are *rightfully* convicted. The wrongfully convicted encounter the same, if not worse, conditions that other prisoners face such as, physical violence and mental health issues. Ground's (2004) found that some wrongfully convicted individuals suffered from physical assaults. The threat or fear of victimization can cause sleep deprivation and may have long-lasting effects once released. For example, Vincent Moto in 1987 was convicted of rape and spent 8.5 years in prison. Eleven years after his release, he still suffered from nightmares and cold sweats, causing him not to sleep at night (Aguirre et al., 2007). Depending upon the severity of the victimization, the exoneree may be physically limited or may need additional medical care. The likelihood of physical violence can cause nonviolent individuals to become violent or find outlets such as gang membership for protective purposes (Campbell & Denvo, 2004; Clarke & McCormack, forthcoming). These learned violent tendencies can become normalized and may continue following release from prison.

Aside from physical violence, which can affect a person's health, there are other health concerns for a wrongfully convicted person during their incarceration. These health problems include contracting hepatitis C (HCV), AIDS (HIV), tuberculosis (TB), and Methicillin Resistant Staphylococcus Aureus (MRSA), or other infectious and deadly diseases that are found in prisons (Dannenberg, 2007). Take for example Roy Brown, of Syracuse, N.Y., wrongfully convicted of murder in 1992, and served 15 years in prison. While in prison during his fifth year, he contracted hepatitis C. Thankfully, he received a liver transplant but only after he had made his funeral arrangements and began to say goodbye to loved ones (Aguirre et al., 2007). In another case, Kirk Odom at the age of 18 was convicted of raping and robbing a woman in 1981. He was a victim of multiple rapes in prison where he contracted HIV. In total, he spent 31 years in prison and on parole (Hsu, 2015). These infectious diseases pose a threat to all inmates, including the innocent. Other common aliments of prisoners include skin rashes, asthma, premature aging, malnutrition, muscular atrophy, heart-related problems and high blood pressure (Innocence Project, 2009; Maruschak, Berzofsky, & Unangst, 2015; Norris, 2012).

Psychological Concerns

A wrongful incarceration can have long-lasting psychological effects that can complicate reentry (Grounds, 2004; Innocence Project, 2009; Konvisser, 2012; Scott, 2010). Darryl Hunt, after serving over 18 years in prison for a murder he did not commit noted: "I'm physically free, but psychologically I'm still confined" (Aguirre et al., 2007). What Hunt is describing is known as institutionalization, an adaptive process that inmates follow in order to handle the prison environment (Innocence Project, 2009). Institutionalization can lead to a personality change, where the person must learn how to adapt to the rigid institutional routine and learn to survive the hostile prison environment. Once released, these adaptive personality tendencies become difficult to discard. John Kogut, convicted in 1986 of a rape and murder, explains that his 17 years spent in prison led him be wary of people even after his release. Kogut while incarcerated kept to himself. This is how he felt safer, rather than joining a gang or focusing on religion, like his fellow inmates. His reclusive personality often caused him to think that people are lying to him. Learning to trust is difficult for him (Aguirre et al., 2007).

Post-traumatic stress disorder (PTSD) is another consequence of the wrongfully convicted person's incarceration. Ground's (2004) study of 18 wrongfully convicted men found that although PTSD is common among war veterans, the wrongfully convicted who are victimized, or who witness victimization can also suffer from PTSD. These memories after are re-traumatizing. Exoneree William Greggory explains he struggles with post-traumatic stress disorder as a result of serving time for a crime he did not commit. He explains at times he breaks down or gets paranoid (Aguirre et al., 2007). Post-traumatic stress disorder can cause difficulty with sustaining relationships and with maintaining employment. Both are important for successful reentry to everyday life. When PTSD is left untreated, the exoneree may be less employable. Without insurance the cost to seek help can be daunting. Counseling and a state health plan should be offered without charge.

According to the Innocence Project (2009) "A 50-year-old prisoner has been found to have the health of a 60-year-old in the free world" (p. 8). The substandard healthcare provided in prison result in untreated health problems. These nonmonetary services are small consolation for a wrongful conviction.

Although most research has focused on men, the health impact and the struggles of reentry apply to female exonerees as well. Konvisser (2012) examined the unique issues women face when entering the free world. Females also, have to learn how to cope with their imprisonment and being away from their family, but there is a key difference. Most exonerations for females are not a result of DNA evidence. Therefore, women exonerees must show that they are in fact innocent. According to the National Registry of Exonerations (NRE) there have been 196 females that have been exonerated.[1] Of these, DNA evidence was used to exonerate only 11 of the women (6%). Of the 196 female's exonerees, 133 (68%) were convicted of crimes that never occurred. Meaning that DNA evidence, the strongest evidence used to assist with exoneration and to help expunge one's record, would never be available. As a consequence, women exonerees may experience considerable difficulty when seeking compensation. There are also unique medical and emotional needs that must be addressed for women to successfully reenter society (Konvisser, 2012). The longer the length of incarceration, the greater the psychological impairment and deterioration of health.

---

1. As of June 27, 2017, for more information see: National Registry of Exonerations. Retrieved from https://www.law.umich.edu/special/exoneration/Pages/about.aspx.

Most prisoners are typically released with the same psychological issues they had when first incarcerated. Due to prison budget cuts few prisoners receive psychological assistance while incarcerated (Clarke & McCormack, Forthcoming). Other long-lasting consequences of wrongful convictions include coping with the stigma and the refusal of victims, family and community members to believe in one's innocence.

Fear of Being Rearrested

The fear of being rearrested can become intensified after release as seen in the case of Scott Hornoff, a detective in Rhode Island, whom was convicted of first degree murder of an old girlfriend. After serving six years, he wants to live every day because he's afraid of being arrested again. The mere presence of a police officer creates anxiety and each time he hears a door slam, he's afraid that the police are coming to get him (Carollo, 2004). This fear obviously affects readjusting into society.

COPING AND ITS CONSEQUENCES

The wrongfully convicted handle their injustices differently while incarcerated and after their release. Campbell and Denov (2004) found there are many different types of coping strategies used in prison. One strategy that may have negative consequences while incarcerated is becoming so preoccupied with their exoneration that they reject the label of being a criminal. When they maintain their innocence and reject the label of being a criminal, this can be perceived by correctional workers, including parole board members that the inmate lacks remorse. The lack of remorse may undermine eligibility for early parole given their perceived higher risk for recidivism. Even when they become eligible, often there is little post-release statutory support or any general preparation for their release.

The case of Ronald Keine highlights possible consequences of an unanticipated release:

> One day, the guards arrived at our cell and announced we had a court date that day. The winter wind blew right through the orange jumpsuit I wore. Underwear would have at least helped a little, but the guard on death row guffawed at the idea of letting us wear any. Underwear was

not allowed because authorities believed we could rip the cloth into strips to make a rope to hang ourselves . . . To us, this was just another court hearing to reject our latest plea to let us show our innocence— there had been many. It was no more to us than a chance to get out of the death row drudgery for a day, to actually experience what most people take for granted- fresh air, trees, landscapes, and new people to talk to . . . it was a total shock, then, when the judge freed us at the hearing that day. We were totally unprepared for it. I can remember standing on those courthouse steps contemplating my next move. I first had to take stock of my situation. I was a twenty-nine-year-old and had nothing. Every asset I owned was sold to raise money for a lawyer who abandoned us after our arraignment, forcing the court to furnish us with a young, inexperienced lawyer. The rumor that the prison would give us clothes and bus fare home was not a reality for we, exonerated men. That was only for paroles and guilty offenders who had maxed out. When someone is exonerated, they are no longer the ward of the court. The penal system has nothing more to do with them. They are done with you. (As cited in Westervelt & Cook, 2013, p. 265)

Even when denied the same reentry services, the wrongfully convicted differs from ordinary long-term prisoners in two ways (Campbell & Denov, 2014). First, some of the wrongfully convicted have an intolerance for injustice. The wrongful conviction has caused a mistrust of authority figures. This intolerance or anger may not occur right after release but is gradually evident, as seen with Walter Smith, who was wrongfully convicted of rape. Smith explains that it took three years after his release to become "mad." He's mad for not only being imprisoned for 10 years but because he realizes how important those 10 years were for building his life. Wrongfully convicted persons also want criminal justice agencies and specific individual within them to acknowledge their errors. Symbolically this acknowledgement can be achieved through compensation. Anger, intolerance, and need for government recognition of its laws can hinder successfully reentry.

The Disadvantages of Being Innocent

There are many services that are available to parolees, including job placement, temporary housing, transportation passes, healthcare, and drug treatment (Innocence Project, 2009; Wilson, 2007). These services are often not available to the innocent because they have not committed a crime and are no longer under the state's control. A parolee and exoneree face the same obstacles and hardship with reentering society; however, the parolee committed an actual crime and is supported by the state, in their reentry into society, the exoneree is not.

HOUSING AND EMPLOYMENT

Housing and employment are two of the more daunting tasks the wrongfully convicted encounter when reentering in society. There are federal housing regulations that can limit the ability of housing agencies to permit convicted individuals to live on their properties (Clarke & McCormack, Forthcoming). The federal government additionally provides incentives to housing agencies to adopt screening polices that deny admission to previous criminals who have ". . . a recent history of criminal activity involving crime to persons or property" (U.S.HUD, 2005). This incentive enhances the public housings agencies ratings and ensures compliance with the federal housing regulations. As a result, the wrongfully convicted may be screened out during the application process, without having a chance to explain their situation.

Currently, 48 states have policies allowing individualized determination of an applicant's housing eligibility. Two states and the District of Columbia deny an application for public housing because of a criminal record. From 2004 to 2009, the number of states making decisions about housing eligibility because of an arrest record, for even the wrongfully arrested, rose from 27 to 30 (Legal Action Center, 2004:2009). Despite this, more than 30 states allow individuals to deny a person who had been arrested, even if the arrest did not lead to a conviction (Legal Action Center, 2009). Even if individuals deny an arrest on a job or housing application, there may be a public record, unless it was expunged or sealed. Expungement of a record is essential but depending on the state, if the record is expunged, this does not necessarily mean that the arrest record will be altered. An expungement rectifies the trial outcome but may not remedy the means by which the offender was arrested. The innocent individual may have to expunge both, arrest and criminal conviction. This process can be time consuming and costly.

Housing authorities use criminal record databases to review an applicant; however, an expungement may have never been received or updated in the database, causing the applicant to be ineligible.

Another setback for the wrongfully convicted is their lack of credit history. This is used to determine eligibility for a mortgage and may be needed for an apartment. When housing is unavailable the wrongfully convicted must rely on family and friends, which can be frustrating and embarrassing. For example, Leo Waters spent 21 years in prison for a rape he did not commit. After being released at age 55, he explained how he felt like a teenager again because he needed his father to co-sign an auto loan. Leo Waters had to live with his parents for two years before he could afford to live on his own. He laments: "I wanted to be my own man instead of being looked after by my parents and relying on other people to take care of me. That was the hardest part" (Aguirre et al., 2007).

Finding employment can be equally if not more difficult for the wrongfully convicted (Westervelt & Cook, 2010). Each day being innocently incarcerated prevents the person from being able to establish themselves professionally. Although there are some prisons that allow prisoners to work, this is not always an option. Again in some states, innocent individuals, who are not yet convicted, can be eliminated from the job pool. Many times, the only identification card the exoneree has is their prison ID card. A driver's license can be difficult to obtain right after release (Innocence Project, 2009). The lack of experience or an employment gap on a resumes further hinders the innocent from finding employment. Kevin Green, who spent 16 years in prison for a murder he did not commit, explains that when he would apply for a job he would provide a copy of the newspaper highlighting his innocence (Aguirre et al., 2007). Without employment, the wrongfully convicted are penniless and dependent on others. Furthermore, housing becomes unlikely; without family or friends, homelessness becomes a daunting fear.

IMPORTANCE OF AN EXPUNGEMENT

A way to help with housing and employment is to expunge a record, both arrest and conviction. Legislation has been proposed that improves the prospects for expunging a criminal record. Between 2004 and 2009, New York and Nebraska allowed for the sealing/expungement of a criminal record. Nebraska also limited criminal records on the Internet (Legal Action, 2009). Despite this progress, nine states[2]

---

2. The nine states include: Alaska, Washington D.C., Hawaii, Maine, Minnesota, Missouri, Pennsylvania, Tennessee, and Vermont.

implemented policies that increase access of criminal records on the Internet. As technologies continue to advance and the courts become digitized, nearly anyone with access to the Internet will be able to search criminal histories without consent. Unexpunged arrest records of the wrongfully convicted are available to three in four households with Internet access (File & Ryan, 2014). Without a mandatory state expungement and/or sealing provision, the wrongfully convicted persons will have a difficult time rebuilding their lives.

Currently an expungement is a separate legal process. Several states and the federal government do not allow for criminal records to be expunged. Even states that do allow for expungement do so under limited circumstances (Shlosberg, Mandery, West, & Callaghan, 2014). A record can be expunged through a pardon or by judicial determination. An attorney will be needed for getting a record expunged. If the individual is unable to find employment, hiring a lawyer may not be an option unless; they receive financial support from family or friends or through compensation statutes. A criminal record can also affect the police's response to the wrongfully convicted, as seen in the case of Douglas Echols, who was wrongfully convicted of rape and served five years in prison. One day, Douglas was stopped for a traffic violation. As a result of his record, he was held by police until it was determined that the charges were dismissed. Shlosberg et al. (2014) finds that exonerees with an unexpunged criminal record committed more post-exoneration offenses (50%) than those who had their record expunged (31.6%). Their findings were consistent with labeling theory. The wrongfully convicted who are unable to get their record expunged maybe be stigmatized, which causes a barrier for reentry, possibly leading to future criminality.

THE IMPACT OF WRONGFUL CONVICTION ON REENTRY

The wrongfully convicted can struggle with rekindling family ties. This inexcusable mistake has led to divorce, termination of parental rights, loss of friends and family support. For years, the wrongfully convicted has been deprived meaningful relationship with loved ones. Fixing this ruptured relationship may be important for successful reentry. This is especially important for persons wrongfully convicted of sexually offending a family member, as seen with the Kern County child abuse cases. Husband and wives were separated from each other and their children. Six Bakersfield parents were wrongfully convicted of child sexual abuse and related charges in the 1980s (McNamara, 2009). Shattered relationships such as these will possibly require counseling to help mend the fractured relationship.

Another struggle that is sometimes overlooked is how some of the wrongfully convicted feel guilty for having their family and friends pay legal fees to help with their exoneration process. Anthony Hick who spent four and half years in prison for a rape he did not commit explains, how one of his biggest disappointments was not being able to pay his father back for spending more than $100,000 on legal fees (Aguirre et al., 2007). Both the exoneree and the family suffer monetarily. Wrongful imprisonment does not only affect the innocent offender but the family as well.

The length of time served can negatively affect an exoneree's reentry. Practical life skills may have to be relearned. This can include, grocery shopping, cooking, using public transportation, personal financial management, use of technology in everyday life, and general time management (Westervelt & Cook, 2013). Getting used to the unregimented lifestyle can also take time. Furthermore, the stigma of incarceration and the type of offense can haunt the innocent. Dan Simon, a professor of law at University of Southern California explains that "Even if people honestly believe that this person was truly innocent, there is a certain stigma that comes with the mere fact that you were in prison" (as cited in Seward, 2012).

SPECIAL POPULATIONS

Juveniles who were wrongfully convicted deserve compensation and reentry services. Juveniles are particularly susceptible to false confessions. A false confession is damaging and most incriminating. Incarcerated youth have unique needs that must be addressed once exonerated. Take for example Jeffrey Deskovic, who was 17 years old when he was convicted of raping and murdering a fellow classmate. He spent 16 years in prison for a crime he did not commit. Deskovic explains that he was overwhelmed emotionally and psychologically. He assumed like others have, that if he gave the officers what they wanted to hear – a confession, they would release him from police custody. He also believed by admitting to the crime he would only serve a short time in a mental hospital. Mr. Deskovic was labeled a sex offender and a murderer. He was placed in a system where sex offenders are not treated compassionately. Once released, he struggled with how the world had evolved without him. He had to learn how to live on his own, figuring out how to pay bills and budget his income. He explains how sorting through junk mail was difficult as was learning how to read body language and social cues (Williams, 2015).

Other consequences of a juvenile wrongful conviction, include missing out on attending prom, graduation, driver's education, college, attending weddings of their friends, obtaining employment, starting a family, buying a house and many more significant activities that emerge in early adulthood. Their release for some may be a delayed beginning, occurring when they are much older. Once released they will have to make up for lost time for example, by learning simple tasks such as cooking, paying bills, buying groceries, learning to live on their own, applying for employment and possibly applying to college. Typically, these events are learned and experienced at various stages, not all at once. The lost time additionally requires them to cope with the milestones they missed.

PROPOSED MODEL LEGISLATION

The Innocence Project has developed a model legislation concerning compensation statutes, which details services that should be granted to the wrongfully convicted. These services should be prompt and follow directly after release. Services include food, transportation, and financial support for necessities, housing assistance, medical and healthcare services, assistance with education and employment and legal services to help expunge criminal records and for regaining custody of children (Innocence Project, n.d.c). The Innocence Project has recommended that the standard of proof for eligibility of services and compensation should be preponderance of the evidence, following tort law. Additionally, those that have been pardoned or when a sentence has been vacated or reversed should also be eligible. Eligibility of the material goods and services mentioned above should be provided for three years. However, physical and mental health care services should be provided throughout one's life.

Concerning compensation, the Innocence Project recommends a minimum of $62,500 per year served, an additional $62,500 granted to offenders on death row, and a minimum of $31,000 per year for those who unjustly served time on parole, probation or those that were mandated to register as a sex offender (as cited in Trivelli, 2016, p. 265). This award should not be capped nor treated as taxable income, which was a common practice until 2015, when President Obama signed the Wrongful Convictions Tax Relief Act. The Act barred states from taxing the monetary award. The law is retroactive; but, the exonerated person has a time restriction for filing (White, 2016).

CURRENT STATE'S COMPENSATION STATUTES

There are 32 states, the District of Columbia and the federal government that have enacted compensation statues, which hold states liable for wrongful convictions. The first compensation statute for wrongful convictions was enacted in 1913 in Wisconsin (Norris, 2012). The federal compensation statute was enacted in 2004, adjusted for inflation, the statute provides $63,000 per year of wrongful incarceration and an additional $63,000 per year spent on death row (Norris, 2012). There are also several states that have bills introduced supporting compensation legislation. Compensation is granted based upon eligibility requirements.[3]

Restriction with Current Statutes

Since states do not enact uniformed legislation governing compensation, there are many discrepancies as to who is eligible and how one becomes eligible. Most compensation statutes do not automatically provide a monetary award. In addition, several states grant a specific time frame for the individual to demonstrate their innocence. Depending on the state, innocence must be proven by the preponderance of evidence, clear and convincing evidence, or a pardon from the governor (Acker & Redlich, 2011). Several of the states prohibit compensation if the individual "contributed" to their wrongful conviction, possibly meaning that they falsely confessed or accepted a plea deal. Due to the high rate of plea bargained convictions and an inordinate

---

3. See the – Current State Compensation and Reentry Statutes Table in the Appendix.

number of false confessions, especially by juveniles and the mentally ill, it is important that contributing factor clauses are eliminated. Another restriction found in some states is the barring of convicted felons from receiving compensation (Innocence Project, n.d.c; Mungan & Klick, 2014; Norris, 2012). These restrictions provide further hardships that can prevent the innocent from successful reentry.

Arbitrariness of Compensation and Reentry Statutes

When discussing the death penalty, Justice Potter Stewart (1972) stated that "These death sentences are cruel and unusual in the same way that being struck by lightning is cruel and unusual." That is, death sentences were being applied arbitrarily and capriciously. There were just as many cases where similar offenses occurred but mainly minorities were being sentenced to death. The statement came after the 5-4 *Furman* decision, which held that the imposition of the death penalty in certain cases constituted cruel and unusual punishment, highlighting how there was improper criteria being selectively applied in death penalty cases. In general, death sentences were being imposed, "unevenly, infrequently, and often selectively against minorities" (Death Penalty Information Center, n.d.). The arbitrariness of the death penalty also applies to the various compensation statues. Studies have shown that race may lead to a wrongful conviction: black defendants are more likely than whites to be wrongfully convicted (Stubbs, 2012). Race might also explain why states provide compensation unevenly: geographical location also affects compensation for a wrongful conviction. Compensation appears to be as random as being "struck by lightning" because uniform statutes do not exist. In the same way that death penalty sentences were being arbitrarily applied so are compensation and reentry assistance.

The various avenues for relief, the limitations of who can make claims and the amount of reparations by state statues can lead to preferential treatment. Monetary compensation and reentry services may be based on individual characteristics, such as a person's race, gender, age, or class. Without set standards, legislators could use their personal opinions for eligibility. This may further add insult to injury. In order to prevent disparities, uniform statutes should provide economic and noneconomic support, consistently and fairly through all states and the federal government.

RECOMMENDATIONS FOR COMPENSATION AND REINTEGRATION SERVICES

A wrongful incarceration may negatively impact the exonerees' health. Services that target and treat post-traumatic stress disorder and personality change need to be provided for the exoneree. Family members should also have access to these services to help them cope with the wrongful conviction and to teach them how to best assist their loved ones with reentry. Health services should be available to determine if the wrongfully convicted contracted a disease. If so, free health-care should be provided to care and treat the illness. Counseling services should also be afforded to the exoneree to help them cope with the violent acts that they may have encountered or witnessed in prison.

There are many wrongfully convicted individuals who are coming out of the prison system with significant legal debt accrued during the appeal process. Even though more states have begun to enact statutes granting compensation, these statutes are not automatically provided to the wrongfully convicted. The individual must show evidence of innocence. Many times this evidence is in the control of the state. Thus, obtaining the evidence and then relinquishing the evidence to the courts with assistance of hired counsel can take years before compensation is granted to the wrongfully convicted. One recommendation proposed by the Innocence Project to alleviate this problem would be to develop a statute that includes immediate provisions for funds and services to assist with successful reentry. This should include the necessities of life: food, medical and dental care, housing, education, psychological counseling, and any other needs to help rebuild their life (Innocence Project, n.d.c). Another area that has been rarely examined, which possibly compensation statues should begin to address is the debt acquired by the exoneree's family members, including taking time off of work to visit their loved ones in prison and hiring investigators or lawyers to help prove innocence. They may never be repaid for the financial hardship.

The Innocence Project recommends a yearly amount for the wrongful incarceration and for time spent on death row, parole, probation or on a sex offender registration list, untaxed, per year (Innocence Project, 2016b). Based on Norris's (2012) and Simms (2016) study and the data in the Appendix,[4] Texas's compensation statute is

---

4. See the table in the appendix. Current State Compensation and Reentry Statutes.

the most advantageous for an innocent individual. The statute affords the wrongful convicted with the highest monetary value and includes other forms of assistance to help with reentry and with establishing oneself. Still, no statute meets all of the Innocence Project's recommendation for what the wrongfully convicted should be provided. Aside from monetary compensation, immediate services should be granted, including: financial support such as food, transportation, and subsistence funds to assist with life's basic necessities. Assistance should be provided for securing affordable housing. The Innocence Project suggests that prioritization should be granted to the wrongfully convicted as a category within each state's Section 8 Housing Voucher Program (2009). Workforce's skills and assistance with employment should be available. Employment can be an important factor for mitigating various psychological issues such as PTSD, depression and anxiety (Konvisser, 2012). Counseling services, medical and dental care should be provided. States should assist with educational degrees and legal services should also be provided to help expunge a criminal record, regain custody of children and to obtain any other public benefits (Innocence Project, n.d.c).

CONCLUSION

Although many wrongfully convicted individuals are ecstatic with their release there is still a long road ahead for these unfortunate exonerees without compensation. Money although beneficial, still may not fully restore an exoneree to a viable life style. There are other problems in which the exoneree faces that need to be addressed, such as physical and mental health aliments, lack of job skills, trust in the justice system, damaged reputation, lack of education, and a lack of social ties. Two ways the justice system, particularly a state, can remedy their wrongdoings are by instituting compensation statutes and by assisting with post-release services. Compensation provides a means to help build a new life. For many a completely new life from what they were used to prior to their wrongful incarceration.

Additionally, compensation and post-release services begin to account for the systemic injustices. If reentry services are provided for the actual convicted criminal, then it should also be provided for the innocent. Readjusting into society is challenging. Holistic statutes restore the public's confidence in the justice system, by acknowledging their wrongs and assists with the person becoming whole again.

Post-release comprehensive services and compensation statutes need to consider their restrictive natures and look at the greater repercussion of a wrongful conviction. Having restrictions that do not provide compensation or assistance because the wrongfully convicted "contributed" to their wrongful conviction by accepting a plea bargain or falsely confessing needs to be reconsidered. There is considerable evidence that juveniles and the mentally ill are the most vulnerable to falsely confessing. Age when incarcerated or illnesses may contribute to an inability to find employment, housing, and even the ability to begin the process of expunging their record. Expungement can be needed for both employment and housing. Additionally, especially for the juvenile population their imprisonment may have occurred during the years when the person was a student or would have attended college. These populations have unique needs and have been deprived of life opportunities, which should be considered in compensation and post-release statutes.

Further, state statutes should consider the marked undervaluation of some exonerees. Uniform and consistent statutes should be enacted. Therefore, all states should either follow the most generous state's compensation and post-release statute or evaluate all of the state's current statutes and determine collectively what would be the most beneficial.

Since Norris's (2012) comprehensive analysis of compensation statutes, five states have implemented statutes (e.g., Colorado (2013), Washington (2013), Minnesota (2014), Hawaii (2016), Michigan (2016)). These new state legislations appear to be similar to Texas's compensation statute (2009) and to the Innocence Project's Model, offering compensation for the incarceration, an additional amount for death row, while on probation, parole or on a registered sex offender list. Furthermore, these statutes offer other assistance such as education assistance, repayment for attorney fees, and repayment for child support. Hopefully, other state statutes will update their current legislation to match that of Texas or of the Innocence Project's proposed model.

Chapter 9

REFORMING INJUSTICE: THE FUTURE OF WRONGFUL CONVICTION

Justice is Truth in Action

– Benjamin Disraeli

THE CASE OF LEDELL LEE

Time was running out. The drugs used to execute the condemned in Arkansas were about to expire. The lethal drugs–midazolan to make the condemned unconscious; vecuronium bromide to prevent breathing; and potassium chloride to arrest the heart–had to be used soon. Arkansas scheduled eight executions to be carried out in the two week period before the expiration date of the lethal drugs. Ledell Lee had been on death row for 24 years; he would be the first to be executed.

Ledell Lee, a 27-year-old mentally challenged black man, was convicted of the 1993 murder and sexual assault of Debra Reese, a 26-year-old white woman in Jacksonville, Arkansas. She was struck 36 times with a tire iron her husband had given her for protection. Ledell Lee was identified as a person near the scene of the crime. He was taken into custody three days later. Soon thereafter, he was charged with the 1989 murder and rape of Christine Lewis, a 22-year-old resident of Jacksonville. The trial resulted in a hung jury, so the prosecutors then focused on Ledell Lee's involvement in the death of Debra Reese.

The evidence to convict him was an eyewitness who identified him as ringing door bells in Debra Reese's neighborhood, and microscopic analysis of a few strands of hair and a drop of blood. Lydell Lee's

192

defense counsel's arguments were so incoherent that he was removed from the trial. An all-white jury deliberated for three hours, found him guilty of first degree murder and sexual assault and sentenced him to death.

His claim of innocence had been repeatedly rejected by the Arkansas appellate courts. In his final days, the American Civil Liberties Union filed a motion to stay the execution on the grounds that he suffered from a mental disability resulting from fetal alcohol syndrome present at the time of his trial and requested that DNA testing be conducted on the blood sample found at the scene of the crime. The motion was denied by Pulaski County Circuit Judge Herbert Wright who argued DNA testing was unnecessary because "there would still be sufficient proof presented by the state at trial for the jury to reach a guilty verdict" (Ferrando & Buckner, 2017). The Innocence Project in New York then joined with the ACLU to file a motion with the Arkansas Supreme Court for a stay of execution to conduct DNA testing. Innocence Project attorney Nina Morrison argued: "The state is rushing to put him to death without giving him the opportunity to do the DNA testing that could prove who actually committed the crime" (Ferrando & Buckner, 2017). The motion was again denied and the execution date was set.

The decision that Lee Ledell was guilty and deserved to die was made soon after his arrest. A heinous crime had been committed: the public expected that "justice" would be served without delay. The prosecutor referred to Lee Ledell as a "super predator": he, then, became eminently convictable. The processing of the case by the police and prosecutors, while following legal procedures, was driven by the presumption of guilt. Skepticism, deliberation, and the possibility of evidentiary error were ruled out. The assumption that procedural fairness constituted justice was defended. Ledell Lee was lethally injected at 11:56 p.m. on April 20, 2017. He was the first person put to death in Arkansas in 12 years[1].

Wrongful convictions emerge as a mirror image of the criminal justice system. Insights are gained into the workings of our justice

---

1. For more information see: Blinder, A. & Fernandez, M. (2017, April 21). Arkansas puts Ledell Lee to death in its first execution since 2005. *New York Times.* Retrieved from https://www.nytimes.com/2017/04/21/us/arkansas-death-penalty-ledell-lee-execution.html. And, Ferrando, E. & Buckner, M. (2017, April 20). 24 years later, Ledell Lee maintained his innocence in death of Debra Reese. *WWM13.* Retrieved from http://www.wzzm13.com/news/local/ledell-lee-24-years-later/433035718.

system that may lead to the conviction of an innocent person. The outcome of the criminal justice process reflects the decision-making of key agents in the system. It is incumbent upon the police, prosecutors and members of the judiciary to alleviate the societal concern for protection against criminal victimization. It is as important for the criminal justice system to ensure the constitutional rights of the accused. There is then a need to create the perception that crime is effectively addressed while justice is being served.

The appearance of control underlies the processing of a criminal case. Criminal behavior, particularly that which engenders fear and outrage in the public, must be quickly, effectively and finally dealt with. The crime control perspective typically drives the processing of a criminal case (Packer, 1968). Misguided intentions often are masked by the commonplace activities of the agents of the criminal justice system. Wrongful convictions then reflect routine flaws in the everyday workings of the criminal justice system. As we have noted earlier, to Lofquist (2001) "wrongful convictions are often the product of the normal, day-to-day routine operations of decision-makers acting free of conspiratorial intent or wrongdoing; the outcome was generated by the structures and routines in which actors act" (p. 192).

Wrongful convictions in the United States have long been recognized (Borchard, 1932). Borchard (1932) documents the leading precipitants of wrongful conviction—eyewitness misidentification, false confessions, police and prosecutorial misconduct, flawed expert witness, and, by implication, and inadequate defense counsel—that are currently considered critical to the conviction of the innocent. An understanding of wrongful convictions as the consequences of flawed decision-making, albeit unintentional, by key agents of the criminal justice is central to system reforms. Attempts to remedy the precipitants of wrongful convictions provide insight into our perception of justice and the risks we take in pursuing it.

Wrongful convictions in the United States and around the world are not aberrations (Huff & Killias, 2010). Since 1992 when DNA testing was introduced in post-conviction proceedings, the Innocence Project in New York has documented the exoneration of 350 factually innocent persons largely convicted of murder or rape. The National Registry of Exonerations has widened the scope of wrongful convictions to include cases for which DNA evidence is not available. As of July 18, 2017, the National Registry of Exonerations reported that 2,066 cases of wrongful convictions were known, the vast majority did not include DNA evidence.[2]

The need for criminal justice reform is indisputable. Effective reforms are premised on a fundamental understanding of the precipitants of wrongful conviction. Leo (2005, 2017) notes that the "causes" of wrongful conviction have largely been identified by legal scholars and journalists; therefore, a consideration of the root cause of wrongful convictions has been overlooked. Acker (2017, p. 15) points out that while criminal justice "mistakes" may be identified as the immediate reason for a wrongful conviction typically initial errors in judgment give rise to a process characterized by the "ratification of error" in a series of faulty decisions, each compounding the adverse effects of those which preceded it (Huff, Rattner, Sagarin, & MacNamara, 1986). The likelihood of a wrongful conviction becomes progressively more likely.

While recognizing that wrongful convictions can be traced to human error, Acker (2017) argues:

> justice systems and the people within them function in complex institutional and social environments and are not immune to their influences. The potential for large-scale structural and contextual factors to influence the perceptions, attitudes and behaviors of actors within criminal justice systems, and help shape the roles that are most immediately responsible for producing wrongful convictions should not be minimized. (p. 15)

Similarly, Doyle (2014) points out that: "No single error can cause an organizational accident independently; the errors of many individuals ('active errors') converge and interact with system weaknesses ('latent conditions'), increasing the likelihood that individual errors will do harm." Doyle argues that analyses of wrongful convictions should broaden their scope to include "sentinel events" not simply the conviction of the innocent. Sentinel events are: "'near misses' acquittals and dismissals of cases that at earlier points seem solid; cold cases that stayed cold too long: 'wrongful releases' of dangerous or factually

2. For more information see: Innocence Project. (n.d.a). *All cases*. New York: Innocence Project. Retrieved from https://www.innocenceproject.org/all-cases/#exonerated-by-dna. And, the National Registry of Exonerations. Retrieved from http://www.law.umich.edu/special/exoneration/Pages/detaillist.aspx?View={FAF6EDDB-5A68-4F8F-8A52-2C61F5BF9EA7}&FilterField1=MWID&FilterValue1=8_MWID.

guilty criminals or vulnerable mentally handicapped arrestees; and failure to prevent domestic violence within at-risk families" (p. 4).

In sum, effective reforms must take into account not only the immediate "cause" of the wrongful conviction, but also the decision-making process that made it possible for the "causes" to occur. Simply put, effective reforms depend on analyses of the systemic context of faulty decision-making that led to the wrongful conviction

The theme of the book incorporates a consideration of the relationship between the root cause and the immediate reasons for the wrongful conviction. That is, systemic flaws in the processing of a criminal case give rise to errors in decision-making that result in a wrongful conviction. The theme then argues for a balance between the need to control criminal activity and the protection of the due process rights of the accused. To strike a balance between two seeming competing value systems (Packer, 1968), reforms must be undertaken on three levels: (1) personal responsibility, (2) systemic, and (3) cultural.

CRIME CONTROL

The overarching focus of the crime control perspective is to efficiently and unquestionably reach a final resolution to a criminal matter. An arrest should be made without delay and evidence gathered to affect the conviction of the accused. The emphasis on expedience gives rise to faulty decision-making initially by the police and subsequently by prosecutors. Dan Simon (2012) argues that just criminal justice outcomes depend on the accuracy of evidence gathering, which is enhanced by the transparency of the activities of the criminal justice agents.

Personal Responsibility

The accuracy of evidence gathering depends on the recognition of the psychological biases inherent in process of decision-making, e.g., confirmation bias, hindsight bias, coherence effect, and so on.[3] The need to have our decisions validated blinds us to common biases experienced in everyday lives. Decisions made by police and prosecutors, however well-intentioned, may have unintended conse-

---

3. For a further discussion, See Chapter 2.

quences. Training should then be made mandatory in police academies, law schools, and criminology and criminal justice academic programs that provide the students with an understanding of the common psychological biases involved in decision-making and ways to guard against them. Training programs should be designed to alert members of the law enforcement community to the dangers of common psychological biases in the process of making decisions. These programs should consider typical situations that require immediate decisions often clouded by a sense of urgency and need for a final resolution to the matter. Techniques for avoiding the pitfalls of psychological biases are an essential part of the training program

The curriculum should focus on an understanding of the crucial stages in the decision- making process where errors are more likely to occur and provide strategies for handling high-risk situations. High-risk situations in the investigatory process include gathering eyewitness/victim testimony, obtaining confessions, and evidentiary decision-making. The framing of the evidence for submission to the prosecutor is often the final distillation of the unobserved biases that shaped the investigation.

Systemic Reforms

Systemic reforms within the law enforcement community focus on policies and procedures that maximize the accuracy of the evidence gathered and the transparency of the investigatory process (Simon, 2012). A series of interconnected and interdependent steps are involved in the initial identification of a suspect, methods of evidence gathering, e.g., interviews with witnesses, unique methods for gaining information from eyewitness, particularly crime victims, the use of photo and physical lineups, and techniques for securing confessions from viable suspects. The expressed intent of the evidence gathering policies and procedures should be to ensure that all the evidence is scrutinized for its accuracy before being presented to a prosecutor. Conflicting testimonial, circumstantial, and physical evidence must be included in the report to prosecutor's office for an evaluation of the merits of the case.

Often law enforcement agencies promote its members on their history of clearing crimes by arresting a suspect. This practice may lead to arresting a suspect based on incomplete, and often inaccurate, evidence simply to make a case for promotion. Policies should be implemented that base promotions on the accuracy of the evidence gathered, and its legal admissibility, rather than on how quickly an arrest is made.[4]

Finally, the transparency of the investigatory process should be encouraged. Transparency should never jeopardize the ability of law enforcement agencies to carry out their work. However, independent oversight of the investigatory process should be done before the evidence is presented to the prosecutor. This oversight may be done by review board within an agency whose members are not involved in the investigation.

DUE PROCESS

Personal Responsibility

The protection of the constitutional rights of persons accused of crime is essential to the just outcome of the case. The myriad of decisions made by prosecutors directly affect the constitutional safeguards provided to defendants. Since these decisions are made outside of public view, prosecutors are free to make decisions that may compromise the defendant's legal rights. Therefore, a renewed focus on adhering to the American Bar Associations Code of Professional Conduct should be part of the training for all members of District Attorney's Offices. Ethical breaches should be grounds for dismissal from service as a prosecutor or related staff member.[5]

Related to the adherence to the American Bar Associations ethical standards is the transparency of the process of prosecutorial decision-making. Procedures should be established that make possible the oversight of prosecutorial decisions from the initial assessment of the evidence, charging the suspect, seeking an indictment, and opting to plea bargain or try the case. An internal review process can be established, similar to one advocated for law enforcement agencies, and carried out by prosecutors not involved in the case. Identifying potential ethical or procedural flaws in the case before a plea is negotiated or the trial has begun may prevent a wrongful conviction.

Similarly, a prosecutor's job security and career advancement

---

4. For a further discussion See Chapter 7.
5. For a further discussion See Chapter 4.

should not be tied to the rate of convictions. Emphasis should be placed on a personal commitment to a just outcome of a case, rather than simply securing a conviction. The ability of the prosecutor to show that the defendant is legally culpable for a crime should be rewarded, rather than engaging in manipulative practices to gain an advantage in the plea bargaining process, or to affect the outcome of the trial.

Systemic Reforms

The establishment of Conviction Integrity Units across the country signals District Attorneys' growing recognition that wrongful convictions are quite possible and that their remedy lies, in part, within the office responsible for the conviction. Since 2003, Conviction Integrity Units have been established in selected District Attorneys' offices to conduct reviews of post-conviction claims of wrongful conviction (Center for Prosecutorial Integrity, 2014). Members of the District Attorneys' office are uniquely positioned to review each decision that led to prosecution of the defendant. A reconstruction of each step in the decision-making process is essential to understand the strategy used to convict the defendant. The rationale for each decision and its effect on subsequent decisions can be scrutinized, and either affirmed or challenged. In this way the danger of the ratification of error (Huff, Rattner, Sagarin, & MacNamara, 1986) may be averted and its cumulative effect on the possibility of a flawed prosecution prevented.

Since 2003, the number of Conviction Integrity Units has grown to 29, having markedly increased each year since 2009 and, from 2014 on has accounted for "a majority of all exonerations . . . largely because of the high number of drug possession guilty plea cases" (National Registry for Exonerations, 2017).

ADVOCACY PROJECTS AND COMMISSIONS

Various advocacy groups, principally the NAACP, local churches, journalists and civic organizations, have been involved in assisting persons thought to be wrongfully convicted. However, the exoneration of the wrongly convicted is largely made possible by the network of Innocence Projects in the United States and elsewhere around the world. The first Innocence Project was established in 1992 by attorneys Peter Neufeld and Barry Scheck at Yeshiva University's Cardozo Law School. Their intent was to use DNA testing to prove the innocence of persons found guilty of crimes they could not have committed. However, if sufficient DNA evidence was not available to be tested, then the Innocence Project would not be able to assist the convicted person. In its first 25 years of service, the Innocence Project has documented 350 cases of wrongful conviction.

The efforts of the Innocence Project in New York have sparked the development of an Innocence network across the United States and in places around the world. From its inception in 2005 with 15 members, the Innocence Network has grown to 69 member organizations–56 in the United States and 13 in Australia, Canada, Ireland, the United Kingdom, the Netherlands, Taiwan, Argentina, South Africa, Italy and France. Many of these organizations are affiliated with law schools, thereby providing their students with invaluable experience with wrongful conviction and the process of exonerating the innocent.[6]

OBSTACLES TO THE ADOPTION OF EFFECTIVE REFORMS

Resistance to Change

There is an inherent resistance for agents of the criminal justice system – police, prosecutors, and members of the judiciary – to change longstanding policies and procedures thought to serve the interests of justice and enhance public safety. Unless there is a compelling reason to alter current practices, a culture of stability and predictability of action will tend to be maintained. Reforms instituted in other agencies or jurisdictions are often considered of limited value. External political pressure, invariably prompted by public outrage, is more likely to prompt policy and procedural changes than internally initiated reforms.

Public Attitudes

The public response to a case of wrongful conviction is often a sense of shock and dismay that an innocent person would have spent decades

---

6. For more information see: The Innocence Network. (n.d.). *About the Innocence Network.* Retrieved from http://innocencenetwork.org/about/.

in prison, narrowly escaping execution. For the most part, these intense emotions are quickly overshadowed by the belief that wrongful convictions are anomalies—random events while unfortunately, are an inevitable consequence of the operation of a complex system of justice.

Fragmented, Autonomous, and Jurisdictionally Bound System of Justice

For the most part, the criminal justice system is autonomous, fragmented, jurisdictionally bound. Justice is administered at the federal, state, and local levels by autonomous agencies, separated by jurisdictions and only loosely tied to one another. The fragmentation of the criminal justice system imbedded in a diffuse governmental structure undermines reform efforts.

Further, the lack of uniformity in training of law enforcement agents and prosecutors, particularly at the local and state levels, further lessens the effective flow of information about reform measures and their impact on wrongful convictions. Innovations in investigatory practices and the adoption of Conviction Integrity Units to the possibility of prosecutorial error are impeded by the fundamental nature of the criminal justice system.

Psychological biases

Unrecognized psychological biases commonly affect decision-making in everyday life. The coherence effect is explained by our need for all the parts of our assessment of a situation to fit together. Confirmation bias is driven by our need to have our decisions validated by selectively focusing on evidence that is consistent with our conclusion. Similarly, hindsight bias – the belief that we were right all along – serves to affirm our decisions retroactively. And, tunnel vision eliminates any evidence that may undermine our confidence in our decision. Key agents of the criminal justice system should recognize the possibility that these psychological biases may well influence their decision-making. Decisions made with accurate and unbiased information is key to the prevention of wrongful convictions (Simon, 2012).

CULTURAL CHANGE

Public expectations for protection against crime and the conviction of its perpetrators underlie a pervasive culture of expedience across the criminal justice system. Legally supported procedural policies directly affect the processing of a criminal case. Criminal justice decision-making is shaped by the organizational policies and performance expectations of law enforcement and prosecutorial offices.

The criminal justice system is intended to be deliberate, skeptical, and protective of the constitutional rights of the accused. However, in practice, the crime control demands imposed on an overburdened criminal justice system require decision-making to be efficient, expedient, and successful. Law enforcement agencies are expected to provide the prosecutor with evidence sufficient to convict the defendant. The prosecutor, in turn, is expected to bring about a successful resolution of the case. In short, the cultural values and organizational demands of the criminal justice system give rise to the conditions that lead to wrongful convictions.

The presumption of guilt is at the heart of the need for cultural change in the processing of a criminal case. While verbally adhering to its opposite – the presumption of innocence – agents of the criminal justice system tend to pursue the conviction of the accused as if the person is, in fact, guilty. The decision-making of the police and prosecutors is premised on the belief that the accused is convictable and, therefore, all their efforts should be directed toward ensuring a conviction. Convictability means that in the judgment of the police and prosecutors that a jury is most likely to find the defendant guilty. The reasonable assurance of a guilty verdict significantly influences police and prosecutorial decision-making. Police investigators gather evidence, conduct analyses, and present the findings to the prosecutors to justify their going forward with the case. Exculpatory evidence may be simply overlooked by the police. Perhaps unwittingly, the prosecutors selectively organize the evidence to construct a case against the accused that is most likely to convince a potential jury of the defendant's guilt.

The lack of pretrial transparency provides a decided advantage to the agents of the criminal justice system. The discovery process is often compromised by the selective evidence gathering of the police and the unwillingness of the prosecution to interpret evidence known to them as exculpatory. Denial of access to exculpatory evidence requires the defense to conduct its own investigation of the case. Most criminal defendants must rely on representation by either a public defender or court appointed attorney. The limited resources available to indigent defense attorneys preclude any independent investigation of the case or the opportunity to secure expert witnesses for the defense. In sum, the combined effects of the lack of transparency and the limited resources of the defense result in a decided disadvantage for the defendant.

In addition, justice should not be limited to "procedural fairness" but should depend on the strength of the evidence and the totality of circumstance in the case. Deliberate skepticism must guide the decision-making of the police and prosecutors. Conscious efforts should be made to guard against a premature belief in the perceived convictability of the accused. Fairness in the processing of a criminal case should replace the willingness to reduce justice to the commonly accepted belief in "procedural fairness" alone.

A fundamental cultural change in the administration of justice is needed to overcome the obstacles to reforms designed to reduce wrongful convictions. This cultural change must extend from the initial criminal investigation to the final disposition of the case. That is, each stage in the decision-making process must be guided by certain principles of conduct at the individual and systemic levels that are specifically intended to minimize the odds of a wrongful conviction. A culture of truth seeking rather than expedience, of skepticism rather than unfounded conclusions, of a focus on personal and systemic integrity rather than on career advancement and organizational efficiency must guide the processing of a criminal case. The value of truth seeking should supersede minimally following "procedural fairness" as the accepted standard for justice.

CONCLUSION

The future of reforms depends on the challenge to integrate the various streams of reform efforts to affect a change in the fundamental nature of the administration of justice. Criminal justice is compromised by an emphasis on either a model of crime control or due process. An integrated model must emerge that incorporates the need for public

safety and ability to redress criminal wrongdoing with the protection of
the constitutional rights of the accused guided by adherence to professional ethical standards. Wrongful conviction reforms do not require a
wholesale revamping of the criminal justice system, but rather a reaffir-
mation of its philosophical and utilitarian underpinnings and their rein-
troduction to the public at large.

Three hallmarks of a wrongful conviction reform are central to their
success. An integrated and sustainable approach is needed to reform
the criminal justice system (Zalman, 2011; Zalman & Carrano, 2014).
Reforms that effectively reduce wrongful convictions must address the
entire spectrum of criminal justice decision-making process from the
initial investigation to the final disposition of the case. Simply altering
the policies and procedures of the law enforcement community without
simultaneously addressing the decision-making flaws of prosecutors
and the constraints of indigent criminal defense can only fail. A
comprehensive approach to criminal justice reform is necessary to
reduce the potential for wrongful convictions.

Zalman (2011) sets forth an integrated justice model to advance the
wrongful conviction reforms. To Zalman (2011) an integrated justice
model is "a functional, organizational, and ideational map that includes
the innocence movement's reform efforts, but goes beyond them to
propose a way of "seeing" justice system reform keyed to innocence
issues" (p. 1507). Zalman (2011) concurs with Findley (2012) that a
fundamental issue faced by the innocence movement is the need to
reduce the conviction of the innocent while protecting the community.
Zalman's integrated justice model includes five domains: *Adversarial*
(due process protections), *Law Enforcement* (community safety), *Polity/
Policy* (governance bases on democratic ideals), *Psychology* (scientific
insight), and *Science* (Scientific methods). Each of these domains in
concert contributes to resolving the need to balance public safety with
the prevention of the conviction of the innocent. However, Zalman
(2011) argues that the Polity/ Policy Domain is key to the success of the
innocence movement. To Zalman (2011) the Integration Justice Model
is "organized around the policy work of the innocence movement, and
policy change and ratification ultimately takes place in or through
institutions of government" (p. 1509). The Innocent movement's recommendations for policy reform depend on the support of legislative
bodies to be put into effect. The Integrated Justice Model may, however, serve to maintain the positive aspects of the criminal justice

system while enhancing organizational and political support system reforms. Zalman (2011) concludes that Integrated Justice Model is "a heuristic offered to help anyone interested in criminal justice, not only those concerned with wrongful convictions, to see criminal justice in ways that facilitate justice system reform" (p. 1519).

The five domains of Zalman's Integrated Justice Model are consistent with the theme that runs through this book. An integrated approach to wrongful conviction reforms is premised on a balance between ensuring the due process rights of the accused and the need for public safety. A balanced integrative approach to criminal justice reform is facilitated by theoretically-driven, scientifically sound empirical research that addresses the systemic flaws that led to an erroneous conviction. Gould and Leo 2010; and Gould, Carrano, Leo, and Hail-Jares (2014) argue that the rigorous social science research can underpin legal analyses of wrongful conviction. Political support for criminal justice reforms depend on the development of convincing evidence that systemic changes that markedly reduce wrongful convictions can be instituted. In sum, efficacy of an integrated, and sustainable approach to criminal justice reform depends on a scientifically valid understanding of the structural processes lead to wrongful convictions and the political will to put those reforms into effect.

Beyond being integrative, criminal justice reforms must be sustainable. Reforms that are short-lived tend to discourage further efforts to combat flaws in the criminal justice system. Sustainability of criminal justice reforms is inextricably tied to the integration of the reforms with the existing system. By integration is meant that wrongful conviction reforms do not compete with the ability to hold criminal offenders accountable and ensuring public safety and well-being. Zalman and Carrano (2014) concludes that: "Reducing the number of wrongful convictions and exonerating innocent defendants will generally also mean increased efficiency in convictions, safer communities, and a more professional and respected system" (p. 1003).

Public knowledge about wrongful convictions is largely fragmented, based on sensational case reporting, and lacking any lasting effect. By providing a coherent understanding of wrongful conviction to the public, a genuine interest in criminal justice reforms will be enhanced and political support will become more likely. The work of the Innocence Projects and Commissions will also benefit from a widespread appreciation of the corrosive effects of wrongful convictions on the justice system.

In sum, the erosion of injustice will be accelerated by the development of integrated, sustainable, theoretical grounded and empirical supported reforms. The efficacy of these reforms must be understood and accepted by law enforcement, prosecutorial and judicial organizations across the country.

A fundamental cultural change in the decision-making process will help to restore the public's trust and confidence in the criminal justice system. The recognition of a need for change in the values and motives of criminal justice agents will serve to counter the perception of racism, socio-economic bias, and regional inequities in the administration of justice.

APPENDIX
CURRENT STATE COMPENSATION AND REENTRY STATUTES[1]

State & Statutes	Compensation	Extra Services	Restrictions
Alabama *ACT 2001-659, SB166*	Only innocent persons convicted of a felony are eligible for $50,000 each year.		Only receive compensation if legislature appropriates funds, a new felony conviction does not arise, and did not contribute to own wrongful conviction.
Alaska *HB 55*[*2]	Would give up to $50,000 per year. Maximum $2 million can be awarded.		Would require the attorney general to pardon or approve the deal. The claim must be filed within two years.
Arizona	No Statute		
Arkansas	No Statute		

1. For more information on the statutes and restrictions see: Cooper & Elliot. (n.d.). State statutes. Retrieved from http://www.wrongfulconvictionlawyers.com/state-statutes/. And, Norris, R. (2012). Assessing compensation statues for the wrongly convicted. *Criminal Justice Policy Review, 23* (3), 352-374.
2. *Asterisk refers to a House Bill's proposal for compensation statutes.

California SB 635 & AB 672 Chapter 403	Maximum $140 per day of incarceration, including jail time.	Help with obtaining an identification card and with transitional services – job training, housing assistance, and mental health services (i.e. Obie's Law).	Services would be provided for 6 months to a year. Convicted person did not contribute or bring about arrest or conviction. This may prevent people who falsely confessed or accepted a plea deal.
Colorado Chapter 409-13-65-101	$70,000 for each year incarcerated. In addition, $50,000 each year awaiting execution & $25,000 each year year on parole, probation, or registered as a sex offender.	Tuition waivers, compensation of child support, reasonable attorney fees, and any fees paid by exonerated person as a result of wrongful conviction.	Needs to be exonerated for minimum of three years to receive tuition waiver. The wrongfully convicted must have not pled guilty to avoid prosecution for another crime in which the person has not been deemed innocent.
Connecticut Public Act 08-143	Relevant factors are considered for determining the amount of compensation.	Tuition at state system of higher education, employment training and counseling.	
Delaware	No Statute		
District of Columbia D.C. Code Ann. §2-421(2002)	Courts determine fair and appropriate amount.		Wrongfully convicted must demonstrate that he did not contribute to his prosecution, therefore, could not have pled guilty unless it was an Alford Plea.
Florida Chapter 961.06	$50,000 annually with a maximum $2 million.	120 hours of tuition at career center or community, state college or university and reimbursed fines that were imposed during sentence.	The innocent person cannot have any prior felony convictions.

Georgia	No Statute		
Hawaii-HB 1046	Provides a minimum of $50,000 per year of actual confinement (includes time spent awaiting trial). Can be additionally compensated if a pardon or if court finds by preponderance of the evidence extraordinary circumstance the court may award maximum of $100,000 in additional compensation	Award reasonable attorneys' fee not to exceed $10,000.	
Idaho	No Statute		
Illinois 705 ILCS 505/8	$85,350 for those who served up to five years; $170,000 for those who served between five and 14 years; $199,150 for those who served more than 14 years.	Fixed attorney fees not to exceed 25% of the compensation awarded, job assistance and placement	
Indiana	No Statute		
Iowa Chapter 663A. 1	$50.00 per day of wrongful incarceration, plus loss of wages up to $25,000 a year.	Pay attorney fees.	Person must not have pled guilty.
Kansas	No Statute		
Kentucky	No Statute		

Louisiana RS 15:572.8	$25,000 per year and a maximum of $250,000.	May be granted compensation for loss of life opportunities resulting from incarceration but cannot exceed $80,000. Pay cost of job skills for three year, pay for counseling and medical services for six years, pay tuition at state system of higher education.	
Maine Chapter 747 §8243	Maximum $300,000.		
Maryland Md. State Fin. & Proc. §10-501	Amount is determined by the Board of Public Works.	Amount is determined by the Board of Public Works.	Only pardon persons eligible
Massachusetts MASS GEN. LAWS ch. 258D	Maximum of $500,000.	50% discount for tuition at any state or community college and physical and emotional services.	Cannot have pled guilty (unless plea was withdrawn, vacated, or nullified) Claims must be brought within two years of conviction being overturned.
Michigan Act 343 of 2016- Wrongful Imprisonment Compensation Act	$50,000 for each year plantiff was imprisoned.	50% discount for tuition at any state or community college and physical and emotional services.	
Minnesota Minn. Stat. §611.365	Individualized but entitled to not less than $50,000 for each year of imprisonment, and not less than $25,000 for each year on super-vised released on a registered offender list.	Entitled to reimburse-ment for all restitution, fees, court costs, and assessment paid by claimant. Eligible for economic damages, loss of wages, reimbursement for medical and dental expenses. Tuition and fees paid for each semester successfully completed or employment skills and development training up to the equivalent value of a four year degree at a	Eligibility depends on prosecutor and the court to determine if exoneree is eligible for compensation.

		public university. Reimbursement for paid and unpaid child support and reimbursement for reasonable costs of paid and unpaid reintegrative services upon exoneration and release.	
Mississippi *Chapter 44 §11-44-7.*	50,000 each year with a maximum of $500,000.	Reasonable attorney fees (10%) of amount awarded for preparing to file and (20%) for litigation if claim is contested by Attorney General, & (25%) if the claim is appealed.	Cannot have fabricated evidence or did not suborn perjury. People who falsely confessed or pled guilty may not receive compensation.
Missouri *SB 1038[3]*	$50.00 per day The act would change the amount the individual could $50,000 and $100,000 when sentenced to death.		Wrongfully convicted person needs to be exonerated by DNA.
Montana *§53-1-214*	No financial compensation	Education aid	Conviction needs to be overturned by post-conviction forensic DNA testing.
Nebraska *LB 260*	$25,000 per year and a maximum of $500,000.	Reasonable attorney fees. Tuition for education and employment skills development training, compensation for child support payments, compensations for reasonable cost such as housing, transportation, reentry services and up to five years of physical and mental healthcare.	
Nevada	No Statute		
New Hampshire *NH Rev Stat. §541-B:14*	Maximum of $20,000.		

---

3. Updates previous statute by changing amount of restitution awarded.

New Jersey *NJ A2910*	Eligible to receive $50,000 for each year wrongfully convicted.	Services may include counseling and vocational training, housing assistance, health insurance, and tuition assistance.	
New Mexico	No Statute		
New York *Court of Claims Act §* *8-b*	The Court of Claims determines reasonable compensation.		Did not bring about or cause conviction. This may prevent a person from receiving compensation if they pled guilty or falsely confessed.
North Carolina *G.S. 148-82 through* *G.S. 148-84*	$50,000 for each year of wrongful incarceration with a maximum of $750,000.	Education tuition waivers and Job skills training.	
North Dakota	No statute		
Ohio	$40,330 per year or an adjusted amount.	Any loss of wages, salary or other earned income that directly resulted from wrongful incarceration.	Individual could not have pled guilty.
Oklahoma *OK ST T. 22 § 1371*	$175,000 maximum.		Individual must show that he played no role in his wrongful conviction including pleading guilty.
Oregon **SB 291 and HB* *5815*	Would provide $50,000 for each year of wrongful incarceration.	Would provide housing and other services	
Pennsylvania	No Statute		
Rhode Island **2016-H 7749*	Would earn the state's median single person income at the time of release and paid for each year. Award can be expanded at the discretion of the court.	Release from child support during the time served. Reasonable attorney fees at a (15%) of the total amount awarded, housing, transportation, reentry services, mental and physical healthcare cost for the period of time from release until claimant is awarded.	

South Carolina	No Statute		
South Dakota	No Statute		
Tennessee	Maximum of $1,000,000	Board of claims shall consider the person's physical and mental suffering and loss of earnings when determining the amount of compensation.	
Texas *Sec. 103.001*	$80,000 per year of wrongful incarceration and $25,000 per year spent on parole or registered as a sex offender, plus annuity.	Compensation for child support payment, tuition for up to 120 hours at a state college or university, reentry and reintegration services (includes life skills, job & vocational training). State additionally provides a state ID card and financial assistance to cover living expenses, mental and health treatment as long as necessary. Also entitled to a case manager to assist with reentry.	
Utah 78-17a-106	Not less than $40,000 for each year and additional $30,000 for each year served on death row.	Physical and mental health care and reasonable attorney fees calculated at 10% of the award under this chapter but cannot exceed $75,000.	
Vermont	Between $30,000 and $60,000 per year of wrongful incarceration.	Economic damages (include loss of wages) and reimbursement for attorney fees. Eligible for up to 10 years of state healthcare, reasonable reentry services and mental and physical health care costs for the time between his or her release date of award.	The person should not have suborn perjury or fabricate evidence during any proceedings related to the crime or charges. This might prevent someone who falsely confessed or pled guilty from receiving compensation.

Virginia § 8.01-195.11	May be awarded up to 90% of Virginia per capita personal incomes for 25 years.	Receive a transition assistance grant of $15,000 (later be deducted from the final award) & entitled to $10,000 for tuition in the Virginia community college system.	Cannot have pled guilty, unless pled guilty when being charged of a capital offense. Any new felony convictions terminate the right to compensation.
Washington Chapter 4.100 RCW	Awarded $50,000 per year of actual confinement (includes time spent awaiting trial), an additional $50,000 for each year spent on death row, & $25,000 for each year on parole, community custody or registered as a sex offender.	Compensation for child support and attorney fees shall be calculated at 10% of monetary damages awarded but expenses cannot exceed $75,000.	Claimant cannot be incarcerated for any offense and did not commit or suborn to perjury to bring about his or her convictions. However, a guilty plea or confession does not automatically constitute perjury.
West Virginia §14-2-13a	No amount specified- court deems "fairly and reasonably" for compensation.		Must show that conduct did not contribute to conviction. This might prevent those that falsely confessed or pled guilty from receiving compensation.
Wisconsin *Wis. Stat. §775.05*	Amount cannot exceed $25,000 or $5,000 per year for the imprisonment.	Attorney fees	Must show that conduct did not contribute to conviction. This might prevent someone who falsely confessed or pled guilty from receiving compensation.
Wyoming	No Statute		

REFERENCES

18 U.S.C. § 201 (c) (2) (2007).

28 U.S.C § 2255.

28 U.S.C § 2241.

28 U.S.C § 2254.

725 Ill. Comp. Stat. 5/115-21 (2009).

Acker, J. R. (2017). Taking stock of innocence: Movements, mountains, and wrongful convictions. *Journal of Contemporary Criminal Justice, 33* (1), 8–25.

Acker, J. R., & Redlich, A. D. (2011). *Wrongful conviction: Law, science, and policy.* Durham, NC: Carolina Academic Press.

Aguirre et al. (2007, November 25). Exonerated, freed, and what happened then. *The New York Times.* Retrieved from http://www.nytimes.com/interactive/2007/11/25/nyregion/20071125_DNAI_FEATURE.html?personId=150.

Agurs v. United States, 427 U.S. (1976).

Ake v. Oklahoma, 470 U.S. 68 (1985).

Albanese, A. (2008, December 16). PATRIOT Act's national security letter gag provisions ruled unconstitutional. *Library Journal Archive Content.* Retrieved from http://lj.libraryjournal.com/2008/12/managing-libraries/patriot-acts-national-security-letter-gag-provisions-ruled-unconstitutional/#_.

American Bar Association. (1983). *Model rules of professional conduct.* Retrieved from https://www.americanbar.org/groups/professional_responsibility/publications/model_rules_of_professional_conduct/rule_3_8_special_responsibilities_of_a_prosecutor.html.

American Bar Association. (2015). *Criminal justice standards for the defense function.* Retrieved from https://www.americanbar.org/groups/criminal_justice/standards/DefenseFunctionFourthEdition.html.

American Bar Association. (2002). *Ten principles of public defense delivery system.* Retrieved from https://www.americanbar.org/content/dam/aba/administrative/legal_aid_indigent.

American Bar Association. (2012). *Resolution 101c- Factors to considering which expert testimony should be presented to a jury.* Approved February 6, 2012. Retrieved from https://www.americanbar.org/content/dam/aba/directories/policy/2012_hod_midyear_meeting_101c.authcheckdam.doc.

Apodaca v. Oregon, 406 U.S. 404 (1972).

Apprendi v. New Jersey, 503 U.S. 466 (2000).

Argersinger v. Hamlin, 407 U.S. 25 (1972).

Armbrust, S. (2008). Reevaluating recanting witnesses: Why the red-headed stepchild of new evidence deserves another look. *Boston College Third World Law Journal, 28* (1), 75–104.

Avery, M. (2009). Obstacles to litigating civil claims for wrongful conviction: An overview. *Public Interest Law Journal, 18,* 429–451.

Balko, D. (2013). Justice delayed is justice denied: Wrongful convictions, eyewitness-expert testimony, and recent developments. *Suffolk University Law Review, 46* (4), 1087–1109.

Bedau, H., Radelet, M., & Putnam, C. (1992). *In spite of innocence: Erroneous convictions in capital cases.* Boston: Northeastern University Press.

Benner, L. (2009). The presumption of guilt: Systemic factors that contribute to ineffective assistance of counsel in California. *California Western Law Review, 45* (2), 263–372.

Benner, L. (2011). *Eliminating excessive public defender workloads.* Retrieved from http://www.americanbar.org/content/dam/aba/publications/criminal_justice.

Benner, L. (2011a). *Excessive public defender workloads violate the sixth amendment right to counsel without a showing of prejudice.* Washington, DC: American Constitution Society Law & Policy.

Bergmann, J. L. (2010). *Section 2255 motions and other federal postconviction remedies* § 1.01.Supplement to Defending A Criminal Case. Retrieved from http://www.rashkind.com/dfcc/Chapter%2016%202255s.pdf.

Berman, G. l., Narby, D. T., & Cutler, B., L. (1995). Effects of inconsistent eyewitness statements on mock-jurors' evaluation of the eyewitness, perceptions of defendant culpability and verdicts. *Law & Human Behavior, 19* (1), 79–88.

Bernhard, A. (2009). A short overview of the statutory remedies for the wrongly convicted: What works, what doesn't and why. *Public Interest Law Journal, 18,* 403–425.

Bernstein, D. E (2013). The misbegotten judicial resistance to the Daubert revolution. *Notre Dame Law Review, 89* (1), 27–70.

Berry v. State, 10 Ga. 511 (1851).

Bittner, E. (1970). *The functions of the police in modern society.* Chevy Chase, MD: National Institute of Mental Health, Center for Studies of Crime and Delinquency.

Blacks, D. (1976). *Behavior of law.* New York, NY: Academic Press.

Black, D. (1983). Crime as social control. *American Sociological Review, 48* (1), 34–45.

Black, D. (1993). *The social structure of right and wrong.* San Diego, CA: Academic Press.

Blackstone, Sir William. (1765). *Commentaries on the laws of England* (Book IV: 27). London: Strahan.

Blinder, A. & Fernandez, M. (2017, April 21). Arkansas puts Ledell Lee to death in its first execution since 2005. *New York Times.* Retrieved from https://www.nytimes.com/2017/04/21/us/arkansas-death-penalty-ledell-lee-execution.html.

Bluhm Legal Clinic, Center on Wrongful Convictions. (n.d.a). *First Wrongful Conviction.* Retrieved from http://www.law.northwestern.edu/legalclinic/wrongfulconvictions/exonerations/vt/boorn-brothers.html.

Bluhm Legal Clinic, Center on Wrongful Convictions. (n.d.b). *Julia Rea.* Retrieved from http://www.uis.edu/illinoisinnocenceproject/exonores/jrea/.

Blume, J. H., & Helm, R. K. (2014). The unexonerated: Factually innocent defendants who plead guilty. *Cornell Law, 157*, 1–44.

Borchard, E. (1932). *Convicting the innocent: Errors of criminal justice.* Hamden, CT: Archon.

Bradfield, A. L., Wells, G. L., & Olson, E. A. (2002). The damaging effect of confirming feedback on the relation between eyewitness certainty and accuracy. *Journal of Applied Psychology, 87*, 112–120.

Brady v. United States, 397 U.S. 742 (1970).

Brennan, M. (2008). Interpreting the phrase "newly discovered evidence": May previously unavailable exculpatory testimony serve as the basis for a motion for a new trial under Rule 33?. *Fordham Law Review, 77* (3) 1095–1145.

Brigham, J. C., & Wolfskeil, M. P. (1983). Opinions of attorneys and law enforcement personnel on the accuracy of eyewitness identification. *Law & Human Behavior, 7*, 337–349.

Bromwich, M. R. (1997). *The FBI laboratory: An investigation into laboratory practices and alleged misconduct in explosives-related and other cases.* Washington, DC: U.S. Department of Justice, Office of the Inspector General. Buckley, J. P. (n.d.). The Reid Technique of interviewing and interrogation. Retrieved from http;//law.wisc.edufjr/clinicals/ip/wcjsc/files/buckley_chapter_on_reid_techniques.doc.

CAL. PENAL CODE § 1127a(b) (2004).

Campbell, K., & Denov, M. (2004). The burden of innocence: Coping with a wrongful imprisonment. *Canadian Journal of Criminology & Criminal Justice, 46*, 139–163.

Carollo, K. (2004, December 12). Finding solace after wrongful conviction. *ABC NEWS.* Retrieved from http://abcnews.go.com/US/story?id=315686.

Cassidy, R. M. (2005). *Prosecutorial ethics.* St. Paul, MN: Thompson-West.

Cates, P. (2011, August 24). *New Jersey Supreme Court issues landmark decision mandating major changes in the way courts handle identification procedures.* New York: Innocence Project. Retrieved from http://www.innocenceproject.org/news-events-exonerations/press-releases/new-jersey-supreme-court-issues-landmark-decision-mandating-major-changes-in-the- way-courts-handle-identification-procedures.

Center for Prosecutor Integrity. (2013). *An epidemic of prosecutor misconduct.* Retrieved from http://www.prosecutorintegrity.org.

Center for Prosecutor Integrity. (2014). *Roadmap for Prosecutorial Reform.* Retrieved from http://www.prosecutorintegrity.org.

Chambers v. Mississippi, 410 U.S. 284 (1973).

Chan, Sau. (1994, August 21). Sources of convictions reviewed as chemist faces perjury accusations: Forensics: Fred Zain's expert testimony and law tests helped put scores of rapists and murderers behind bars. But college transcript shows he flunked somechemistry classes' and barely passed others. He is also accused of evidence-tampering. *The Associated Press.* Retrieved from http://articles.latimes.com/1994-08-21/news/mn-29449_1_lab-tests-fred-zain-double-murder.

Chicago police found to dismiss cases erroneously. (1983, May 2). *New York Times.* Retrieved from http://www.nytimes.com/1983/05/02/us/chicago-police-found-to-dismiss-cases-erroneously.html.

Clarke, K., & McCormack, P.D. (forthcoming). Wrongful Convictions. In C. Marcum & L. Carter (Eds.), *Female offenders and reentry: Pathways and barriers to returning to society*. Boca Raton, FL: CRC Press.

Cole. S. (2005). More than zero: Accounting for error in latent fingerprint identification. *Journal of Criminal Law & Criminology, 95* (3), 985–1078.

Cole. S. (2014). The innocence crisis and forensic science reform. In M. Zalman & J. Carrano (Eds.), *Wrongful conviction and criminal justice reform: Making justice* (pp.167–185). New York: Routledge.

Cole, S. A., & Thompson, W. C. (2013). Forensic science and wrongful convictions. In, C. R. Huff & M. Killias (Eds.), *Wrongful convictions & miscarriages of justice: Causes and remedies in North American and European criminal justice systems* (pp.111–135). New York, NY: Routledge.

Coleman, C. T. (1919). Origin and development of trial by jury. *Virginia Law Review, 6* (2), 77–86.

Comer, D. R., & Vega, G. (2011). *Moral courage in organizations: Doing the right thing at work*. Armonk, N.Y: M.E. Sharpe.

Commonwealth v. Gomes, 470 Mass. 352 (2015).

Connick v. Thompson, 131 S. Ct. 1350 (2011).

Cooper & Elliot. (n.d.). State statutes. Retrieved from http://www.wrongfulconvictionlawyers.com/state-statutes/.

Covey, R. D. (2011). Longitudinal guilt: Repeat offenders, plea bargaining, and the variable standard of proof. *Florida Law Review, 63* (2), 431–456.

Criminal Jury Instructions 2.6-4 identification of Defendant (2013) Retrieved from http://www.jud.ct.gov/ji/criminal/part2/2.6-4.htm.

Cutler, B. L. (2009). *Expert testimony on the psychology of eyewitness identification*. New York: Oxford University Press.

Cutler, B. L., Penrod, S. D., & Dexter, H., R. (1990). Juror sensitivity to eyewitness identification evidence. *Law & Human Behavior, 14* (2), 185–191.

Daftary-Kapur, T., Dumas, R., & Penrod, S. D. (2010). Jury decision-making biases and methods to counter them. *Legal & Criminological Psychology, 15* (1), 133–154.

Dannenberg, J. (2007, August 15). Prisons as incubators and spreaders of disease and illness. *Prison Legal News*. Retrieved from https://www.prisonlegalnews.org/news/2007/aug/15/prisons-as-incubators-and-spreaders-of-disease-and-illness/.

Daubert v. Merrell Dow Pharmaceuticals, 509 U.S. 579 (1993).

Death Penalty Information Center. (n.d.). Arbitrariness. Retrieved from http://www.deathpenaltyinfo.org/arbitrariness?did=1328.

Deffenbacher, K. A., Bornstein, B. H., & Penrod, S. D. (2006). Mugshot exposure effects: Retroactive interference, mugshot commitment, source confusion, and unconscious transference. *Law & Human Behavior, 30* (3), 287–307.

De Melker, S. (2014, November 9). Four wrongfully convicted men, four very different outcomes. *PBS Newshour*. Retrieved from http://www.pbs.org/newshour/updates/life-exoneration/.

De Montesquieu. C. (1734). *Considerations on the causes of the greatness of the Romans and their decline*. Translated by Lowenthal, D. (1965). *Constitution Society*. New York: The Free Press.

Dervan, L. E., & Edkins, V. A. (2013). The innocent defendant's dilemma: An innovative empirical study of plea bargaining's innocence problem. *Journal of Criminal Law & Criminology, 103* (1), 1–43.

Devers, L. (2011). *Plea and charge bargaining: Research Summary*. Bureau of Justice Assistance, U.S. Department of Justice. Retrieved from https://www.bja.gov/Publications/PleaBargainingResearchSummary.pdf.

Devine, D. J., Clayton, L. D., Dunford, B. B., Seying, R., & Pryce J. (2000). Jury decision making 45 years of empirical research on deliberating groups. *Psychology, Public Policy, & Law, 7* (3), 622–727.

Disraeli, B. (1851). *Agricultural Distress*. Speech in House of Commons.

Dist. Attorney's Office for Third Judicial Dist. V. Osborne, 557 U.S. 52 (2009).

Dodd v. State, 993 P2d 778 (Okla. Crim. App. 2000).

Donahue, C. (1999). Biology and the origins of the English jury. *Law & History Review, 17* (3), 591–596.

Doyle, J. (2014). *Mending justice: Sentinel event reviews*. Washington, DC: National Institute of Justice. Retrieved from https://ncjrs.gov/pdffiles1/nij/247141.pdf.

Drizin, S. A., & Leo, R. (2004). The problem of false confessions in the post-DNA world. *North Carolina Law Review, 82* (3), 891–1008.

Dufraimont, L. (2008). Regulating unreliable evidence: Can evidence rules guide juries and prevent wrongful convictions? *Queen's Law Journal, 33*, 261–326.

Duncan v. Louisiana, 391 U.S. 145 (1968).

Dunning, D., & Perretta, S. (2002). Automaticity and eyewitness accuracy: a 10-to 12-second rule for distinguishing accurate from inaccurate positive identifications. *Journal of Applied Psychology, 87* (5), 951–962.

Durose, M. R., & Langan P. A. (2003). "Felony sentences in state courts, 2000." *Bureau of Justice Statistics Bulletin*. Washington, DC: U.S. Department of Justice, Office of Justice Programs.

Ellement, J. (2015, May 18). SJC ruling limits charges, jail time in fallout from state drug lab scandal. *The Boston Globe*. Retrieved from https://www.bostonglobe.com/2015/05/18/sjc-caps-prison-time-for-people-whose-convictions-are-impacted-dookhan-drug-lab-scandal/EwSxVoP95wVBCBYGPaaENM/story.html?comments=all&sort=OLDEST_CREATE_DT.

Elwork, A., Sales, B. D., & Alfini, J. J. (1982). *Making jury instructions understandable*. Charlottesville, VA: Michie.

Epstein, J. (2007). The great engine that couldn't: Science, mistaken identification, and the limits of cross-examination. *Stetson Law Review, 36*, 727–787.

Ex parte Robbins, 360 S. W. 3d 446,470 (Tex. Crim. App. 2011) (Cochran, J., dissenting).

Farole, D. J. Jr., & Langton, L. (2010). *County-based and local public defenders offices, 2007*. Washington, DC: Bureau of Justice Statistics, U.S. Department of Justice. Retrieved from https://www.bjs.gov/content/pub/pdf/clpdo07.pdf.

Federal Bureau of Investigation. (2016). *Crime in the United States*. Washington, DC: USGPO. Retrieved from http://www.fbi.gov/ucr/ucr.htm.

Fed. R. Crim. P. 33.

Fed. R. Evid. 403.

Fed. R. Evid. 702.

Fed. R. Evid 704.

Ferrando, E. & Buckner, M. (2017, April 20). 24 years later, Ledell Lee maintained his innocence in death of Debra Reese. *WWM13*. Retrieved from http://www. wzzm13.com/news/local/ledell-lee-24-years-later/433035718.

File, T., & Ryan, C. (2014). *Computer and Internet Use in the United States: 2013.* Washington, DC: United States Census Bureau. Retrieved from https://www.census. gov/history/pdf/2013computeruse.pdf.

Findley, K. A. (2012). Tunnel vision. In B.L. Cutler (Ed.), *Conviction of the innocent: Lessons from psychological research* (pp. 303–323). Washington, DC: American Psychological Association.

Findley, K. A., & Scott, M. S. (2006). The multiple dimensions of tunnel vision in criminal cases. *Wisconsin Law Review,* 291–397.

Fox, A. (2017, January 24). Proposed house bill to remove time limit for new trial based on actual innocence. *The Sheridan Press.* Retrieved from http://thesheridan-press.com/proposed-house-bill-remove-time-limit-new-trial-based-actual-innocence/.

Fradella, H. (2006) Why judges should admit expert testimony on unreliability of eyewitness testimony. *Federal Courts Law Review.* Retrieved from http://www.fclr. org/fclr/articles/html/2006/fedctslrev3.pdf.

Frohmann, L. (1997). Convictability and discordant locales: Reproducing race, class, and gender ideologies in prosecutorial decision-making. *Law & Society Review, 31* (3), 531–555.

Frye v. United States, 293 F. 1013 (D.C. Cir. 1923).

Gabel, J. D. (2014). Realizing reliability in forensic science from the ground up. *Journal of Criminal Law & Criminology, 104* (2), 283–352.

Gabel, J. D., & Wilkinson, M. D. (2008). Good science gone bad: How the criminal justice system can redress the impact of flawed forensics. *Hastings Law Journal, 59,* 1001–1030.

Gardner, T., & Anderson, T. (2016). *Criminal evidence: Principles and cases* (9th ed.). Boston, MA: Cengage Learning Inc.

Garrett, B. L. (2008). Judging innocence. *Columbia Law Review, 108,* 55–142.

Garrett, B. L. (2011). *Convicting the innocent: Where criminal prosecutions go wrong.* Cambridge, MA: Harvard University Press.

Garrett, B. L. (2012). Eyewitnesses and exclusion. *Vanderbilt Law Review, 65* (2), 451–506.

Garrett, B. L., & Neufeld, P. J. (2009). Invalid forensic science testimony and wrongful convictions. *Virginia Law Review, 95* (1), 1–97.

General Electric Co. v. Joiner, 522 U.S. 136 (1997).

Gershman, B. L. (2007). *Trial error and misconduct* (2nd ed.).Charlottesville, VA: LexisNexis.

Giannelli, P. C. (2007a). Regulating crime laboratories. The impact of DNA evidence. *Journal of Law & Policy, 15* (1) 59–92.

Giannelli, P. C. (2007b). Wrongful convictions and forensic science the need to regulate crime labs. *North Carolina Law Review, 86,* 163–235.

Giannelli, P. C. (2010). Independent crime laboratories. the problem of motivational and cognitive bias. *Utah Law Review, 10* (2) 247–266.

Gideon v. Wainwright, 372 U.S. 335 (1963).

Giglio v. United States, 405 U.S. 150 (1972).

Godsey, M. A., & Pulley, T. (2003). The innocence revolution and our "evolving standards of decency" in death penalty jurisprudence. *University of Dayton Law Review, 29* (2), 265–292.

Goldin, D. (1995, April 8). 5th state trooper pleads guilty in scandal. *New York Times,* Retrieved from http://www.nytimes.com/1995/04/08/nyregion/5th-trooper-pleads-guilty-plea-in-scandal.html.

Goldstein, R. M. (2011). Improving forensic science through state oversight. *Texas Law Review, 90,* 225–258.

Goldstein, A. G., Chance, J. E., & Schneller, G. R. (1989). Frequency of eyewitness identification in criminal cases: A survey of prosecutors. *Bulletin of the Psychonomic Society, 27* (1), 71–74.

Gould, J. B., & Leo, R. (2010). One hundred years later: Wrongful convictions after a century of research. *Journal of Criminal Law & Criminology, 100* (3). 825–868.

Gould, J. B., Carrano, J., Leo, R., & Hail-Jares, K. (2014). Predicting erroneous convictions. *Iowa Law Review, 99,* 471–522.

Graham, F. (2009). *Anatomy of a jury trial.* U.S. Department of State, 14 (7), 1–45. Retrieved from http://iipdigital.usembassy.gov/media/pdf/ejs/0709.pdf

Gregory, L. W., Mowen, J. C., & Linder, D. E. (1978). Social psychology and plea bargaining: Applications, methodology, and theory. *Journal of Personality & Social Psychology, 36* (12), 1521–1530.

Grisham, J. (2006). *The innocent man: Murder in a small town.* New York: Doubleday.

Grometstein, R. & Balboni, J. (2012). Backing out of a constitutional ditch: Constitutional remedies for gross prosecutorial misconduct post Thompson. *Albany Law Review, 75* (3), 1243–1281.

Gross, S., Jacoby, K., Matheson, D., Montgomery. N., & Patil, S. (2005). Exonerations in the United States, 1989 through 2003. *Journal of Criminal Law & Criminology, 95* (2), 523–560.

Gross, S. R., O'Brien, B., Hu, C., & Kennedy, E. H. (2014). Rate of false conviction of criminal defendants who are sentenced to death. *Proceedings of the National Academy of Science, 111* (20), 7230–7235.

Gross, S., & Shaffer, M. (2012). *Exonerations in the United States, 1989-2012: National Registry of Exonerations.* Retrieved from https://www.law.umich.edu/special/exoneration/Documents/exonerations_us_1989_2012_full_report.pdf.

Grounds, A. (2004). Psychological consequences of wrongful conviction and imprisonment. *Canadian Journal of Criminology & Criminal Justice, 46* (2), 165–182.

Gudjonsson, G. H. (2003). *The psychology of interrogations and confessions: A handbook.* Chichester, England: Wiley.

Haney, C., & Lynch, M. (1994). Comprehending life and death matters: A preliminary study of California's capital penalty instructions. *Law & Human Behavior, 18,* 411–436.

Hans, V. P. (2002). U.S. jury reform: The active jury and the adversarial ideal. *St. Louis University Public Law Review, 21,* 85–97.

Hansen, M. (1994). Lab evidence questioned; Exonerated ex-con wins $1 million judgement, spurring investigation. *ABA Journal, 80* (7), 16.

Hastie, R., Penrod, S. D., & Pennington, N. (1983). *Inside the jury.* Cambridge: Harvard University Press.

Hertwig, R., Gigerenzer, G., & Hoffrage, U. (1997). The reiteration effort in hindsight bias. *Psychological Review, 104*, 194–202.

Hirschy, T. (2003). Usual suspects: Do solvability factors predict case investigation outcomes for the Dublin, Ohio Division of Police. Retrieved from https://www.ncjrs.gov/App/Publications/abstract.aspx?ID=209221.

Horry, R., Halford, P., Brewer, N., Milne, R., & Bull, R. (2014). Archival analyses of eyewitness identification test outcomes: What can they tell us about eyewitness memory? *Law & Human Behavior, 38* (1), 94–108.

Hsu, S. S. (2012, April 16). Convicted defendants left uniformed of forensic flaws found by Justice Dept. *The Washington Post.* Retrieved from http://www.washingtonpost.com/local/crime/convicted-defendants-left-uninformed-of-forensic-flaws-found-by-justice-dept/2012/04/16/gIQAWTcgMT_story.html.

Hsu, S. S. (2015, February 28). D.C. to pay $9.2 million in wrongful conviction. *The Washington Post.* Retrieved from https://www.washingtonpost.com/local/crime/judge-orders-dc-to-pay-record-91-million-in-wrongful-conviction-case/2015/02/27/f54edaa6-beea-11e4-8668-4e7ba8439ca6_story.html?utm_term=.f7a1172c5f47.

Huber, P. W. (1991). *Galileo's revenge: Junk science in the courtroom.* New York: Basic Books.

Huff, C. R., & Killias, M. (2010). *Wrongful conviction: Perspectives on miscarriages of justice.* Philadelphia: Temple University Press.

Huff, C. R., Rattner, A., & Sagarin, E. (1996). *Convicted but innocent: Wrongful conviction and public policy.* Thousand Oaks, CA: SAGE.

Huff, C. R., Rattner, A., Sagarin, E., & MacNamara, D. (1986). Guilty until proven innocent: Wrongful conviction and public policy. *Crime & Delinquency, 32* (4), 518–544.

Imbler v. Pachtman, 424 U.S. 409 (1976).

Innocence Project. (n.d.a). *All cases.* New York: Innocence Project. Retrieved from https://www.innocenceproject.org/all-cases/#exonerated-by-dna.

Innocence Project. (n.d.b). *Chester Bauer.* New York: Innocence Project. Retrieved from http://www.innocenceproject.org/cases-false-imprisonment/chester-bauer.

Innocence Project. (n.d.c). *Compensating the wrongfully convicted.* New York: Innocence Project. Retrieved from http://www.innocenceproject.org/compensating-wrongly-convicted/.

Innocence Project. (n.d.d). *Eddie Joe Lloyd.* New York: Innocence Project. Retrieved from http://www.innocenceproject.org/cases-false-imprisonmenteddie-joe-lloyd.

Innocence Project. (n.d.e). *How is your state doing?* New York: Innocence Project. Retrieved from http://www.innocenceproject.org/how-is-your-state-doing.

Innocence Project. (n.d.f). *Ohio.* New York: Innocence Project. Retrieved from http://www.innocenceproject.org/how-is-your-state-doing/OH.

Innocence Project. (n.d.g). Nathan Brown. New York: Innocence Project. Retrieved from http://www.innocenceproject.org/cases/nathan-brown/.

Innocence Project. (n.d.h). *North Carolina*. New York: Innocence Project. Retrieved from http://www.innocenceproject.org/how-is-your-state-doing/NC.

Innocence Project. (n.d.i). *Michael Marshall*. New York: Innocence Project. Retrieved from http://www.innocenceproject.org/cases/michael-marshall/.

Innocence Project. (n.d.j). *The case-Curtis McCarty*. New York: Innocence Project. Retrieved from http://www.innocenceproject.org/cases-false-imprisonment/curtis-mccarty.

Innocence Project. (n.d.k). *The causes of wrongful conviction*. New York: Innocence Project. Retrieved from http://www.innocenceproject.org/causes-wrongful-conviction.

Innocence Project. (n.d.l). *Unvalidated or improper forensic science*. New York: Innocence Project. Retrieved from http://www.innocenceproject.org/causes-wrongful-conviction/unvalidated-or-improper-forensic-science.

Innocence Project. (2007a). *After 21 years in prison- including 16 on death row- Curtis McCarty is exonerated based on DNA evidence*. New York: Innocence Project. Retrieved from http://www.innocenceproject.org/news-events-exonerations/press-releases/after-21-years-in-prison-including-16-on-death-row-curtis-mccarty-is-exonerated-based-on-dna-evidence.

Innocence Project. (2007b). *Criminal justice reform commissions: Case studies*. New York: Innocence Project. Retrieved from http://www.innocenceproject.org/criminal-justice-reform-commissions-case-studies/.

Innocence Project. (2009). *Making up for lost time: What the wrongfully convicted endure and how to provide fair compensation*. New York: Innocence Project. Retrieved from http://www.innocenceproject.org/wp-content/uploads/2016/06/innocence_project_compensation_report-6.pdf.

Innocence Project. (2014). *Louisiana exoneree reflects on his 17 years of wrongful imprisonment and on vindication*. New York: Innocence Project. Retrieved from http://www.innocenceproject.org/louisiana-exoneree-reflects-on-his-17-years-of-wrongful-imprisonment-and-on-vindication/.

Innocence Project. (2015a). *Access to post-conviction DNA testing*. New York: Innocence Project. Retrieved from http://www.innocenceproject.org/free-innocentimprove-the-law/fact-sheets/access-to-post-conviction-dna-testing.

Innocence Project. (2015b). *False confessions and recording of custodial interrogations*. New York: Innocence Project. Retrieved from http://www.innocenceproject.org/free-innocent/improve-the-law/fact-sheets/false-confessions-recording-of-custodial-interrogations.

Innocence Project. (2016, March 29a). *Prosecutorial oversight: A national dialog in the wake of Connick v. Thompson*. New York: Innocence Project. Retrieved from https://www.innocenceproject.org/prosecutorial-oversight-national-dialogue.

Innocence Project. (2016, May 31b). *New York Times Op-ed Calls for Wrongful Conviction Compensation Reform*. New York: Innocence Project. Retrieved from http://www.innocenceproject.org/op-ed-new-york-times-compensation/.

Innocence Project. (2016, August 1c). *Incentivized informants*. New York: Innocence Project. Retrieved from https://www.innocenceproject.org/causes/incentivized-informants/.

Innocence Project. (2017). *Eyewitness misidentification.* New York: Innocence Project. Retrieved from https://www.innocenceproject.org/causes/eyewitness-misidentification/.

Johnson v. Louisiana, 406 U.S. 356 (1972).

Jost, K. (2011). Eyewitness testimony. *CQ Researcher, 21* (36), 853–876.

Joy, P. (2006). The relationship between prosecutorial misconduct and wrongful convictions: Shaping remedies for a broken system. *Wisconsin Law Review, 2,* 399–429.

Joy, P. A., & McMunigal, K. C. (2011). Contingent rewards for prosecutors? *Faculty Publications.* Paper 36. Retrieved from http://scholarlycommons.law.case.edu/cgi/viewcontent.cgi?article=1035&context=faculty_publications.

Judicial Council of California. (2015). *California criminal jury instructions.* Retrieved from www.courts.ca.gov/partners/312.htm.

Justice for All Act of 2004, Pub. L.108-405.

Justice Policy Institute. (2011). *System overload: The costs of under-resourcing public defense.* Retrieved from http://www.justicepolicy.org/systemoverload.

Karman, A. (2016). *Crime victims: An introduction to victimology* (9th ed.). Boston, MA: Wadsworth Cengage.

Kassin, S. M., Dror, I. E., & Kukucka, J. (2013). The forensic confirmation bias: Problems, perspectives and proposed solutions. *Journal of Applied Research in Memory and Cognition, 2,* 42–52.

Kassin, S. M., & Gudjonsson, G. H. (2004). The psychology of confessions. *Psychological Science in the Public Interest, 5* (2), 33–67.

Kassin, S. M., Drizin, S. A., Grisso, T., Gudjonsson, G. H., Leo, R., & Redich, A. D. (2010). Police-induced confessions: Risk factors and recommendations. *Law & Human Behavior, 34,* 3–38.

Kassin, S. M., & Wrightman, L. (1985). Confession evidence. In S. Kassin & L. Wrightman (Eds.), *The psychology of evidence and trial procedure* (pp. 6794). Beverly Hills, CA: Sage.

Katz v. United States, 389 U.S. 347 (1967).

King John. (1215). *Magna Carta.* Retrieved from http://www.constitution.org/eng/magnacar.htm.

King, N. J. (2013). Enforcing effective assistance after Martinez. *The Yale Law Journal, 122,* 2428-2458.

King, N. J. (2014). Judicial reviews: Appeals and postconvcition proceedings. In A. D. Redlich., J. R. Acker, R. J. Norris., & C. L. Bonventre (Eds.), *Examining wrongful conviction. Stepping back, moving forward* (pp. 217–236). North Carolina: Carolina Academic Press.

King, N. J., & Hoffman, J. L. (2011). *Habeas for the twenty-first century: Uses, abuses and the future of the great writ.* Chicago, IL: University of Chicago Press.

Konvisser, Z. (2012). Psychological consequences of wrongful conviction in women and the possibility of positive change. *DePaul Journal for Social Justice, 5* (2), 221–294.

Krane, D. E., Bahn, V., Balding, D. J., Barlow, B., Cash, H., Desporters, B., et al. (2009). Time for DNA disclosure. *Science, 326* (5960), 1631-1632.

Kumho Tire Co. v. Carmichael, 119 s. Ct. 1167 (1999).

Larrison v. United States, 24 F.2d 82 (7th Cir. 1928).

Lafler v. Cooper, 132 S. Ct. 1376 (2012).

Laurin, J. E. (2013). Remapping the path forward: Toward a systemic view of forensic science reform and oversight. *Texas Law Review, 91* (5), 1051–1118.

Lavoie, D. (2013, January 31). Ex-state chemist pleads not guilty. *The Boston Globe.* Retrieved from http://www.bostonglobe.com/metro/2013/01/31/chemist-annie-dookhan-pleads-not-guilty-obstruction/8LSlUcGVCpXkSHYred9omI/story. html#.

Lefstein, N. (2011). *Securing reasonable caseloads: Ethics and law in public defense.* Chicago: American Bar Association.

Legal Action Center. (2004). *After prison: Roadblocks to reentry. A report on state legal barriers facing people with criminal records.* New York, NY. Retrieved from http://lac. org/roadblocks-to-reentry/upload/lacreport/LAC_PrintReport.pdf.

Legal Action Center. (2009). *After prison: Roadblocks to reentry. A report on state legal barriers facing people with criminal records: 2009 Update Executive Summary.* New York: NY. Retrieved from http://lac.org/roadblocks-to-reentry/upload/lacreport/ Roadblocks-to-Reentry--2009.pdf.

Leo, R. (2005). Rethinking the study of miscarriages of justice. *Journal of Contemporary Criminal Justice 21* (3), 201–223.

Leo, R. (2017). The criminology of wrongful convictions: A decade later. *Journal of Contemporary Criminal Justice, 33* (1), 82–106.

Leo, R. A., & Liu, B. (2009). What do potential jurors know about police interrogation techniques and false confessions? *Behavioral Science & the Law, 27,* 381–399.

Levs, J. (2013, December 4). Innocent man: How inmate Michael Morton lost 25 years of his life. *CNN.* Retrieved from http://www.cnn.com/2013/12/04/justice/ exonerated-prisoner-update-michael-morton/index.html.

Lindsay, D. S., & Johnson, M. K. (1989). The eyewitness suggestibility effect and memory source. *Memory & Cognition, 17,* 349–358.

Lindsay, R. C. L., & Wells, G. L. (1985). Improving eyewitness identifications from lineups: Simultaneous versus sequential lineup presentation. *Journal of Applied Psychology, 70* (3), 556–564.

Lindsay, R. C. L., Wells, G. L., & O'Connor, F. J. (1989). Mock-juror belief accurate and inaccurate eyewitnesses. *Law & Human Behavior, 13* (3), 333–339.

Lindsay, R. C. L., Wells, G. L., & Rumpel, C. M. (1981). Can people detect eyewitness identification accuracy within and across situations? *Journal of Applied Psychology, 66,* 79–89.

Loftus, E. (1979). *Eyewitness testimony.* Cambridge, MA: Harvard University Press.

Loftus, E., Doyle, J. M., & Dysart, J. E. (2007). *Eyewitness testimony: Civil and criminal* (4th ed.). Charlottesville, VA: Lexis Law Publishing.

Loftus, E. F., Loftus, G. R., & Messo, J. (1987). Some facts about "weapons focus." *Law & Human Behavior, 11,* 55–62.

Lofquist, W. (2001). Whodunit? An examination of the production of wrongful convictions. In S. D. Westervelt & J. A. Humphrey (Eds.), *Wrongly convicted: Perspectives on failed justice* (pp. 174--196). New Brunswick, NJ: Rutgers University Press.

London, K., & Nunez, N. (2000). The effect of jury deliberations on jurors' propensity to disregarded inadmissible evidence. *Journal of Applied Psychology, 8* (6), 932–939.

Longergan, J. R. (2008). Protecting the innocent: A model for comprehensive, individualized, compensation of the exonerated. *Legislation & Public Policy, 11*, 405–452.

Marder, N. S. (2006). Bringing jury instruction into the twenty-first century. *Notre Dame Law Review, 81 (2), 449–512.*

Maruschak, L. M., Berzofsky M., & Unangst, J. (2015). *Medical problems of state and federal prisoners and jail inmates, 2011-12.* Washington, DC: US Department of Justice, Bureau of Justice Statistics. NCJ 248491.

Mason v. Brathwaite, 432 U.S. 98, 110 (1977).

McNamara, M. (2009, April 11). 'Witch Hunt' Falsely imprisoned Bakersfield parents are profiled in the frustrating MSNBC documentary. *Los Angeles Times.* Retrieved from http://articles.latimes.com/2009/apr/11/entertainment/et-witch hunt11.

Medwed, D. S. (2010). Brady's bunch of flaws. *Washington & Lee Law Review, 67* (4), 1533–1567.

Medwed, D. S. (2012). *Prosecution complex: America's race to convict and its impact on the innocent.* New York: New York University Press.

Melson, K. E. (2010). Embracing the pat forward: The journey to justice continues. *New England Journal on Criminal and Civil Confinement, 36* (2), 197–232.

Merton, R. (1948). The self–fulfilling prophesy. *Antioch Review, 8* (2), 193–210.

Miceli, M. P., & Near, J. P. (1992). *Blowing the whistle: The organizational and legal implications for companies and employees.* New York: Lexington.

Miniño, A, M. (2010, May). Mortality among teenagers aged 12-19 years: United States, 1999-2006. *NCHS data brief, 37,* 1–8.

Miranda v. Arizona, 384 U.S. 436 (1966).

Missouri v. Frye, 132 S. Ct. 1399 (2012).

Mnookkin, J. L. (2015). Constructing evidence and educating juries the case for modular, made-in-advance expert evidence about eyewitness identifications and false confessions. *Texas Law Review, 93* (7) 1811–1848.

Mnookin, J. L., Cole, S. A., Dror, I.E., Fisher, B., Houck, M. M., Inman, K., et al. (2011). The need for a research culture in the forensic sciences. *UCLA Law Review. 58* (30), 725–780.

Moschzisker, R. (1921). The historic origin of trial by jury. *University of Pennsylvania Law Review & American Law Register, 70* (10), 1–13.

Mostaghel, D. (2011). Wrongly incarcerated, randomly compensated: How to fund wrongful-conviction compensation statutes. *Indiana Law Review, 44,* 503–544.

Mungan, M. C., & Klick, J. (2016). Reducing guilty pleas through exoneree compensations. *Journal of Law & Economics, 59* (1), 173–189.

Murphy, B., & Lavoie D. (2012, October 13). For Mass. Lab chemist Annie Dookhan, an unlikely road to scandal. *The Associated Press.* Retrieved from http://www.masslive.com/news/index.ssf/2012/10/for_mass_lab_chemist_annie_dookhan.html.

Natapoff, A. (2006). Beyond unreliable: How snitches contribute to wrongful convictions. *Golden Gate University Law Review, 37* (1), 107–129.

National Academy of Sciences. (2009*). Strengthening forensic science in the United States: A path forward.* Washington, DC: National Academies Press.

National Conference of State Legislatures. (2013). *Post-conviction DNA testing.* Retrieved from http://www.ncsl.org/Documents/cj/PostConvictionDNATesting.pdf.

National Institute of Justice (2009). *Projects funded under fiscal year 2009 solicitations.* Retrieved from http://www.nij.gov/funding/awards/pages/2009.aspx.

National Registry of Exoneration. (2017). *Current exonerations.* Retrieved from https://www.law.umich.edu/special/exoneration/Pages/about.aspx.

Neil v. Biggers, 409 U.S. 188 (1972).

Neufeld, P., & Scheck, B. (1996). Commentary. In E. Connors, T. Lundregan, N. Miller, & T. McEwen, *Convicted by juries, exonerated by science: Case studies in the use of DNA evidence to establish innocence after trial* (NCJ 161258, pp. xxviii-xxxi). Washington, DC: National Institute of Justice.

N. H. Criminal Jury Instructions 3.06 identification. (1985). Retrieved from http://federalevidence.com/node/1382/.

Nolan, T. (2007). Depiction of the "CSI effect" in popular culture: Portrait in domination and effective affectation. *New England Law Review, 41,* 575–589.

Norris, R. J. (2012). Assessing compensation statues for the wrongly convicted. *Criminal Justice Policy Review, 23* (3), 352–374.

Norris, R. J., Bonventre, C. L., Redlich, A. D., & Acker, J. A. (2011). "Than that one innocent suffer": Evaluating state safeguards against wrongful convictions. *Albany Law Review, 74* (3), 1301–1364.

North Carolina Innocence Inquiry Commission. (2016). *NC Innocence Inquiry Commission case statistics.* Retrieved from http://www.innocencecommission-nc.gov/about.html

Office of the Inspector General. (2006). Special report. *A review of the FBI's handling of the Brandon Mayfield case (unclassified and redacted).* Washington: DC: U.S. Government Printing Office.

Ofshe, R., & Leo. R. (1997). The decision to confess falsely: Rational choice and irrational action. *Denver Law Review, 74,* 979–1122.

Ostendorff, J. (2011, July 18). States look to right wrong convictions. *USA Today.* Retrieved from http://usatoday30.usatoday.com/news/nation/2011-07-17-dna-evidence exonerates-innocent-prisoners-wrongful-convictions_n.htm.

Packer, H. (1968). *The limits of the criminal sanction.* Stanford, CA: Stanford University Press.

Palmer, S. (1970). *Deviance and conformity: Roles, situations and reciprocity.* New Haven, CT: College and University Press.

Peel, R. (1829). *Nine principles of policing.* Retrieved from: www.gov.uk/government/publications/Policing-by-consent/definition-of-policing-by-consent.

People v. McDonald, 37 CAL. 3D 351 (1984).

People v. Petschow, 119 P.3d 495 (2004).

Perez-Pena, R. (1997, February 4). Supervision of Troopers faulted in evidence-tampering. *New York Times.* Retrieved from http://www.nytimes.com/1997/02/04/nyregion/supervision-of-troopers-faulted-in-evidence-tampering-scandal.html.

Perry v. New Hampshire impact: The role of eyewitness identification jury instruction (2012, January 18).Retrieved from http://federalevidence.com/node/1382/.

Peters, J. (2013, January 20). No national crime lab standards. *The Republican Lifestyle Desk*. Retrieved from http://www.masslive.com/living/index.ssf/2013/01/no_national_crime_lab_standards.html.

Peterson, J. L., & Hickman, M. J. (2005). *Census of publicly funded forensic crime laboratories, 2002.* Washington, DC: U.S. Department of Justice, Bureau of Justice Statistics.

Peterson, J. L., Mihajovic, S., & Bedrosian, J. L. (1985). Capabilities, use and effects of the nation's criminalistics laboratories. *Journal of Forensic Sciences, 30* (1), 10–23.

Possley, M. (2014). *Nathan Brown.* Retrieved from https://www.law.umich.edu/special/exoneration/pages/casedetail.aspx?caseid=445   7.

Poveda, T. (2001). Estimating wrongful convictions. *Justice Quarterly, 18* (3): 689–708.

Powell v. Alabama, 287 U.S. 45 (1932).

Rakoff, J. S. (2014). When innocent people plead guilty. *The New York Review of Books.* Retrieved from nybooks.com/articles/2014/11/20/why-innocent-people-plead-guilty/.

Ramsey, R. & Frank, J. (2007). Wrongful conviction: Perceptions of criminal justice professionals regarding the frequency of wrong conviction and the event of systems errors. *Crime & Delinquency, 53* (3), 436–470.

Reid Company. (n.d.). Company information. Retrieved from http:// www. reid. com/.

Repaka, J. (1986). Rethinking the standard for new trial motions based upon recantations as newly discovered evidence. *University of Pennsylvania Law Review, 134*, 1433–1459.

Rigby, M. (2013, January 15). Scientific advances in arson investigations reveal wrongful convictions. *Prison Legal News.* Retrieved from https://www.prisonlegalnews.org/news/2013/jan/15/scientific-advances-in-arson-investigations-reveal-wrongful-convictions/.

Ridolfi, K., & Possley, M. (2010). *Northern California Innocence Project, Preventable Error: A Report on Prosecutorial Misconduct in California 1997–2009.* Northern California Innocence Project Publications. Retrieved from http://digitalcommons.law.scu.edu/ncippubs/2.

Risinger, D. M. (2007). Convicting the innocent: An empirically justified wrongful conviction rate. *Journal of Criminal Law & Criminology, 97* (3), 761-806.

Risinger, D. M., & Saks, M. J. (2003). A house with no foundation. *Issues in Science & Technology, 20* (1), 35–39.

Rizer III, A. L. (2003). The race effect on wrongful conviction. *William Mitchell Law Review, 29* (3), 845–867.

Russano, M. B., Meissner, C. A., Narchet, F.M., & Kassin S. M. (2005). Investigating true and false confession with a novel experimental paradigm. *Psychological Science, 16*, 481–486.

Salassi, H.D., Jr. (1996). Post-conviction remedies and waiver of Constitutional rights. *Louisiana Law Review, 26* (3), 705–718.

Saltzman, J., & Daniel, M. (2004, January 24). Man freed in 1997 shooting of officer judge gives ruling after fingerprint revelation. *Boston Globe.* Retrieved from http:www.boston.com/news/local/articles/2004/01/24/man_freed_in_1997_shooting_of_officer/?page=full.

Sarasohn, D. (2005, September 8). The Patriot Act on trial. *The Nation.* Retrieved from http://www.thenation.com/article/patriot-act-trial/.

Scheck, B. (2010). Professional and conviction integrity programs: Why we need them, why they will work, and models for creating them. *Cardozo Law Review, 31* (6), 2215–2256.

Scheck, B. (2013). Four reforms for the twenty-first century. *Judicature, 96* (6), 323–336.

Scheck, B., Neufeld, P., & Dwyer, J. (2000). *Actual innocence: Five days to execution and other dispatches from wrongly convicted.* New York: Doubleday.

Schmechel, R. S., O'Toole, T. P., Easterly, C., & Loftus, E. F. (2006). Beyond the Ken? Testing juror's understanding of eyewitness reliability evidence. *Jurimetrics Journal, 46,* 177–214.

Scott, L. (2010). "It never, ever ends": The psychological impact of wrongful conviction. *American University Criminal Law Brief, 5* (2), 10–22.

Severance, L., & Loftus, E. (1982). Improving the ability of jurors to comprehend and apply criminal jury instructions. *Law & Society Review, 17,* 153–198.

Seward, C. (2012, May 21). Researches: More than 2,000 false convictions in past 23years. *NBC News.* Retrieved from https://usnews.newsvine.com/_news/2012/05/21/11756575-researchers-more-than-2000-false-convictions-in-past-23-years?lite.

Shell, E. (2013). A recipe for mistaken convictions: Why federal rule of evidence 403 should be used to exclude unreliable eyewitness-identification evidence. *Suffolk University Law Review, 46,* 263–285.

Sherr, L., Redmond, L., & St. John, C. (2007, May 8). Untangling a murder mystery. ABC News. Retrieved from http://www.abc.news.go.cpm/20/20/story/id.2931404&page.

Shlosber, A., Mandery, E. J., West, V., & Callaghan, B. (2014). Expungement and post- exoneration offending. *Journal of Criminal Law & Criminology, 104* (2), 353–388.

Siegel, L., Schmalleger, F., & Worrall, J. (2011). *Courts and criminal justice in America.* Upper Saddle River, NJ: Pearson Education, Inc.

Siegel, L., & Worrall, J. L. (2013). *Essentials of Criminal Justice* (8th ed.). Belmont, CA: Wadsworth Cengage.

Siegel, L., & Worrall, J. L. (2015). *Introduction to Criminal Justice* (15th ed.). Boston, MA: Wadsworth Cengage.

Simms, T. (2016). Statutory compensation for the wrongly imprisoned. *Journal of Social Work, 61* (2), 155–162.

Simon, D. (2012). *In doubt: The psychology of the criminal justice process.* Cambridge, MA: Harvard University Press.

Singer, E. (1981). Reference groups and social evaluations. In M. Rosenberg & R. H. Turner (Eds.), *Social psychology: Sociological perspectives* (pp. 66-93). New York: Basic Books.

Slifer, S. (2014, March 27). How the wrongfully convicted are compensated for years lost. *CBS News.* Retrieved from http://www.cbsnews.com/news/how-the-wrongfully-convicted-are-compensated/.

Smalarz, L., & Wells, G. L. (2015). Contamination of eyewitness self-reports and the mistaken identification problem. *Current Directions in Psychological Science, 24* (2), 120–124.

Smith, B., Zalman, M., & Kiger, A. (2011). How justice system officials view wrongful convictions. *Crime & Delinquency, 57* (5), 663–685.

Smith, R. P. (2012). Instructing deadlocked juries: Use of second Allen charge not error per se (United States v. Robinson). *St. John's Law Review, 52* (2), 285–296.

Sneha. S. (2015, January 24). Joseph Sledge, North Carolina man wrongful convicted of murder, freed after 37 years in jail. *International Business Time.* Retrieved from http://www.ibtimes.com/joseph-sledge-north-carolina-man-wrongly-convicted-murder-freed-after-37-years-jail-1793724.

Speed, A. K. (2014, January 26).Victim recantations prove weak in most criminal cases. *Daily Press.* Retrieved from http://articles.dailypress.com/2014-01-26/news/dp-nws-witnesses-recant-20140126_1_recantation-virginia-court-montgomery-case.

Spencer, B. D. (2007). Estimating the accuracy of jury verdict. *Journal of Empirical Legal Studies, 4* (2), 305–329.

Spencer, H. (2015, April 18). FBI admits flaws in hair analysis over decades. *The Washington Post.* Retrieved from http://www.washingtonpost.com/local/crime/fbi-overstated-forensic-hair-matches-in-nearly-all-criminal-trials-for-decades/2015/04/18/39c8d8c6-e515-11e4-b510-962fcfabc310_story.html.

Starr, D. (2013, December 9). The interview: Do police interrogation techniques produce false confessions? *The New Yorker.* Retrieved from http://www.newyorker.com/magazine/2013/12/09/the-interview-7.

State v. Cabagbag, 277 P.3d 1027 (2012).

State v. Guilbert, 49 A.3d 705 (2012).

State v. Grimes, 982 P.2d 1037 (1999).

State v. Henderson, 27 A.3d 872 (2011).

State v. James, No. 96-CA-17, 1998 WL 518135 (Ohio Ct. App. Mar.25, 1998).

State v. Jimmy Ray Bromgard, No. 88108 (Minn. Dist. CT. Nov. 16, 1987).

State v. Lawson, 291 P.3d 673 (2012).

State v. Marallo, No. 1468-10-98 RdCr. (2004).

State v. Mitchell, 275 P.3d 905 (2012).

State v. Patterson, 886 A. 2d 777 (2005).

State v. Spiller, No. 00-2897-CR, 2001 WL 1035213 (Wis. App. Sept. 11, 2001).

Steblay, N. (1997). Social influence in eyewitness recall: A meta-analytic review of lineup effects. *Law & Human Behavior, 21* (3), 283-297.

Steblay, N., Dysart, J., Fulero, S., & Lindsay. R. (2001). Eyewitness accuracy rates in sequential and simultaneous lineup presentations: A meta-analytic comparison. *Law & Human Behavior, 25* (5), 459-473.

Strickland v. Washington, 466 U.S. 668 (1984).

Strickler v. Greene, 527 U.S. 263,281-82 (1999).

Stubbs, C. (2012, April 19). Wrongful convictions, wrongful bias. *American Civil*

Liberties Union. Retrieved from https://www.aclu.org/blog/wrongful-convictions-wrongful-bias.

Sudnow, D. R. (1965). Normal crimes: Sociological feature of the penal code in a public defender office. *Social Problems, 12* (3), 255–276.

Tallent, L. (2011). Through the lens of Federal Evidence Rule 403: An examination of eyewitness identification expert testimony admissibility in the Federal Circuit Courts. *Washington and Lee Law Review, 68* (2), 765–809.

Tepfer, J. A., & Nirider, L. H. (2012). Adjudicated juveniles and collateral relief. *In* Balancing fairness with Finality: An examination of post-conviction review. Symposium in *Maine Law Review, 64,* 553–574.

The Center for Holistic Defense. (n.d.). Bronx defenders. Retrieved from http://wwwbronx-denders.org/programs/center-for-holistic-defense/.

The Declaration of Independence. (U.S. 1776).

The Innocence Network. (n.d.). About the Innocence Network. Retrieved from http://innocencenetwork.org/about/.

The Justice Project. (2007). *Jailhouse snitch testimony: A policy review.* Washington, D.C. Retrieved from http://www.pewtrusts.org/~/media/legacy/uploadedfiles/wwwpewtrustsorg/reports/death_penalty_reform/Jailhouse20snitch20testimony-20policy20briefpdf.pdf.

Thomas, S. (2015). Addressing wrongful convictions: An examination of Texas's new junk science writ and other measures for protecting the innocent. *Houston Law Review, 52* (3), 1037–1066.

Thomas, S. A. (2014). Blackstone's curse: The fall of the criminal, civil, and grand juries and the rise of the executive, the legislature, the judiciary, and the states. *William & Mary Law Review, 55* (3), 1195–1239.

Thomas, W. I. (1923). *The unadjusted girl: With cases and standpoint for behavior analysis.* Boston: Little Brown and Company.

Thomas, W. I., & Thomas, D. S. (1928). *The child in America: Behavior problems and programs.* New York: A. A. Knopf.

Thompson, S. G. (2009). Judicial blindness to eyewitness misidentification. *Marquette Law Review, 93,* 639–669.

Thompson, S. G. (2010). Eyewitness identification and state courts as guardians against wrongful conviction. *Ohio State Journal of Criminal Law, 7,* 603–635.

Trivelli, A. (2016). Compensating the wrongfully convicted: A proposal to make victims of wrongful incarceration whole again. *Richmond Journal of Law & the Public Interest, 29,* 257–282.

Truman, J., & Morgan, R. (2016). Criminal Victimization, 2105 (NCJ 250180). *Bureau of Justice Statistics Bulletin.* Washington, DC: U.S. Department of Justice, Office of Justice Programs.

U.S. Const. amend. V.

U.S. Const. amen. VI.

U.S. Const. amend. XIV.

United States Department of Housing and Urban Development. (2005). *Instruction Guidebook for Completing Public Housing Assessment System Management Operations Certification Form HUD-50072: Management Operations Assessment Sub-System*

(MASS). "Sub-Indicator #5: Security". Retrieved from http://portal.hud.gov/hud-portal/documents/huddoc?id=DOC_26260.pdf.

United States Department of Justice. (2002). Principles of federal prosecutors. Retrieved from http://www.justice.gov/usao/eousa/foia_reading_room/usam/title9/27mcrm.htm#9-27.420.

United States v. Ash, 413 U.S. 300 (1979).

United States v. Bagley, 473 U.S. (1985).

United States v. Cervantes-Pacheo 826 F.2d 310,216 (5th Cir. 1987).

United States v. Cresta, 825 F.2d 538, 541 (1st Cir. 1987).

United States v. Fuentes, 988F. Supp. 861 (ED Pa. 1997).

United States v. Hoffa, 385 U.S. 293 (1966: 310-312).

United States v. Kaufman, 858 F.2d 994 (5th Cir. 1988).

United States v. Mathis, 264 F.3d 321 (3d Cir. 2001).

United States v. Singleton, 144 F.3d 1343 (10th Cir. 1998).

United States v. Singleton, 165 F.3d 1297 (10th Cir.1999).

United States v. Telfaire, 469 F .2D 552 (D.C. Cir. 1972).

United States v. Wade, 388 U.S. 218 (1967).

Van de Kamp et al. v. Goldstein, 129 S. Ct. 855 (2009).

Walters, C. M. (1985). Admission of expert testimony on eyewitness identification. *California Law Review, 73*, 1402–1430.

Warden, R. (2004). *The snitch system: How incentivized witnesses put 38 innocent Americans on death row.* Chicago: Northwestern University School of Law Center on Wrongful Convictions.

Wells, G. L. (1978). Applied eyewitness-testimony research: System variables and estimator variables. *Journal of Personality & Social Psychology, 36* (12), 1546–1557.

Wells, G. L., & Bradfield, A. L. (1998). "Good, you identified the suspect." Feedback to eyewitnesses distorts their reports of the witnessing experience. *Journal of Applied Psychology, 83*, 360–376.

Wells, G. L., & Bradfield, A. L. (1999). Distortions in eyewitnesses' recollections: Can the post-identification feedback effect be moderated? *Psychological Science, 10*, 138–144.

Wells, G. L., & Olson, E. A. (2003). Eyewitness testimony. *Annual Review of Psychology, 54* (1), 277–295.

Wells, G. L., & Murray, D. (1984). Eyewitness confidence. In G. Wells and E. Loftus (Eds.), *Eyewitness testimony: Psychological perspectives* (pp. 155–170). New York: Cambridge University Press.

Wells, G. L., Small, M., Penrod, S., Malpass, R. S., Fulero, S. M., & Brimacombe, C. A. E. (1998). Eyewitness identification procedures: Recommendations for lineups and photospreads. *Law & Human Behavior, 22* (6), 603–647.

Wells, G. L., & Quinlivan, D. S (2008). Suggestive eyewitness identification procedures and the Supreme Court's reliability test in light of eyewitness science: 30 years later. *Law & Human Behavior, 33*, 1–24.

Wells, G. L., & Quinlivan, D. S (2009). The eyewitness post-identification feedback effect: What is the function of flexible confidence estimates for autobiographical events? *Applied Cognitive Psychology, 23*, 1153–1163.

Wertheimer, M. (1944). Gestalt theory. *Social Research, 11*, 78–99.

West, E. M. (2010). *Court findings of ineffective assistance of counsel claims in post-conviction appeals among the first 255 DNA exoneration cases.* New York: Innocence Project. Retrieved from www. innocenceproject.org/wp-content/uploads/2016/05/Innocence_Project_IAC_Report.pdfconviction appeals.

Westervelt, S. D., & Cook, K. J. (2010). Framing innocents: The wrongly convicted as victims of state harm. *Crime Law & Social Change, 53,* 259–275.

Westervelt, S. D., & Cook, K. J. (2012) *Life after death row: Exonerees' search for community and identity.* New Brunswick, NJ: Rutgers University Press.

Westervelt, S. D., & Cook, K. (2013). Life after exoneration: Examining the aftermath of a wrongful capital conviction. In C. R. Huff & M. Killias (Eds.), *Wrongful conviction and miscarriages of justice: Causes and remedies in North America and European criminal justice systems* (pp. 261–281). NY: Routledge.

Westervelt, S. D., & Humphrey, J. A. (2001). *Wrongly convicted: Perspectives of failed justice.* New Brunswick, NJ: Rutgers University Press.

White, G. B. (2016, February 22). Taxing the wrongfully convicted. The Atlantic. Retrieved from http://www.theatlantic.com/business/archive/2016/02/taxing-the-wrongfully-convicted/470397/.

Williams, B. L. (2015, May 8). Wrongfully convicted teen finds new challenges in freedom. *Juvenile Justice Information Exchange.* Retrieved from http://jjie.org/2015/05/08/wrongfully-convicted-teen-finds-new-challenges-in-freedom-as-a-man/.

Williams v. Florida, 399 U.S. 78 (1970).

Williams v. Reynolds, 904 F. Supp. 1529 (F.D. Okla. 1995).

Wilson, K. J. (2007). State policies and procedures regarding "gate money": A report prepared for: California Department of Corrections and Rehabilitation. *Center for Public Policy Research, University of California, Davis.* Retrieved from http://www.cdcr.ca.gov/Adult_Research_Branch/Research_Documents/Gate_Mo ney_Oct_2007.pdf.

WIS. STAT. § 809.30(2)(h) (2013-2014).

Wise, R. A., Sartori, G., Magnessen, S., & Safer, M. A. (2014). An examination of the causes and solutions to eyewitness error. *Frontiers in Psychiatry, 5,* 1–8.

Wolitz, D. (2010). Innocence commissions and the future of post-conviction review. *Georgetown University Law Center,* 1-82. Retrieved from http://scholarship.law.georgetown.edu/cgi/viewcontent.cgi?article=1336&context=facpub.

Wren, J. (2011). *Proving damages to the jury.* Costa Mesa, CA: James Publishing, Inc.

Zalman, M. (2011). An integrated justice model of wrongful convictions. *Albany Law Review, 74* (3), 1465–1524.

Zalman, M., & Carrano, J. (2014). Sustainability of innocence reform. *Albany Law Review, 77* (3): 955–1003.

Zalman, M., Smith, B., & Kiger, A. (2008). Official estimates of the incidence of "actual innocence" convictions. *Justice Quarterly, 25* (1), 72–100.

Zimmerman, C. (2001). From the jailhouse to the courthouse: The role of informants in wrongful convictions. In S.D. Westervelt & J. A. Humphrey (Eds.), *Wrongly convicted: Perspectives on failed justice* (pp. 55–76). New Brunswick, NJ: Rutgers University Press.

NAME INDEX

SUBJECT INDEX